Evolution, Creation, Intelligent Design & Hybrids:
Which Ones Are Scientific?

Published by
American University & Colleges Press™
American Book Publishing
5442 So. 900 East, #146
Salt Lake City, UT 84117-7204
http://www.american-book.com

Printed in the United States of America on acid-free paper.

Evolution, Creation, Intelligent Design & Hybrids: Which Ones Are Scientific?
Designed by Jana Rade, design@american-book.com

Publisher's Note: This publication is designed to provide accurate and authoritative information in regard to the subject matter covered. It is sold or distributed with the understanding that the publisher and author is not engaged in rendering legal, accounting, or other professional service. If legal advice or other expert assistance is required, the services of a competent professional person in a consultation capacity should be sought.

ISBN-13: 978-1-58982-601-4
ISBN-10: 1-58982-601-9

Library of Congress Cataloging-in-Publication Data

Grebens, George, 1943-
 Evolution, creation, intelligent design & hybrids : which ones are scientific? / George Grebens.
    p. cm.
 Includes bibliographical references and index.
 ISBN-13: 978-1-58982-601-4
 ISBN-10: 1-58982-601-9
 1. Evolution--Religious aspects--Catholic Church. 2. Intelligent design (Teleology) 3. Creationism. 4. Religion and science. 5. Catholic Church--Doctrines. I. Title. II. Title: Evolution, creation, intelligent design, and hybrids.
 BX1795.E85.G74 2010
 231.7'652--dc22

2009051639

Special Sales: These books are available at special discounts for bulk purchases. Special editions, including personalized covers, excerpts of existing books, and corporate imprints, can be created in large quantities for special needs. For more information e-mail orders@american-book.com or call 801-486-8639.

Evolution, Creation, Intelligent Design & Hybrids: Which Ones Are Scientific?

George Grebens, PhD

Dedication

Dedicated:

To my wife and

To the countless saints who have dedicated their lives and offered the ultimate sacrifice during the twentieth century.

Foreword

For over 150 years the Evolution vs. Creation debate has continued in the USA, Europe and the world. This debate has expanded from the 1980s to include two other debaters: the Intelligent Design and the Progressive Creation, or Old Earth Creation views. Recent American State and Federal court decisions have not helped resolve the debaters' scientific issues. If it were simply an issue of implementing the scientific method, it should have been easy to solve. Instead, the debate diversified on both sides of the original Evolution vs. Creation debate.

Classical Darwinism launched its movement at the end of the nineteenth century. It solidified itself with an evolutionary synthesis in the 1930s while making some detours through Marxism and Nazism. Then evolution continued its path to emerge as Neo-Darwinism or neo-evolution in the 1940s. Evolution received a marketing face-lift to appear as 'methodological naturalism' in 1983. It reinvented itself in the form of a modern evolutionary synthesis in the 1980s and 1990s. In the 1980s a new group of scientists emerged, the intelligent design (I.D.) scientists. These scientists used new high–tech lab equipment to discover complex information processes at the sub-chromosome levels. It became evident that the theory of evolution did not predict, nor was able to explain, this level of complexity. Because of this, many neo-evolution scientists shed their nineteenth century evolution umbilical cord. They sought alternate explanations and causes.

Scientists who did not adhere to the Darwinian view were recognized as being creation flood or teleology scientists. In the late nineteenth and early twentieth centuries, some of these scientists succumbed to the Darwinian long-ages theory. To explain their positions, they created several hybrid uniformitarian explanations: the day-age[1], gap theory[2], and theistic evolution[3]. The attempt to reconcile the Genesis account of creation with the Darwinian interpretation of scientific data is particularly noticeable in the struggle that led to Vatican II[4]. Prior to 1950, very little scientific research had been done which would have helped confirm any particular position. In the 1950s, the American government invested heavily in scientific research. This investment produced a myriad of new empirical data that was interpreted within the evolutionary scientific model. In the 1960s, a group of creation scientists developed the modern creation scientific model that helped provide an alternate explanation and predictions for this new empirical data. These creationists then compared their model's results with those produced by the evolution scientific model. This comparison was publically debated at high levels during the 1970s and early 1980s. Here, creation[5] and neo-evolution scientists compare the various interpretations and predictions of scientific empirical evidence. This debate continues today in creation scientific journals. In the late 1980s, there re-emerged the earlier theistic evolution group under new names: progressive creation or old-age creation. Together with neo-evolution scientists, these hybrid uniformitarian scientists challenge scientific interpretations offered by the original young earth creation model. During the 1980s and 90s, among Neo-Evolutionists, many scientists, upon examining data produced by high-tech electronic/atomic microscopes, have recognized information-rich and nano-robotic processes[6] and features that the uniformitarian/evolutionary scientific model simply could not predict.

This debate outcome has raised several questions. What is the true

---

[1] The day-age view holds that, in the Bible, each day in the Genesis creation week represents undetermined ages.

[2] The gap theory view holds that there is an undetermined amount of time between the Biblical Gen.1:1 and 1:2.

[3] Theistic evolutionists have several interpretations of God's creation schedule. They use the uniformitarian long-age view, and schedule in several divine interventions. Mini-special-creation adjustments correspond with the gaps identified in the geologic column.

[4] O'Connell, Fr. Patrick, B.D., 'Science of Today And The Problems of Genesis' Tan Books and Publishers, Inc. Rockford, Illinois, 1959, 1993

[5]http:// www.icr.org.

[6] Meyer., Stephen, "Signature in the Cell," HarperCollins e-books, 2009

nature of the scientific method presented to us? Had the original scientific method been improperly defined? Had the method or the nature of science changed with time? Wasn't the scientific method supposed to provide a constant - an authoritative anchor? Has science and the scientific method been misapplied by scientists? Has content been misunderstood, blended or mutated into economics, philosophy, or ideology? Perhaps it had not been designed to fulfill a role that most thought it should have fulfilled? Has it expanded beyond its procedural scope? Does it now provide evidence for scientific misconduct or intellectual dishonesty? Has it been hijacked by influential forces and led to fulfill other purposes?

It will be shown that today all of these questions coexist with the proper use of the scientific method. For the most part, scientific literature, textbooks, and the media promote the simplified, linear, three- to seven-step scientific methods. Some philosophers of science offer more steps and new definitions of the scientific method only to meet counter proposals. At the same time, it has been shown that during the twentieth and twenty-first centuries states and empires have interlaced their ideology with Darwinian concepts to promote Malthusian-based social re-engineering and population control schemes.

Throughout this century's turbulent events, few remember that for thousands of years the original concepts of science and of the scientific method have progressed at an incremental pace. In contrast to the twentieth century's view, the millennial development emphasized a different set of priorities. The ancients made tremendous discoveries and applications. Their scientific method may initially have been blended with other subjects – astronomy with astrology, or chemistry with alchemy – however, this duality helped maintain interest and scientific initiative. For example, how far would Plato and Aristotle have gone with their inquiries had their interest in mathematics not been blended with philosophy? We can also find, in this early history, the rudiments of modern evolution were blended with pantheism and polytheism.

It will be seen that physical and mathematical tool refinement has in large measure contributed to the development of scientific disciplines. These tools helped us move from uncertainty to conditional certainty. The Babylonians, Egyptians, Persians, Greeks, Christians, and Muslims clearly understood, used and developed these basics. Explanations of origins either rested with God, gods or some version of a changing materialistic steady state. These views seem to still remain with us.

There are many modern and historical definitions of the scientific method and science. However, the scientific method that led to our modern time must have contained some basic features that currently have been obscured by a relativistic approach. Whether builders aligned their pyramid with mathematical precision with the zodiac; ship builders incorporated engineering standards and codes; or aviators met aerodynamic requirements, their scientific method would include:

(a) Start with an accurate knowledge-base that contains law-based, quantifiable standards and codes that would help manage a knowledge base of conditional certainty' (see 3DMM).

(b) Use investigative techniques, tools, and procedures to identify specific areas of uncertainty. Uncertainty may be located in the knowledge-base and/or the environment.

(c) Conduct the decision-making and problem-solving (DMPS) process with the objective of converting specific uncertainty to conditional certainty - i.e., improve and qualities guarantee the accuracy of the knowledge base.

Yet, today many areas of society, academia, and courts are tied to an effort to substitute and truncate the management of the historical knowledge base. This effort is to replace, redefine, and reduce the investigative processes without realizing that relativized uncertainty leads to naïve realism. The modern aim is to narrow opportunities for out-of-box creative thinking. This reprioritizes the qualitative filters within the DMPS process. These modernizing steps suggest that an original qualitative world-view is being replaced by one that is linear and economically expedient. This challenge and cultural war can be seen in the evolution versus creation debate. This war doesn't affect scientific methodology, but also affects our awareness, policies, education, constitutional and legal priorities.

To visualize the extent of this process, a brief historical perspective is necessary.

Over time, definitions may vary with preferences and taste. Such changes may be gradual or drastic. For example, the twentieth century's neo-modernist view did not emerge as a logical outgrowth of the age of enlightenment. Instead, neo-modernism arbitrarily dismissed the former.

This is also true with the recent emergence of scientificism[7] with regards to Catholicism. Catholicism and scientificism have much in common. Each represents a practical approach to life, has a knowledge-base, has a methodology for conditional certainty, and is authoritative. Both reflect purpose, objectives, strategy, and a world-view.

For example, from the first century within Christendom, it had been important to have considered oneself to be a Catholic Christian. This was true throughout Eastern and Western Europe, Middle East and Carthage. Saint Ignatius was first to mention the concept of Catholicism (i.e., universal) in his letter to Christians in Smyrna[8] in 106 AD. And even after the great schism in 1054 AD, both the Western Roman Catholic Church and Eastern Catholic Orthodox Church[9] had retained the notion of being Catholic. During the sixteenth century in Western Europe, Martin Luther at first saw himself as a Roman Catholic reformer who wished to update and improve the Roman Catholic Church and its institutions. Various concepts of Catholicity had remained among some post-reformation groups.[10] This is also true of some breakaway Roman Catholic groups.[11] This designator was a key component of one's identity. An alternate position would have meant being less than Christian - possibly a heretic.[12] Or worse, that one

---

[7] Scientificism is a specific word that reflects our current condition. Scientism is a subgroup of scientificism.

[8] Ignatius, "Letter to the Smyrnaeans" 7 & 8 (http://www.earlychristianwritings.com/srawley/smyrnaeans.html). Some trace the concept's beginning to Matthew 16:18-19 where Jesus Christ told Peter that "He would build His Church upon this rock, that He will give Peter the keys of the kingdom of heaven…" See also St. Cyril of Jerusalem (circa 315-386), "Catechetical Lectures, XCIII" (http://www.newadvent.org/fathers/310118.htm).

[9] See "The Longer Catechism of the Orthodox, Catholic, and Eastern Church" (http://www.tserkovnost.org/catechism_filaret/catechism_filaret-1.html).

[10] High Anglican and others who subscribe to the clauses: "One Holy Catholic and Apostolic Church" (Nicene creed); "the Catholic faith" (Athanasian creed); and "holy Catholic church" (Apostles' creed).

[11] This would also include: independent Catholics, ancient Catholics, liberal Catholic churches, Polish National Catholic Church and Society of Saint Pius the X (SSPX).

[12] Ignatius, "Letter," 7, where he distinguished between Christians and the

has reverted to the paganism of the ancient Roman Empire, or one who entertains views of those who subscribed to the various pluralistic beliefs that were common among the surrounding people.

Non-Catholic world-views began to appear with the emergence of the Reformation in the fourteenth to fifteenth centuries. A hundred years later, other non-Catholic worldviews emerged that were established upon the rationalistic and empiricist philosophies.[13] By the nineteenth century the latter view began to replace both Catholic and post-Reformation views. In addition to borrowing and promoting the scientific method[14] the latter movement also redefined and embellished the scientific method with notions such as: reductionism, uniformitarianism, and modernism. Cryptically this movement also promoted a concerted effort to replace Christianity – specifically the notion of Catholicism.

Christianity inherited a knowledge base of geometric natural law upon which Creation had been established. Christianity had been set within the Roman Empire. This empire had its own knowledge base of conditional certainty. This dual knowledge base empowered Christendom (Byzantium and Rome) to continue with the effective conversion process of the

---

heretics who, for example, negated "the Eucharist to be the flesh of our Savior Jesus Christ, and which the Father, of His goodness, rose up again." Saint Augustine (354-430 AD), "Against the Epistle of Manichaeus called Fundamental," (Chapter 4: Proofs of the Catholic Faith), (http://www.ccel.or/ccel/schaff/npnf104.iv.viii.1.html).

[13] It is necessary to include the emergence of Masonic/Freemasonry lodges in Scotland in the sixteenth century and Grand Masonic lodges in England on 24 June, France in 1728 and America in 1730 (see David Stevenson, *The Origins of Freemasonry: Scotland's Century 1590-1710* (Cambridge: Cambridge University Press, 1988); http://www.masonicsites.org ("The Regises Manuscript"); Steven C. Bullock, *Institute of Early American History and Culture* (Williamsburg, VA, 1996); and *Revolutionary Brotherhood: Freemasonry and the Transformation of the American Social Order, 1780-1840* (Chapel Hill: University of North Carolina Press). Similarly, the influence of Talmudism which begins from the fourteenth century, after making its way to Western Europe from East Europe after the disintegration of the Khazar Empire during the eleventh century, see Joseph Bau, *Modern Varieties of Judaism* (New York: Columbia University Press, 1972) (http://www.JewishVirtualLibrary.or/jsource/judaism/Haskalah.htlm); also www.khazaria.com.

[14] Others have included: dialectical materialism, coupled with materialism, atheism, and skepticism.

natural world's uncertainty (scientific method) into an increasingly accurate knowledge base (science). Here is a comparison of Catholicity and scientificity:

Figure 1. Comparison: Catholicism and scientificism.

CATHOLICISM	SCIENTIFICISM
CERTAINTY	
Christianity has traced its certainty on legally historical precedents, established within and corroborated within the structure of geometric natural law. This historic documented legal content reveals three singularities: (a) special creation; (b) energy-density drop one cycle down the qualitative infrastructural cone; (c) record of a recent global hydro-tectonic catastrophe, followed by environmental and biological adjustments.	Scientificism provides a synthetic construction of origins and history based on the doctrine of uniformitarianism: (a) Current events, rates, processes are used to: (b) reconstruct history based on the principle of simple to complex; (c) algebraic axioms, theorems, empirical materialism, methodological naturalism, and reductionism. This creates a closed system (no external participation), whose origins may be a big bang or steady state.
SCIENTIFIC METHOD	
Scientific method distinguishes between conditional certainty and uncertainty. It identifies the pursuit for accurate knowledge-base (science), thus laying the foundation for conditional certainty. Providing investigative techniques, tools, processes to help resolve uncertainty (decision-making and problem solving – DMPS – the scientific method.)	Preconditioned filtering (5th step in DMPS) affects all decision-making and problem- solving phases. This results in promoting 'naïve realism' through reductionism and modernism (uniformitarian ideology) and 'luxury effect.'
AUTHORITY	
Two law-based holy/sacred traditions and Christian scriptures, which reflect: ecumenical councils (at least the initial seven councils that establish the original executive functions: purpose, objectives, strategies; and the supervisory functions: policy, procedures, and rules. With the authority of bishops, the church created a favorable environment not only for management style (ethics, attitude, culture—see management style in 3DMM) but also for the patronage	Rationalist and empiricist philosophies stand in contrast to, and enhance a replacement policy towards, the Catholic option. Recently, there developed scientific communities, establishment-sponsored organizations, economics groups, marketing syndicates, university offices. Peer review, academic councils, seek overwhelming scientific consensuses. Editorial boards on various publications, journals, newsletters; econ-

and development of the arts, sciences, technology, and commerce. This also included the development of centers of study, monasteries, universities, and centers for the refinement of knowledge accuracy (e.g., Vatican library), through studies, scientific, medical and ethics groups under the magisterium. Various Protestant authorities created environments for the development of sciences and arts. Continuously, scientific conferences and institutions, scientific editorial boards, publications, journals, and newsletters help propagate information from the general knowledge-base.

omic communities, third-party interest groups, state legal organizations, and international agencies.

What we know today as the scientific method is nothing more than a decision-making and problem-solving tool that had been in development for millennia. It is from the Renaissance through to the nineteenth century that scientists, who professed to be Christians, have refined the accuracy of the knowledge base. The aim of this refinement was to help improve mankind (made in the image of God), society (made in the image of the Kingdom of God), and the state (designed to improve righteous management and ensure development). These scientists included many members of the clergy. Whether alone, under patronage, or with state support, they established all of the scientific branches, taxonomies and made major scientific breakthroughs before World War I.

During the last 100 years, however, notions of science have changed. The change introduced notions of: uniformitarianism, reductionism, behaviorism, secularism, and notions like dialectical materialist economics (DIAMAT) and racial eugenics.

During the early twentieth century dramatic events occurred: world wars, revolutions, economic collapses, and the devastating applications of radical scientific social sciences. All of this made many people weary and skeptical of the sciences. So a new class of modern scientists set out to sanitize this metamorphosing scientific method that seemed to have been in the middle of all the turmoil. These modern scientists purged the new method of all ideological derivatives. This was supposed to render science as objective as possible – i.e., ethics-free. In other words, the new science and also atheism (e.g., R. Dawkins) were not to be seen as a contributing factor to ideological excesses. Instead, these were to project an objective neutral image of rationality.

The approach changed the new science's definitions and terminology. All disciplines and subjects have been and are being reframed. For example, evolution is now to be limited only to biology. Paleontology and astronomy are considered to be outside evolution's parameter. However, these disciplines are still viewed through uniformitarian eyeglasses.[15] In school, students are taught science i.e., biology, physics, chemistry, astronomy, etc., but are not shown that these subjects can be viewed through a scientific lens, as well as, through artistic, economic, agricultural, project, religious, and management lenses. Science policymakers, while taking the extra step to segregate science from pseudoscience, have demonized all that is anti-scientific: religion, ideology, cultism and race – thus rendering whole branches of knowledge less relevant. In a similar manner, materialism is now to be perceived as naturalism.

It soon became apparent that there was more to these reductionist policies and notions of uniformitarian science:

In 1940 and 1995, science executives convened two key '*scientificist ecumenical councils*' to formulate the modern evolutionary synthesis *creed.*

At the dawn of the twenty-first century, the *scientificist magisterium* formulated the *Encyclical of Infallibility.* It proclaimed that 'evolution is almost certainty, and is truth.'

During the past thirty years, establishment scientificist organizations had screened personnel for their purity of thought, intent, and practice. They unceremoniously defrocked, blacklisted, and excommunicated numerous professional scholars, university professors, public school teachers, and government employees who succumbed to non-uniformitarian temptations.[16]

They pointed with a trembling finger at an increasing number of heretics, backsliding and unrepentant reprobates among the 'young earth creation' and 'intelligent design' scientists.

Federal and state courts have been tasked to re-interpret the Articles

---

[15] In Chapter 4 of this book, I analyze the National Academy of Sciences' policy in greater detail.

[16] A partial example of this reality can be seen described in *Expelled: No Intelligence Allowed,* starring Ben Stein, 2008.

of the United States Constitution. Such reinterpretation would allow the passage of judgments on what constitutes true uniformitarian science versus heretical, cultist/religious pseudoscience. This is to set grounds for excommunicating heretical scientists. This will bar heretics from curriculum design, scientific publishing houses, federal grants, access to repositories of scientific documentation, and museum artifacts, determining priorities for scientific research in geologic, paleontological, oceanographic areas, and barred from any institution that is under uniformitarian authority. This court action is modeled on what has passed in support of 'hate laws' and 'untraditional marriages.'

Financed support has been offered to increased scientificist conversions. But this initiative has taken unexpected turns, and still remains an uncontrollably high risk operation.

Establishment evolution scientists of all grades challenge and stir up the masses. These establishment scientists work through public debates, publication, and Internet. Their fingerprints are evident in every science education media programming.

To establish its dogmas (purposes, objectives) and cannons (strategies), the Catholic Church had thousands of years of historic precedents and the certainty of divine law. The scientificist executives magisterium, on the other hand, in spite of its world media outreach, digital networks, and limitless financial support, their reductionist and modernist guidance have only a little over a century. What kind of world would these scientists create if they had thousands of years to produce their reductionist world?

Scientists wished to see evolution as a scientific ethics-free theory. This free evolution is set to achieve almost certainty and truth. Now, increasingly, scientists realize that they have to address scientific ideological issues. These issues increasingly acquire ominous non-scientific content and form

In contrast to these approaches, for thousands of years the Eastern and Western Catholic Church maintained, in spite of the numerous challenges, an environment that sustained a unique civilization. Such an environment allowed for a steady incremental conversion of uncertainty to conditional certainty.

To unravel these approaches to science, this book will address issues of what constitutes true science and the true scientific method:

(a) Both science and the scientific method reflect management content. To better understand this management component, multi-billion dollar engineering project management techniques will be summarized, used and will help test processes and outcomes.

(b) The scientific method helps resolve uncertainty. The scientific method as a management tool is used to move from uncertainty to conditional certainty, thus increasing knowledge base accuracy. This book examines three approaches to the decision-making and problem-solving (DMPS) process. In the real world, DMPS is the successful tool that is used for converting uncertainty to certainty. It will be shown that the true definition of the original scientific method is essentially identical to the DMPS process.

(c) Science and the scientific method have twelve limitations. These limitations in turn allow us to identify an objective and unfettered scientific method.

(d) The true scientific method is a sensitive tool. This book will identify at least twenty-two common pitfalls that scientists encounter and use.

(e) Scientists, teachers, and students must identify and recognize at least twenty common, pseudoscientific methods and assumptions.

(f) Science and the scientific method cannot escape the five models of thinking

(g) As a management tool, science and the scientific method must address five qualitative levels of change (copy, change, re-engineering, re-design, and invention)

(h) We recognize the materialist's definition of what religion is. Yet religion comes in many forms, as cults, philosophies, theologies, and ideologies. Christianity is unique among all of these in that it is established upon geometric natural law, continuous covenantal framework and legal historical documentation. Reflecting verifiable knowledge base accuracy and lawful tools for resolving uncertainty, project management features had been applied for millennia.

The task of this book is to determine which among the four debating groups - evolution, young earth creation, intelligent design, and the hybrid uniformitarians - uses the true scientific method. More specifically, the question is: which of the debaters comes closest to the objective or unfettered scientific method. The thirty-five figures and tables become a scientific score card that readers can use to determine which among the debaters' comes closes to applying the scientific method.

Table of Contents

1. Conditions for Scientific Development 1

2. Scientific Interpretations and Predictions 11

3. Conceptual Formulae 27

4. Certainty from Uncertainty, 5 Change Levels, Models,
 N.A.S - 24 Points 47

5. Religion Everywhere 203

6. Score Cards, Filters and Solutions 243

Appendix 1: Challenging Evidence 265

Appendix 2: 21 Journalistic Assumptions 267

Index 269

About the Author 273

1. Conditions for Scientific Development

This book is the result of several decades of research in different fields. This book reflects the experience and work of thousands of highly qualified people. The output comes from the strategic participation in, and management of, multiple projects. And above all, the book is fixed on the contribution and work accomplished in multiple fields.

During the last sixty years, innovation in science and technology has become the single factor that has helped improve human life around the world. Increasingly, however, undergrowth and tares have also sprung up and suffocated options, where earlier classical foundations had for centuries accelerated and optimistically included everyone in the development and in the benefits. This process has also facilitated a cynical by-product that increasingly destabilizes all original foundations through social re-engineering. The first has helped maintain an environment for social and knowledge incremental growth. The second has limited qualitative infrastructural designs and stressed Malthusian options.

People reacted in three predictable ways. The first continue to cultivate the undergrowth and tares. This approach increased re-engineering in all established structures. The second resisted this focused cultivation of weeds and sought new standards for proper cultivation. These standards were based upon workable scientific models. The third used high-tech labs and made significant discoveries. Here they uncovered fatal oversimplifications and numerous artificial barriers to proper cultivation. They sought new strategies for solutions outside the existing paradigm.

It has been noticed that during the past 500 years European history was being reinterpreted and rewritten. But, at the same time, it has not been forgotten that the European Christian classical foundations have helped to successfully maintain several civilizations. Even when in the fifth century, the Western Roman Empire underwent challenging conditions; it is the Christian classical foundations that sustained the civilizing life line. From that time to Charlemagne's empire, the Christian Celtic culture and the Roman Empire (Byzantium) continued to offer organizational and cultural options for another 1,000 years and beyond – e.g., in Rus' - Russia. The Christian option unified and organized a world-view that reflected discoverable laws in a divinely ordained Creation. This concept of universal lawfulness contributed to the discovery of accurate and certain knowledge. It also led to technological progress. This progress was seen to have been of paramount importance in the continuous improvement and perfection of man and society.

Europe overcame historical, economic, and demographic challenges. The ravages of the black plague in the West during the fourteenth century did not dampen the *optimism* that was attached to discoveries. This hope held that environmental, state, and individual shortcomings would be overcome. Monasteries and then medieval universities contributed to cultural and scientific development. This development was found in every branch - literature, law, architecture, technology, navigation, geography, and celestial mechanics. This then led, before the fourteenth century, to the creation of a small industrial revolution that was based on wood and stone technology. This included inventions such as the windmill, watermill, manufacturing, textiles, transportation, clocks, architecture, shipbuilding, irrigation, etc.[17]

Renaissance spearheaded this momentum. Commercial families, ruling monarchs, and, in the West, the Pope and the magisterium (council of bishops) participated, supported, and were patrons of the arts and sciences. Astronomers calculated, predicted, and adjusted stellar movements and charts. Earlier, Pope Gregory adjusted the calendar. This updating benefited the military, commercial navigation, geographical explorations to China (Marco Polo), and eventually to the New World. This included the invention of the printing press and application of gun powder. Collaboration extended to the refinement and recalibration of stellar calculations in conformity with the long suspected heliocentric view. Architectural designs, building materials, became part of the knowledge-base contained in both the Byzantine and Vatican libraries.

---

[17] See also, http://en.wikipedia.org/wiki/Science_in_the_Middle_Ages.

A longer and wider timeline can help catalog the rise and fall of all civilizations. What is overlooked during this march of history is a constant – the transmission and development of accurate knowledge (science) and technology. European astronomy and mathematics can be traced to Mesopotamia among the Sumerian cuneiforms. Here we find a numeric system based on sexagesimal (base sixty) place value, and a circle divided into 360 degrees of sixty minutes each. The Greek Hipparchus borrowed from all of this – see his 'Almagest,' 'Planetary Hypotheses,' 'Tetrabiblos' and 'Canobic Inscription.' There's evidence that Babylon I and II and Egypt inherited catalogs of stars with constellations. These include forecasted lunar and planetary movements with regards to the horizon. The ancients used, from the earliest times, water clocks, gnomon, shadows, and intercalations. Mathematics included arithmetic, algebra, geometry, and trigonometry[18]. From Babylon to Persia and then transmitted through Alexander the Great's exploits, the Greeks inherited this knowledge. This included the heliocentric model of planetary motions. Seleucus of Seleucia's works[19] documented the heliocentric model, the Metonic cycle – a lunisolar calendar based on nineteen solar years (235 lunar months, synodic month). Hipparchus and later Ptolemy maintained a multi-year, complete list of eclipse observations. These helped track dates from 652 BC to 130 AD. Greek astronomy was a branch of mathematics that reflected geometric models. Plato directed the development of a two-sphere model that represented stellar and planetary phenomena.[20] This Hellenistic knowledge also entered India (Greek-Bactrian city of Ai-Khanoum – third century BC) and was developed in the sixth century as evidenced in the *Romaka Siddhanta* (Doctrine of the Romans).

In the third century BC, Ptolemy II of Egypt established the library of Alexandria. It became the major center of research and learning in the

---

[18] A. E. Berriman, "The Babylonian Quadratic Equation" in C. B. Boyer, *A History of Mathematics*, 2nd Edition (New York:Wiley, 1989).

[19] George Sarton, "Chaldean Astronomy of the Last Three Centuries BC," *Journal of the American Oriental Society*, 75 (3): 166-173.

[20] David C. Linberg, *The Beginnings of Western Science: The European Scientific Tradition in Philosophical, Religious, and Institutional Context, 600 BC to A.D 1450*, (Chicago: University of Chicago Press, 1992.) See also, Plato's *Timaeus* and *Republic.*

Middle East. The library lasted to serve several empires. It was finally moved to Byzantium and Rome.

Later, Islamic astronomy and mathematics had also been based on these early discoveries[21]. For example, in 1030 Al-Biruni in his *Indica* discussed Indian astronomical theories of Aryabhata, Brahmagupta and Varahamihira – specifically about Earth's rotation on its axis, within the scope of two possible views: geo or heliocentric ones. Abu Said Al-Sijzi proposed that the Earth moved around the Sun. Early Christian and Medieval Europe had again access to Greek knowledge through Moslem Spain. In the thirteenth century, this knowledge had contributed to Hindu science also via Arabic translations. One can trace the works of Cardinal Nicholas of Cusa (*Learned Ignorance –De docta ignorantia*) fifteenth century, and references in Nicolaus Copernicus' *De revolutionibus* (1543) that cited theories of Albategni, Arzachel and Averroes.[22] All were additions to the general and historic scientific knowledge-base.

As a matter of interest, it's possible to find the earliest scientific marvel that has been observed by all civilizations around the world. The zodiac had remained a permanent fixture of value throughout history until recent times. The zodiac's design is visible in both hemispheres around the Earth. The design has a set of arbitrarily grouped stars. Each star and constellation has its own distinctive and group meaningful name. The zodiac has been used as a scientific tool to plot a navigational course across seas, deserts, and lands. It was used to forecast lunar, planetary, and stellar pathways. It was .used as a universal calendar that helped date events over time. For example, stellar etchings in the Tara tomb in Ireland – circa 700 BC -- depict a specific date. The zodiac was a source of mythology that helped unify populations under common reference points, ideology, and religious and mystery messages. The zodiac was also a source of scientific knowledge – geometry and celestial mechanics.

The list of scientific and technological achievements through history include: mathematics, geometry, engineering, and financial accounting. This list can include recent discoveries such as: a) the Piri Re'is maps located in the Istanbul Library. The maps outlined - to scale - every

---

[21]   (http://www.muslimheritage.com/topics/default.cfm?ArticleID=482) Khwarizm, Foundation for Science Technology and Civilization.

[22] Richard Covington, "Rediscovering Arabic Science," *Saudi Aramco World*, May-June, 2007: 2-16.

continent around the Earth, including the continent of Antarctica. These ancient maps had been copied by scribes at the library of Alexandria from earlier maps; b) we all may know about the Egyptian's Giza pyramid structures' alignment with geodesic and stellar configurations, but few know about the pyramids' angular wall structural calculations, which have a precision that surpasses that of the modern sky scrapers and contain an impossible vertical angle of fifty-four degrees; c) the Platonic geometric solids – the five convex regular polyhedral (tetrahedron, cube, octahedron, icosahedrons, and dodecahedron) have been found carved in stone in Scotland[23] 1,000 years before Plato described them in his writings – *Timaeus* (360 BC). Plato, himself, had suggested that he had received this knowledge of geometry from the Egyptian monotheistic priests[24].

These stellar navigational maps, calendars, mathematics, geometry, accounting, and other sciences had integrally contributed to the survival of mankind upon this planet. This ancient mathematical knowledge-base had been developed, used, and partially forgotten during the decline of civilizations, but rediscovered as knowledge from a seeming earlier golden age.

With the rise and fall of civilizations, one may inquire as to what conditions had been favorable or detrimental to the development of accurate knowledge.

Favorable conditions for the development of accurate knowledge necessitate a world-view that:

(a) Emphasizes the existence of order and organization. These can be observed and measured on Earth and in the heavens. This order and organization provides proof that certainty is attainable.

(b) Allows for accurate documentation (remembrance) of data and information.[25] This verifiable data becomes a reliable information-base, which:

(c) Contributes to the exercise of qualitative comparisons. Users measure ranges and establish standards. The user then can test

---

[23] Michael Atiyah and Paul and Sutcliffe, "Polyhedra in Physics, Chemistry and Geometry," *Milan JH. Math* 71: 33-58.

[24] James McEvoy, "Plato and The Wisdom of Egypt," *Irish Philosophical Journal* (1984).

[25] Data is any random numbers: 12   6   43; while information is "contextualized data": Day: 12; Month: 6; Year: 1943.

alternatives, make forecasts, and establish detailed plans and schedules for resources loading in order to meet specific objectives. Analysts then use this comparative value to formulate a knowledge-base

(d) Combines knowledge within the scope of a right style – i.e., attitude, motivation, culture, and ethics. Such competitive styles interplay in the setup of predictable and qualitative objectives. This knowledge-base, interlaced with the right style, can be described as wisdom.

The qualities that are favorable to environmental development also contribute to creativity. Here, creativity is expressed in a number of ways: (1) projects (planned & scheduled resources to meet objectives); (2) automation (standardized processes that yield high quality products); and (3) manufacturing (conversion of prime resources to final quality products). Projects, automation, and manufacturing are designed to help identify and resolve uncertainty and to ensure conditional certainty. The 2,000-year-old Christian history demonstrates these qualities. The Creator, God, created the heavens and the Earth that were established upon geometric natural law. This law is discoverable in that it helps identify and resolve uncertainty. In other words, this law contains the necessary management features that help identify and convert uncertainty to conditional certainty. This geometric natural law provides the strategic means to identify workable, measurable, and reproducible solutions. These features then help open the road to further discoveries of lawful, measureable, and recognizable knowledge. These two integral features help establish manageable infrastructures. These management infrastructures, standards, and means for calibration become the foundation for a third level of discoverable infrastructural laws. In this three-layered array, we can identify: ethics, culture, and attitude. These, in turn, are part of and impact society's mission, economic health that sustain and lead to self-perfection.[26] This Christian millennial timeline

---

[26] What eventually became known as modernism had, during the past 400 years of European history, gone to great lengths to disprove the validity, credibility, and reliability of the Christian Biblical knowledge-base. Eventually, modernist interpretations have become part of the curriculum at Christian seminaries and Bible schools. "Science and the Bible" is a typical topic that can be found in any curriculum – e.g., (http://en.wikipedia.org/wiki/Science_and_the_Bible). Here the topic is set within the typical uniformitarian realist (UR) framework. The key objective is to examine to what extent the Bible is unscientific. A UR author would place all reality within the uniformitarian framework: (a) use the present to

exhibited an optimistic and constructive trend that lasted into the Renaissance and into the twentieth century. Scientists like Leonardo DaVinci, Johann Kepler, and Bernard Riemann have spearheaded geometric natural law-based science.[27]

On the other hand, relativism drives the dynamics that are not conducive to the development of civilizations. Here, relativism is instrumental in diluting standards and requirements that help identify and provide solutions for uncertainty, thus ensuring accuracy and knowledge-base conditional certainty. Historically, relativist world-views have oversimplified reality. Such users prioritize algebraic, reductionist, and subjective views. Naïve realism reveals relativism's true objectives. Such an approach effectively removes any pursuits for qualitative conditional certainty from our awareness. Instead of investments into qualitative infrastructural abundance, increasingly we get incremental austerity directives – to do more with less. In science, economics, and government programs, users go to great lengths to promote uncertainty under its many guises.[28] The trend is to reduce complexity to a hands-on appropriate

---

measure the past; (b) simple-to-complex statistical progression; (c) materialist closed systems. History is set within artificial time landmarks: Stone Age, Bronze Age, and Iron Age. UR writers then select convenient and partial descriptions from the Bible. This allows them to focus on "primitive" limitations that existed during these early Biblical times. They then conduct God psychology by speculating on whether a supernatural being would or could not have done. At the same time, UR writers totally ignore the legal format of the Bible: geometric natural law, precedents, and genealogies which allow dating Biblical events and civilizations. They may speculate about a UR defined supernatural entity but fail to notice psychologically-based scientific selective breeding techniques (see Jacob and his father-in-laws' agreement); record of seven-year droughts, which reflect climatic processes that followed an Ice Age (2000-1500 BC). The Bible may not directly describe the pyramids in Egypt, but we know a great deal about Egyptian ruler's protocol, Joseph's influence on the Empire. We also know the scientific cause-effect relationships in personal, social, and civilization's dynamics – the blessings and curses (Deut. 27-28). In contrast, modern 'scientific' relativism reintroduces practices of failed civilizations - phallic worship appeasement for the masses. It becomes clear that modernists simply provide a UR view and not a scientific one.

[27] http://www.emis.de/classics/Riemann.

[28] Uniformitarian definitions of concepts such as: hypothesis, theory, contaminated, inconclusive, "almost certainty," etc.

technology at the lowest common denominator.

The non-conducive method and approach to civilization promotes that:

(a) All perception is not founded on order and organization but that all is relative; all is in constant state of flux.

(b) Current systems, processes, and rates are the only true measure for all that has happened in the past. In other words, history is viewed through the lens of current processes, standards, and rates. This view includes: oversimplification, appropriate technology, and hands-on evidence (smell the coffee syndrome) - the materialistic nature of the modern thinker.

(c) Seeks the illusive notion of perpetual revolutionary change that unifies plurality at ever lower common denominators.

Failed civilizations, declining nations with economic meltdowns, reflect the conditions that are non-conducive with developing civilizations. Such zero-growth civilizations are characterized by subjectivism, increasing disrespect for human rights, cynicism, slavery, collectivism, genocide, population reduction schemes, and secular policies where court decisions protect variations of phallic worship. Such secularism is evident in the twentieth century's Marxist and Nazi empires. Such systems lead to collectivism. Compare the terms: proletariat - human resources, and the consumer. These stand in stark contrast to the view that man is made in the image of God.

European sixteenth century rationalist and empiricist philosophers concluded that certainty is attainable solely through reason. Empiricism suggested that certainty cannot be attained through what it defined as subjective or irrational divine revelation. Certainty was to be attained through reason since it was believed that the reasoning faculty is not subject to the effects of the Second Law of Thermodynamics. Therefore, reason is the source and fountain of true knowledge and certainty.

In the early stages, this approach led to the various notions that existed during the Age of Enlightenment. Soon after the French Revolution, however, the enlightened view was replaced by a more scientific approach. This new approach reflected uniformitarian, reductionist, and dialectical materialist methods. In addition, this new view stressed relative, modernist, and post-modern methods. In this context, the modernists' duty was to purge the historical knowledge-base of its redundancy. This millennia old classical knowledge-base was to be revised, redefined, and reinterpreted within these post-modernist guidelines.

Today, science has been placed within a new modernist framework. However, the same philosophers noticed that today science had not yet been completely divorced from religion (thus the science versus religion issue). Modernists addressed this issue in terms of a demarcation line. They had to find a way to draw this demarcation line. This line was to be set between science and non-science (i.e., pseudoscience, religion, and cultism).

Among the early 'demarcationists' was John William Draper with his book, *History of the Conflict between Religion and Science* (1874). Soon after came Andrew Dickson White who presented his essay *A History of the Warfare of Science with Theology in Christendom.*[29] Both authors re-interpreted history. They cast religion (specifically Christianity) into a new role. This role was that Christianity has always conducted a war against 'science.' The logical positivist group (Vienna circle) continued this trend of thought. Its members reduced all reality and meaning to statements that can reflect empirical observation. In other words, statements that could not reflect empirical observations were viewed to be beyond physical experience, thus reflecting subjective and meaningless value. Karl Popper corrected this 'verificationist' view by expanding this argument from the level of a scientific statement to one that included a scientific theory. Popper proposed the falsification[30] approach, where the scientific statement or theory would prove to be scientific only if it should be falsifiable. However, it soon became evident that: a) the certainty of non-falsifiable statements also played a vital role in the formulation of scientific ideas; b) that there are very few scientific theories that are anomaly-free – i.e., non-falsifiable; and that c) many examples have been discovered where pseudoscience has been falsifiable, verifiable, and revisable.

In addressing the demarcation line, Paul Feyerabend considered post-modernist and post-structuralist views. His eclectic approach blurred the demarcation line. He noted that history of science shows five trends in the manner in which science has practiced. He discovered that there are no exclusive logical or methodological rules of science that are distinct from sound reasoning. There is no special scientific authority to draw upon. Every scientific procedure had been violated at some time. Science (reasoning) is inseparable from the larger body of human thought and

---

[29] See http://www.cscs.umich.edu/~crshalizi/White/.

[30] See http://www.physics.csufreson.edu/rhall/tamII_intro.html.

inquiry. Science is not entirely empirical in practice or in principle. He pointed to the various branches of pure science where theorizing was not established on any objective foundation that can be verified – e.g., the string theory. In response, many scientists and historians have questioned the value of such extreme skepticism and relativism. Feyerabend's observations, however, had been legitimately documented.[31]

---

[31] Alan B. Spitzer, *Historical Truth and Lies about the Past* (Chapel Hill: University of North Carolina Press, 1996). Keith Jenkins, ed. *'The Post-modern History Reader,'* (London: Routledge, 1997).

2. Scientific Interpretations and Predictions

Proponents of the debate have, during the past sixty years, provided millions of pieces of information. This information came in the form of textbooks, articles, websites, DVDs, conferences, high level public debates, and even court cases. Scientists, policymakers, political activists, and third parties have participated in this debate. All have contributed to the progress, and benefited from this highly informative forum. They all have galvanized modern civilization to its core.

The original debates were set between representatives of uniformitarian materialism (Darwinian evolution, neo-evolution) and creation catastrophists. Two other groups provided secondary highlights – teleological and hybrid views that had affinity to the traditional creation view. The uniformitarian materialist view was an outgrowth of the European sixteenth century rationalistic and empiricist philosophical schools. The creation catastrophist group represented the traditional Christian view of a recent special creation and the Earth's worldwide hydro-tectonic events and effects knowledge base

A recent group has re-introduced the teleological view, which in the light of breakthrough discoveries made with the super high-tech labs; hypothesize an intelligent designer to help them interpret the origin of life evidence.

Our modern society is saturated with the uniformitarian (evolutionary) view in every domain. Young Earth Creation (Creation Science), Intelligent Design and Hybrid Uniformitarianism have an uphill battle to prove their science and scientific methodologies. It is therefore necessary to examine the quality of science that all these schools exercise.

The average American has been extensively exposed to the evolutionary view. The educational system, the media, and journalism promote the uniformitarian interpretation of reality. Similarly, in most cases the public also receive an uniformitarian interpretation of what Creation and Intelligent Design positions due to media and educational saturation. At the same time, in a pluralistic setting, Christianity has significantly been diverted from its original roots. Many religious organizations, denominations and churches have adapted to their new pluralistic environment. Many have speciated into unrecognizable forms e.g., hybrid uniformitarian. This is why the Christian view that is presented in this book may appear unfamiliar to some readers. A historical perspective is necessary to help identify favorable conditions that lead to increasing an accurate knowledge base and the means for addressing uncertainty. Christianity did not emerge in a vacuum. Christianity had been set and competed with a myriad of religions, ideologies and cults; existed in world empires; was subjected to influences and invasions; mediated politics, negotiated among warring parties and survived for two millennia.

Every culture has documented myths of origins. Early Greeks absorbed and developed many fields of inquiry that came from previous civilizations. Greeks searched for tools that improved and confirmed accuracy of knowledge. At the same time, early Greek paganism reflected a historical knowledge base, that recently it has been discovered included links to Biblical characters - iconographic artwork representing Adam (Zeus), Cain (Hephaestos), Noah (Nereus), Nimrod (Hercules), and others.[32]

The Christian Bible, however, contains a unique knowledge base. This documented knowledge base, coupled with holy traditions, contain geometric natural law that documents qualitative geometric solids at the core of creation, laws, judgments, statutes; identifies origins, causes, processes, standards, rates, observations, measurable and testable engineering features, climatic, terrestrial conditions, and qualitative infrastructures. These features allow for the re-construction of workable models; for example, the description and design of Noah's Ark. The ark's design standards, codes and construction reveal that the ark was to withstand global accelerating oceanic tidal waves built up through lunar and solar gravitational influence and tectonic activity (see below for details). The Ark, within legal historical documented evidence has become

---

[32] Robert Bowie Johnson, Jr., *The Parthenon Code,* (New York: Praeger Publishers, 1988); and *Noah in Ancient Greek Art* MD: Solving Light Books, 2006).

a laboratory marker for establishing pre-, during and post-worldwide hydro-tectonic conditions. Earlier, the Genesis six-day Creation reveals an engineering project plan with its scheduled activities, strategic resource loading and utilization, performance measures, forecasting, multiple infrastructural setups, quality control and the five geometric solids (see Figures 21 and 26). Infrastructures align the days with geometric golden mean, energy density values, etc. This approach is evident throughout the Biblical content and its history. Similarly, the Ten Commandments in the Old Testament (Exodus 20) are executive laws (not supervisory rules) within the three-dimensional management model (3DMM). This 3DMM is also encapsulated in the Tabernacle in the Wilderness,[33] and in King Solomon's Tabernacle[34]. These management executive laws do not only identify the Creation week, but amplified in individual, family, group, social, and global laws in terms of forecasted cause and effect 'blessings' and 'curses.'[35] The New Testament also reflects the Old Testament features and standards - the seven-day Creation week where St. Paul writes, 'the God who made the world and everything in it;'[36] and that through Christ all things visible and invisible were made.[37] Paul references the Genesis1:1–2:4 account to identify Jesus Christ as the incarnate God of the Old Testament. Clearly no other ancient or modern document contains any of these unique features, since these other works and worldviews are established upon algebraic and not geometric principles.

The geometric law-coded events, standards, reflect measurable conditions within physical and geometric laws are evident and made conscious throughout Christendom's history. This is a certainty that withstood the competitor's knowledge bases – before flood and after - Mesopotamia, Babylon I and II, Egypt, Assyria, and other civilizations. Competition maintained views of *eternal matter* (steady state) (Greeks), *evolution* (Aristotle, Plato), *cyclical expansion and contraction of the universe* (India), and *quasi-historical mythology* that described a great universal battle between gods. Here the victorious god used the body parts of the defeated gods to create the existing universe (Babylonian Talmud).

---

[33] Exod. 25 - 40. See also, Hebrews 8ff.

[34] 1 Chron. 6.

[35] Deut. 27-28.

[36] Acts 17:24-26.

[37] Acts 14:15.

Within this competitive view of origins, we can see that the first Christian Church fathers maintained a Christian Biblical recent six-day Creation view of the created world. Justin Martyr, circa 100 AD, mentions the six-day Creation in his *Dialogue with Trypho.* Theophilus (169 AD) calculates 5,695 years since Creation in his *To Autolycus.* Origen (185 AD) estimates that the world was not yet 10,000 years. Eusebius (263 AD) mentions that several of the fathers wrote about a recent six-day Creation (*Church History; Nicene and Post Nicene Fathers*). Included Basil (330 AD) mentions the recent six days of Creation in his *On the Hexameron.* Augustine (354 AD) suggests less than 6,000 years in his *The City of God.* This view of a recent divine creation week had been central to the Christian knowledge base foundation for two millennia.

knowledge baseMany modern critics attempt to associate the recent Biblical view of Creation exclusively with that promoted by a fundamentalist Protestant fringe group that speculates about the 'inerrancy' of the Bible. But history shows that a recent Creation view had been a long-standing Christian view. What has occurred since the 1960's is that creationists had updated their scientific model and refined their sophisticated scientific instruments, tools, and procedures, in view of the new data that had been made available during the 1950's. It now became evident that Biblical historical events were supported by the correct interpretation of scientific evidence in geology, paleontology, anthropology, demographics, and genealogies. Now, it was possible to reconstruct and supplement reconstituted archives that had originally been maintained in the library of Alexandria, Egypt, where the Septuagint version of the Old Testament had been translated into Greek. The history from Creation had been meticulously documented through parallel and serial genealogies. This method of tracing one's ancestry had also been common throughout European history. It had been common to see that the identity of peoples and nations had been traced through lineage – specifically royal documented lineages –to Noah and his sons - Shem and Japheth. This can also be seen in the Russian literary archives, calendar of saints, and even in the literary works of non-Christian nations. For example, in Arthur Kostler's book, *The Thirteenth Tribe*, Khazar aristocracy and the majority of its population converted to Talmudic Phariseeism (tenth century AD) trace and document their lineage to Noah's son Japheth.

Biblical historical events, origins, and lineages had been very real and well documented by these early people who lived in the Middle East and throughout Europe. The Biblical historical record provides a reliable guide in areas where other histories either corroborate the Biblical event or simply compromise such evidence through sporadic legendary means.

2.1 Brief History of Scientific Concepts

The modern uniformitarian view can be traced to the works of James Hutton's *Theory of the Earth* (1785, and two volumes, 1795) where the author interpreted geology in terms of 'older' geological formations. In 1811, Georges Cuvier and Alexandre Brogniart developed the 'stratgraphic succession' theory. The theory attempted to help explain Earth's geologic layers. Charles Lyell, in his *Principles of Geology Being an attempt to explain the former Change of the Earth's Surface by Reference to Causes now in Operation*, (1830), continued Hutton's and Cuvier's work and formulated the 'uniformitarian' concept for geology. Today, this uniformitarian view suggests at least three concepts: (1) all scientific work must start from existing conditions, processes, and rates (i.e., the present is the measure for the past); (2) everything progresses through random (chance) slow changes from the simple to complex, from primitive to modern; and that (3) the process is a closed system – it excludes all non-materialistic causes (materialism). These three points had then been expanded from geology and paleontology to the subjects of biology, astronomy, demographics, culture, history, linguistics, and even religion.

In 1942, Julian Huxley proposed an *Evolutionary Synthesis*, which more recently has been updated by E. Mayr and W. B. Provine, eds, *The Evolutionary Synthesis: Perspectives on the Unification of Biology*.[38] This last work lists a five-point strategy for the united subjects under an evolutionary synthesis. He thus provides criteria or assumptions for constructing the uniformitarian / evolutionary scientific model.

The rise of the *modern creation science* initiative should be understood within the context of historical and social events that transpired during the early part of the twentieth century in the United States.

• During the last 250 years, the methods, conclusions, and influence of the uniformitarian-based studies had specifically aimed at reducing certainty, via relativism, in much of the education and seminary curricula in Europe and America. This was evident in the interpretation of history, interpretation of geological, paleontological, and archaeological evidence,

---

[38] Harvard University Press, 1998.

as well as, in the linguistics methodologies, anthropology, oral traditions, and specifically those that focused on the various criticisms of Biblical interpretations. During the past 100 years, various schools of thought emerged to solidify an uniformitarian slant. Examples of these schools of thought include: source criticism, redaction, form, canonical, rhetorical, narrative, psychological, socio-scientific, higher and textual criticism, and modernism and post-modernism. All of these criticisms, which on the surface appeared logical and legitimate, in actuality were designed to specifically reduce Christian certainty via relativism, and 'update' education and seminary curricula in Europe and America with the new strategic objectives. Although this initiative has succeeded in mainstream European and American education, this alarmed the more conservative members and authorities in many Protestant denominations in the United States. They saw a clear anti-Christian secular agenda, such as was becoming evident in the Union of Soviet Socialist Republics and eventually in Nazi Germany.

• The Darwinian notion of 'survival of the fittest' has redesigned the European civilization's moral fiber. This redesign contributed to the selfish and immoral momentum that led up to and existed during World War I.[39] The notions of 'struggle for existence' galvanized not only the Bolshevik revolution in Russia, but also the International Socialist view on what constituted economic foundations, justifications for policy, collectivization programs, and emphasis on behavioral sciences.

• In America these two tendencies led, among other things, to the 1920's Pre-Conference on the Fundamentals of Our Baptist Faith (June 21 and 22, 1920) at Delaware Avenue Church in Buffalo, New York. It is here that the original Baptist Biblical fundamentals were established. This included the view on scriptural inerrancy.[40] Also, during the period that

---

[39] Vernon L Kellogg, "Headquarters Nights," *Atlantic Monthly* (1917); Benjamin Kidd, "Science of Power," in L.W. Levine, *Defender of the Faith William Jennings Bryan* (New York: Oxford University Press, 1965), 261-265.

[40] The term 'fundamentalism' was coined at the Niagara Falls Bible Conference and was used to describe a collection of twelve books by Milton and Lyman Steward, *The Fundamentals* (1910) – see Dr. Terry L. Matthew, *Fundamentalism in Religion 166: Religion in America* (Winston-Salem, NC: Wake Forest University, Fall 1996) (http://www.wfu.edu/~matthetl/perspectives/twentyone.html). By the end of World War I, these views spread throughout the Protestant denominations. The

lead up to World War II in Europe, even though Darwinism had been accepted and even promoted by many of the protestant institutions, the pre-Vatican II Catholic Church and its European-based creation scientists, who had been on the defensive, understood the implications of uniformitarianism. The Catholic Church sanctioned Teilhard the Chardin's evolutionary concepts that led to an Omega Point," and issued encyclicals against modernist activities – see the First Vatican Council's *Humani Generis*; and Pope Pius X's, *Pascendi Domenici Gregis* (*Encyclical On Modernism*), par. 10.[41]

• In 1925, uniformitarianists of various persuasions found an opportunity to act against the religious fundamentalist counter-initiative. They took advantage of what became known as the Scopes Trial in Dayton, Tennessee. The initial issue on trial (the Butler Act) expressed concern for teaching perspectives such as struggle for existence and that man has evolved from primates. These two notions had proved to have had adverse effects on moral issues. However, the undercurrents during court proceedings have helped sway national and international opinions. Journalistic analyses published after the trial - specifically those written by the journalist Henry Louis Mencken of the *Baltimore Sun* – had colored events and distorted the standard practices of objective reporting of court proceedings. Mencken not only misrepresented court proceedings but also the events that surrounded the trial and the roles that the various players and personalities played. Mencken did this to force an alternate purpose. It is interesting to note that these ulterior motives, initiatives, and coloring are played out today in the media, school textbooks, and court proceedings. In 1925, the national and international newspapers (media) transmitted whatever the *Baltimore Sun* reported on the trial during that year. This included the new views that evolution is science, enlightenment, and the hope of all future progress. Religion, and specifically Christianity, is a bigoted entity, a pure emanation of cultism, backwardness, and a throwback into the Dark Ages (pseudoscience).

---

content of the books and other related literature was to reaffirm the original tenants of Protestant Christianity and to defend this against the harmful elements of liberal theology, higher criticism, and Darwinism, which were all based on uniformitarian premises.

[41] See also, J.W.G. Johnson, *Evolution?* (CA: Perpetual Eucharistic Adoration, Inc, 1986); and Gerard J. Keane, *Creation: Rediscovered* (IL: Tan Books and Publishers, Inc., 1999).

Since that time, numerous plays, movies, and theatrical pieces reflected the *Baltimore Sun's* perspective. None of these writers, authors, and producers cared to review the actual documented court proceedings. The *Baltimore Sun's* perspective is the view that is still presented today. These plays, videos, literature, and casual conversations continue to suggest that these are the actual events that transpired during the 1925 Scopes Trial. Few notice however, that among other events, during the Scopes Trial, the prosecution brought into evidence a tooth of a newly discovered Nebraska Man. This was to be scientific evidence for evolution. After the trial, scientists traced the tooth to its original location. It was discovered that the tooth was not from a humanoid but from an extinct pig.

The Scopes Trial events led to several undeniable conclusions. That:

(1) The concept of scientific evolution was a highly financed program that had specific objectives. These objectives were to impact the original American constitutional foundations and the Christian foundations of America.

(2) Science labs will increasingly be staffed by professional establishment scientist. These establishment scientists are the ones who will identify, collect, categorize, quantify, test, filter, and document approved and authorized empirical evidence. They will determine what is deemed to be scientific and pseudoscientific.

(3) Parallel to the professional scientist, there's staffing evidence for ideological, social, and legal activists who market, defend, and are willing to go to extremes in order to ensure the dominance of the establishment's world-view and system.

(4) A governing entity supports and authorizes the content of an exclusive and comprehensive educational curriculum. This entity decides issues only within uniformitarian premises and objectives.

(5) A financed and controlled media guides, promotes, and saturates the audience with an exclusively uniformitarian outlook.

(6) A substitution and replacement program for the original Christianity is maintained through policies of pluralism, which are part of the social re-engineering program within the scope of uniformitarian secular initiatives.

Evolutionists synthesized the various branches of biology, paleontology, and Mendel's genetics under a unified and coordinated evolutionary synthesis. However, the Theory of Evolution was scientifically tested in the lab for the first time in the 1950's, when America invested heavily into scientific research as it competed with

Soviet sciences. This highly budgeted decade produced enormous and made significant strides in the sciences. Enormous volumes of data were gathered, tested, published, and interpreted.

It is also within this context that *modern creation science* was born. Until that point there were many European and American science writers, scientists, and American fundamentalist science writers[42] who had formed creation and counter-evolution organizations[43]. However, modern creation science was born in 1961 when Dr. Henry M. Morris and John C. Whitcomb coauthored the books, '*The Genesis Flood*,' (Institute of Creation Research, CA, 1961) offered a 'creation scientific model' that provided an alternate interpretation of the voluminous empirical data that had been gathered during the 1950's. Furthermore, during the 1970's and early 1980's Dr. H. M. Morris, together with Dr. Duane T. Gish published and debated evolution scientists on the contrasting interpretation, prediction and results of the increasing empirical data. The creation scientific model tested geological and paleontological evidence and proved that the Creation Scientific Model provided and predicted better results and explanations of data than that offered by the Evolution Scientific Model. It became evident that the Biblical Old Testament is not only a document of legends, fables, and moral teachings; instead, it is also a unique source of verifiable historical events; contains quantitative value and information that has covered a period of 4,000+ years. Henry Morris demonstrated

---

[42] Swiss-American paleontologist, Louis Agassiz (1807-1873), instead of evolution, proposed that rock fossils suggested the evidence for several catastrophes with divine re-creative intervention at various stages. George McCready Price (1870-1963) continued to develop flood geology view. G.K. Chesterton, in his *The Everlasting Man*, developed creationist ideas and criticized the flaws of evolution. Harold W. Clark described "catastrophism" in his *Back to Creationism* (Angwin, CA: Union Press, 1929).

[43] William Bell Riley founded the "Anti-Evolution League of America" 1924, and was supported by William Jennings Bryan. The 'Religion and Science Association' was formed from by a Wheaton College professor in 1935, which soon fell apart because the three founding creationists viewed three versions of Creation (day-age, gap theory, six-day creation young earth view). Another group, 'Deluge Geology Society,' that published the Bulletin of Deluge Geology and Related Science from 1941-1945, and the 'Creation-Deluge Society' faltered from a similar division. The American scientific affiliation had undergone various changes and eventually supported the old earth creation model.

that, when the original Biblical text is properly interpreted, this documentation can provide significant and key verifiable details for a recent worldwide hydro-tectonic-based flood whose effects can be identified, described, and predicted in the sciences of geology, paleontology, and other scientific disciplines.

2.2 Evolution/Uniformitarian
and the Creation/Catastrophe Scientific Models

Scientists who construct, interpret, and predict scientific data from the *evolution scientific model* include the uniformitarian assumptions: (1) begin with existing physical, chemical, laws of motion, processes, rates, and observations; (2) assume that statistical (chance) processes qualitatively progress from the simple to complex or from primitive to modern; and (3) reconstruct qualitative changes within a materialist concept, i.e., excluding nonmaterial causalities or interventions. In other words, instead of prioritizing and relying on actual historical evidence, evolution scientists attempt to reconstitute a past and a history of origins that is based on the three uniformitarian doctrinal assumptions.

Scientists who construct, interpret, and predict scientific data from the *creation scientific model* also include the same scientific data, evidence, and information as those who use the uniformitarian assumptions[44] but include the creation scientific assumptions, interpretation, and predictions: (a) begin with current to millennial historical evidence as documented and corroborated with the history of the Christian Bible; (b) use existing empirical scientific evidence (all branches), discoverable physical natural laws (e.g., motion, gravitation, biogenesis, geometric), and biological complexity as it adapts to challenging and challenging environments. Recognizing the distinctions between the five change levels: copy, adaptation, re-engineering, redesign; reinvent; and (c) a documented record for three recent historical singularities:

---

[44] Henry M. Morris distinguishes three creationist approaches based on purpose, application and audience (see http://www.icr.org). Creation can be viewed in terms of: "(1) Scientific creationism (no reliance on biblical revelation, utilizing only scientific data to support and expound the creation model); (2) Biblical creationism (no reliance on scientific data, using only the Bible to expound and defend the creation model); (3) Scientific biblical creationism (full reliance on biblical revelation but also using scientific data to support and develop the creation model)."

(1) Divine special creation (prime contractor), which is rationally reflected through geometric natural law. This creation process followed a specific timeline[45] - beginning with the creation of time itself.

(2) A drop of at least one energy-density cycle on the universal infrastructural cone.[46]

(3) Events of an initial, global, hydro-tectonic catastrophe of short duration (twelve months) that was followed by secondary, multiple mega-environmental adjustments in areas of the atmosphere, weather, geology/tectonics, sea levels, volcanic activities, an ice age that began 500 years after the global flood ended, etc. These mega-changes are identified and coded as geologic and paleontological observable and measureable evidence.[47]

A key purpose for the evolution and creation scientific models is to anticipate or make predictions. Based on the criteria in the models' designs, and with the use of the same available, observable, measurable, and reproducible data and conditions, both the evolution and creation scientists can now interpret and make predictions:

Figure 2. Comparison Scientific Predictions: Uniformitarian - Creation.

UNIFORMITARIAN/EVOLUTION	CREATION SCIENCE
ASSUMPTIONS	
Scientific predictions derived from uniformitarian, materialistic, reductionist constructed past and present rules for interpreting empirical data.	Three historically documented singularities, geometric natural law that account for life's original complexity. while the third singularity is evident through empirical scientific methods
TIME	
Prediction: Slow random/chance process requires billions of years to bring the Big Bang events to present conditions.	**Prediction:** Creation events within the context of geometric natural law identifies the creation of time and provides a timeline record for all creation, three universal singularities that affect directly and indirectly all temporal estimations of age and provide evidence for recent age of Creation between 6000 to 12,400 years. (John Morris, *'The Young Earth: The Real History of the Earth – Past, Present and Future,'* Master Books, AR,
Prediction: Time/age of fossils measured via	

---

[45] Gen. 1:1 - 2:4 – documents the perspective of the prime contractor.

[46] Gen. 3, specifically 3:17 "…cursed is the ground on thine account…."

[47] Gen. 6ff.

geologic column, which results from the slow processes of localized sedimentary or episodic catastrophic events (e.g., meteoric impact).

Prediction: Simple creatures found at lower sedimentary layers, and species that are *more complex* found at increasingly higher layers.

Prediction: Various chemical dating methods can ascertain long ages

2007, p. 35)[48]

Prediction: Geologic timeline (column) reflects not long uniformitarian ages but the effects of sedimentation occurring during an initial global hydro-tectonic mega-catastrophic event, with subsequent secondary self-adjusting catastrophes over hundreds of years. Under such conditions geologic sedimentary layers and the fossilization of living creatures' mobility capacities as they attempt to escape flood conditions – slower creatures will be buried first (at lower strata), and faster ones under sedimentary layers at increasingly higher layers. Geologic sedimentary formations are a record of the speed of creatures relative to their environmental conditions, rather than the age of the fossilized creatures.

Prediction: Significant inconsistencies in the chemical dating methods that compromise every dating method, particularly when these methods are compared with each other.

GEOLOGY AND PALEONTOLOGY

Prediction: Geologic column and the fossil record reveal fossilized life forms that developed over generations from simple to complex structures – net basic increase in complexity over time, with unlimited vertical change, with unlimited vertical change.

Prediction: Simple to complex fossilized life forms found in areas

Prediction: Geologic strata, sedimentation and the fossil record reveal recent events of an initial global hydro-tectonic catastrophe and secondary environmentally self-adjusting mega-catastrophes: evident in geology, paleontology, hydrography, atmosphere, ice age, demographics, etc.

Prediction: Geologic and paleontological evidence will reveal that life appeared fully formed (e.g., difference between the so-called pre-/Cambrian age). Clear and sharp boundaries will separate original taxonomic groups.

Prediction: There will be a total absence of intermediate/ transitional forms in the earth strata.[49]

Prediction: Evidence of polystrate tree trunk positions (allegedly standing across billions of years)

---

[48] John Morris, '*The Young Earth: The Real History of the Earth – Past, Present, and Future*' (AR: Master Books, 2007), 35. This document also includes a CD Power Point presentation.

[49] Some evolutionists bring evidence for bird-reptile transitional species; however, such evidence becomes questionable when fossils of fully formed birds are found at lower sedimentary levels.

around the world.

Prediction: Voluminous amounts of intermediate / transitional forms leading from one species to the next will be evident.

are the result of rapid sedimentation under hydro-tectonic effects – this rapid process is currently observed in the events following mount St. Helens volcanic effects.

Prediction: Identified symptoms of 'gigantism' among plant, animal and human fossils when geologic layers reveal specific effects of the initial mega-hydro-tectonic effect.

MICRO & MACRO CHANGE MECHANISMS

Prediction: Universal common ancestry extending from atom to living cell and through various branching of the standard phylogenetic Tree to the emergence of man.

Prediction: Although evolutionary change is too small to observe, measure, predict and reproduce, it can be used to estimate that random beneficial mutations among groups in challenging environments will allow groups of species to not only to adapt (micro-evolution) to their environment, but also change their species (speciation – macro-evolution) over time and environment.

Prediction: Appearance of new species demonstrates new and addition of qualitative infor-mation.

Prediction: Appearance of greater variety of new species.

Prediction: The created original kinds/ syngameons 'species' will vary due to environmental challenges but speciation will be limited within each kind / species. The taxonomical tree simply identifies groups and families, not their change from one species into another.

Prediction: 'Beneficial' random mutations must overcome the significantly greater volume of hazardous mutations. An organism's security programs help prevent or remove anomalous mutations. Biological system is programmed for adaptive change (micro-evolution), but not for higher infrastructural change that involves re-engineering of supervisory systems and re-design (i.e., macro-evolution) unless such 'micro-change' has been programmed into the genetic code (e.g., caterpillar to butterfly).

Prediction: Any significant environmentally challenged adaptive change demonstrates a loss and not a gain of information. All of today's species are descendants of a few original species 'proto-types' - syngameons

Prediction: Evidence shows for the high potential of gradual extinction of species rather than their rise in complexity.

LIFE

Prediction: the axiomatic concept of abiogenesis suggests that life

Prediction: Evidence of biogenesis – is a law that shows that life comes from life. Paleontological evidence shows that all life appears fully formed,

originated from non-life.[50]   and then adapts within the scope of its programmed

---

[50] The general notion of 'spontaneous combustion' (e.g., aphids arise from dew on plants, fleas form from putrid matter, mice from dirty hay, crocodiles from rotting logs at the bottom of lakes and rivers) had been questioned and challenged by: physician Girolamo Fracastoro, who theorized about epidemic diseases caused by nonliving 'spores' (1546); Sir Thomas Browne, *Enquiries into Very many Received Tenets and Commonly Presumed Truths* (1646); Robert Hooke who drew microorganisms ('cells') (1665); Anthony van Leeuwenhoek discovered microorganisms (1676); Francesco Redi proved in 1668 that no maggots emerged in meat if flies were prevented from laying eggs. But it was Louis Pasteur in the nineteenth century who conclusively proved, through conclusive experiments, that living organisms did not arise spontaneously from nonliving matter. But Charles Darwin in 1871, by promoting uniformitarianism, described a 'chemical evolutionary' view (i.e., reintroducing a 'spontaneous combustion' notion). See Francis Darwin, ed., '*The Life and Letters of Charles Darwin*,' including an autobiographical chapter. London: John Murray, 1871), v. 3, p. 18 (http://darwin-online.org,uk/content/frameset?viewtype=texst&itemID=F1452.3&pageseq=30) Since then there have been almost thirty hypotheses on how life could have emerged from nonlife: A.I.Oparin, *The Origin of Life on Earth* (chemical evolution); J.B.S. Halden (pre-biotic oceans giving rise to biopoiesis or biopoesis, life from self-replicating nonliving molecules; Sidney W. Fox (peptide structures); Manfred Eigen and Peter Schuster (transient stages between molecular chaos and self-replicating hypercycle in a preiotic soup); Gunter Wachtershauser (iron-sulfer world theory, 1980s); Morse and MacKensie elaborated on Halden's view; Stanley Miller suggested colder if not freezing conditions where life originated; Steen Rasmussen, Craig Venture have tried their hand at a 'top-down approach.' The famous Stanley Miller and Harold Urey's primordial soup theory, followed by the deep sea vent theory. Zachary Adam considered tidal processes and radioactive grains of uraniums on primordial beaches; homochirality was to address the left-handedness of handamino acids and left right-handedness of nucleic acid sugars; Martin and Russel's views of self-organization and replication with abiotic molecules under proper conditions. Then there were the genes first or metabolism first models (iron-sulfur and others); Leslie Orgel re-examined the limitations and improbability of all previous research and proposed another hypothetical complex bio-chemical formula in *Self-Organizing Biochemical Cycles* (http://dx.doi.org/10.1073/pnas.220406697). The 'bubble theory" (J.Panno, *The Cell: Evolution of the First Organism*, www.cogs.susx.ac.uk/users/ctf20/dphil_2005/publications.htm). Thomas Gold suggested that primitive life developed deep under the surface of the Earth (http://www.microscopy-uk.org.uk/index/.html?). Richard Dawkins suggested two views: autocatalysis (simple molecular replicators) described in *The Ancestor's Tale*, Julius Rebek's

structure.

Dating methods is a key issue of contention in the evolution versus creation debate. The various dating methods are addressed through this book. One example to consider are the comparative results of the various dating methods - radioisotopic, uranium-thorium-lead, and potassium-argon - do not provide uniform or similar ages. Depending on which of the two or three dating methods that a scientist may use, based on the assumptions made, the results among the dating methods for the same rock samples may vary by millions of years. We can also consider the case of the relatively unweathered condition of the Moon's surface. When the Apollo missions brought back lunar surface samples, the test evidence: (a) helped falsify the four, major, evolutionary theories about the Moon's formation;[51] (b) presented some puzzling conclusions when the uranium-thorium-lead and the potassium-argon methods had been used; (c) discovered younger rocks were encased inside older rocks; (d) showed that the common theories and assumptions attached to the various dating methods did not necessarily lead to conclusive, reliable, and probable results, and led, in many cases, to contradictory results.

Some evolution debaters challenged creation scientists by asking to 'just provide conclusive evidence of clear human footprints in rocks that are billions of years old.' Apparently, such evidence would be sufficient for evolutionists to reconsider the evolutionary dating methods. Creationists who advocate a recent history of the universe do not subscribe to the evolutionary geologic column, and it is easy for them to predict and accept that such footprint evidence does exist.[52] When such evidence is produced, it is: (a) never seriously investigated scientifically by establishment scientists because such evidence contradicts the a priori uniformitarian premise; or (b) it is explained away, dismissed offhand, shelved in a museum never to be seen again; or (c) ignored, never

---

experiments; and the clay theory by A. Graham Cairns-Smith. Other scientists (Francis Crick, Jason Dworkin) proposed extraterrestrial origins (near Mars, comets) for life on Earth. And other hypotheses: lipid world, polyphosphate model, PAH world, and multiple genesis. Although the sensation of these theories has been great, the results were unsuccessful or highly inconclusive (unrepeatable).

[51] Conference convened in Kona, Hawaii, Ibid.

[52] See Appendix 2 of this book..

published; finally (d) may be accessible only to establishment authorized personnel and no one else.

At the same time, there are at least a hundred other dating methods that are hardly ever considered in evolutionary scientific literature. These other dating methods include: rate of erosion of continents (e.g., all continents can be washed into the ocean within fifteen million years), the 50,000 volcano remains appear to be recent according to their structural makeup, sodium input-output into the oceans. Then there's the relative strength of electromagnetic fields around the Earth and other planets, explanations for comets, which have a predictable life; helium buildup in the atmosphere; and the missing evidence for meteoric orbit deflections that should orbit the sun at various angles to the solar system's plane, etc.

3. Conceptual Formulae

It was only during the 1950s that the theory of evolution had been tested scientifically in the lab for the first time[53]. Prior to this, for over 100 years, biologists, archeologists, and geologists, as well as the 'social Darwinists' and eugenicists, grouped and positioned themselves to define the scope of a new Darwinian scientific approach. The original pre-Darwinian evolutionists[54] included: Herbert Spencer (survival of the

---

[53] Michael Denton, *Evolution: Theory in Crisis* (Bethesda, MD: Adler & Adler, Publishers, 1986) 79. See also, E. Mayr and W.B. Provine, eds., *The Evolutionary Synthesis*, 54ff. Mayr & Provine provide an early history of genetic theory. On the one hand, evolutionists capitalized on Mendel's hereditary principles to theorize their evolutionary process, but Galton, de Vries, Johannsen, and Bateson saw that selection of small fluctuating differences could not move a population beyond original limits of variability. This contrast of views still exists today in the evolution versus creation and intelligent design.

[54] James Hutton's, *Theory of the Earth* (1785, and two volumes, 1795) is perhaps the first work where interpretations of 'older' geological formations appear. In 1811, Georges Cuvier and Alexandre Brogniart developed the 'stratographic succession' theory to explain Earth's layers. Charles Lyell, *Principles of Geology Being an attempt to explain the former Change of the Earth's Surface by Reference to Causes now in Operation* (1830) followed suit and formulated the 'uniformitarian' concept for geology. Soon, however, uniformitarianism was applied to every other branch of science, history, language development, and even social and political science. The uniformitarian doctrine suggests that one can only start with conditions, physical laws, and rates of change that exist today. Then use these to reconstruct past events. Since current rates of change are slow, and organic change is to be seen in terms of small incremental chance mutations, origins of current reality must include long periods of history in order to accommodate chance (relative statistical progressive methods) to work itself out to the existing conditions.

fittest), Jean Baptiste Lamark (inheritance of acquired characters), and Thomas Malthus (population densities and economics), and they have debated the concepts. It is, however, upon Charles Darwin's natural selection of the species and his followers such as Francis Galton (eugenics) and others who launched the momentum that went beyond geology and biology into all other branches of human endeavor. This progressivist thrust has not only drawn economists such as Karl Marx (struggle of the classes), but also reflected the influence of the eighteenth and nineteenth century philosophers such as Georg W.F. Hegel (dialectics to the ideal/mind), Ludwig Feuerbach (humanized Hegelianism), Henri L. Bergson (creative evolution), and Friedrich Nietzsche (will to power & death of God). Each in turn influenced the others; for example, Nietzsche's foundation branched out to Karl Jung's psychiatry and to the politics of Adolf Hitler (superior versus inferior and parasitic races).

During the early twentieth century, biologists attempted to synthesize several biological specialties under the Darwinian theory of evolution. During the period 1918 – 1932, population geneticists synthesized natural selection with Mendelian genetics. Julian Huxley in his work, *Evolution: The Modern Synthesis,* (1942) documented activities, information, and participating members who from the 1930s and 1940s created the new evolutionary synthesis. This group included R.A. Fisher, Theodosius Dobzhansky, Sewall Wright, Ernst Mayr, George Gaylord Simpson, and other synthesizers. This and similar groups recognized the limitations and uncertainty that the Darwinian theory posed. To remedy this, they defined all terms within the uniformitarian scope. They explored the mechanical, biological, and process alternatives, and formulated an uniformitarian model. This model was to be flexible enough to allow them to collect, describe, filter, interpret, and predict data and information in scientific terms. This allowed them to establish a knowledge-base for further application. This approach had been applied to the definition of proteins and the interpretation of forensic evidence, and definition of species. However, during that time, this evolutionary endeavor also weighed into the implementation of dangerous social engineering projects and techniques such as those conducted in Soviet Russia and Nazi Germany. Each brought dire consequences.

During the 1950s, scientific investigative and experimental strategies, techniques, and tools produced a vast amount of empirical data and information. This data allowed the scientific community to test their scientific models and the derived or implied predictions. The results allowed scientists to adjust their foundational premises. Having received funds to significantly upgrade and staff their labs, scientific results led to the emergence of neo-evolutionary views.[55] These neo-evolutionists went beyond the classical Darwinian ideas of natural selection and gradualism. Neo-evolutionists explored the DNA and genetics through mathematical models, kin selection, altruism, and speciation. Here attempts were made to identify biological levels at which evolution (natural selection of species) occurred. Some hypothesized that the gene is the only true unit of selection (Richard Dawkins, *The Selfish Gene*). Dawkins suggested a wide variety of cross-species migration - a progressive movement across up to five infrastructural levels among the species. The interpretation of the geologic data in this view was to support evidence for uniformitarian, progressive, qualitative, and interrelated (linked) patterns (e.g., homology and cladistic studies)[56].

3.1 The Neo-Evolutionist Formula

Neo-evolutionists updated and positioned their modern evolutionary synthesis[57] as a strategic view. The strategy includes five basic theses:

Here the conclusion was that evolutionary principles and phenomenon can be substantiated and explained through known genetic mechanisms and processes.

Evolutionary principles imply small incremental genetic changes. Natural selection directs these genetic changes. Such selection includes geographical separation, isolation, and extinction. These lead to speciation and not saltation (leaps)[58]

The change mechanism - no matter how small - is caused through environmental phenotypal selection and not through, genetic drift.[59]

---

[55] E. Mayr and W.B. Provine, eds., *The Evolutionary Synthesis*, Ibid.

[56] Michael Denton, *Evolution: Theory in Crisis*, 328ff.

[57] E. Mayr and W.B. Provine, eds., *The Evolutionary Synthesis, Ibid.*

[58] Niles Eldredge and Stephen Jay Gould, "Punctuated equilibria: an alternative to phyletic gradualism," in T.J.M. Schopf, ed., *Models in Paleobiology* (San Francisco: Freeman Cooper, 1972), reprinted in Niles Eldredge, *Time Frames* (Princeton: Princeton University Press, 1985).

[59] T. Dobzhansky and O. Pavlovsky, "An experimental study of interaction between genetic drift and natural selection," *Evolution* 11:311-319 (1957).

Natural population that carries genetic diversity also drives evolution. Ecological factors (e.g., niche occupation, barriers to the gene flow) affect natural selection in the wild.

Historical observations from different levels in paleontology and extrapolations from micro to macro-evolution, and not empirical data, are sufficient to help explain the evolutionary process. This would not necessarily mean a constant rate of changes (gradualism).

Evolutionists agree on each of the five strategic basic points of the modern evolutionary synthesis. These points reflect objectives, strategy, policy, procedures, and rules and regulations and the very nature of the neo-evolutionists' scientific direction, defense, and output. The five points also show that evolutionists use:

• Genetic 'mechanisms' and 'processes' that are limited to mechanical, organic, and possibly process models and do not predict information software, nano-robotic level evidence at the chromosomal nano-engineering levels.[60] Evolutionists must explain evolution's micro and macro-changes, not through indirect scientific conditions while using tools that are applied to larger or bulkier systems, but use tools for information sub-chromosomal management levels.[61] Sub-microscopic magnitudes and information technology would affect all modern synthesis' points.

• The five points do not empirically address macro-change or transpacific evolution. Scientific testing must foresee cross-informational infrastructures[62].

• Comparative anatomy, such as the analogous resemblance between existing, fossilized, and intermediate forms (limbs and vestigial organs), are not really limited to single interpretation or explanations. For example, Beverly Halstead affirmed that no species can be considered ancestral to any other[63].

---

[60] Michael Denton, *Evolution: Theory in Crisis*, 79.

[61] Summary: http://en.wikipedia.org/wiki/Natural_selection

[62] E. Mayr, *Animal Species and Evolution* (Cambridge: Harvard University Press, 1963.) Mayr includes geneticist Goldschmidt, paleontologist Schindewolf, and zoologists Jeannel, Cuenot, and Cannon, among those who also maintained that neither evolution within species nor geographic speciation could explain the phenomena for "macro-evolution," page 351 in the 1970 edition.

[63] B. Halstead, "Halstead's Defense Against Irrelevancy," *Nature* 292 (1981):

• As stated above, numerous theories have been proposed for natural selection - genetic mutation mechanics and processes, but simulation processes conducted in the lab still do not provide reliable or valid measurements. Nor do such techniques help improve predictions. Such simulations must go beyond linear and adaptive change. These must account for up to five categories of change (copy, adaptation, re-engineering, redesign, invention) and various levels of their supervisory infrastructures.

The basic neo-evolution methodology and data relationships are summarized in the following formula:

$$\frac{C + M + T + V}{L + E + R} = A + K + S + P$$

C = Chance (e.g., genetic mutation, flow, mechanisms)
M = Matter
T = Time
V = Environmental stress
E = Uniformitarianism
L = Relativism
R = Reductionism
A = Simple (primitive) to complex (natural selection)
 (across five infrastructural change levels: micro-/macro-evolution)
K = Knowledge-base (materialism, uniformitarianism)
S = Standards
P = Scientific Process (evolutionary realism) (dialectical materialism)

This neo-evolution model formula is compared with those of the creation and intelligent design scientific models below.

Looking at this evolutionary formula, some scientists as early as the 1960s and later in the 1980s sought to provide alternate interpretations of the scientific data. The evolution formula had at least four inherent theoretical weaknesses. Present conditions, standards, and rates are not at all representative of what might have existed in the past. There is evidence that conditions and structures in the past had been much more robust than they are today. It is premature to scientifically consider that a closed materialistic system is the only alternative or source for scientific evidence.

403-04..

The earlier group of scientists recognized these limitations of the evolution formula. The new generation of creation scientists did three things: (1) they re-examined the many aspects of the scientific method, scientific assumptions, scope, evidence, data and structures;[64] (2) they participated in medium-to-high level public debates with evolutionists. During these debates the results of the two scientific models were compared; and (3) the Institute of Creation Research (ICR) scientists published genuine and serious scientific research.[65]

During the 1970s and 1980s, the evolutionists re-examined their positions and repositioned themselves on many scientific points.

3.2 The Creation Formula

As seen above, neo-evolution scientists provided five biology-based points through their evolutionary modern synthesis. If creation scientists were to provide their own biology-based creation modern synthesis points and run it parallel with that of the evolutionist synthesis, the creation modern synthesis would run something as follows:

Creation principles and phenomena can best be substantiated and explained through the cellular genetic infrastructural and information technology within each species at the chromosome level in life forms. This discovery has been discovered and promoted by the intelligent design group.

Living species provide evidence for 'preprogrammed' capability to copy and adapt to/within environmental conditions within the specie scope. Differentiation from a prototype or parent provides evidence for the species' ability to retain and replicate genetic information and to adapt to environmental conditions within the preprogrammed genetic scope. At each stage of change, there is evidence of a loss and not a gain of genetic information. In other words, it is inconceivable that a collection of all of

---

[64] Example: Dwain Gish, 'The Fossils Still Say No!' Both Dr. Dwain Gish and Dr. Henry Morris of the Institute of Creation Research (www.icr.org) have led the high profiled and highly successful evolution-creation debates during the late 1970s and 1980s.

[65] RATE (Radioisotopes and the Age of the Earth), see www.ICR.org, "Thousands...Not Billions" and others. Also, John Baumgardner, at Los Alamos (New Mexico) National Laboratory from 1984, was expert in the design of computer models for planetary catastrophes, Earth's 3-D computer simulation of plate tectonics movement (funded by NASA).

today's species types can be repackaged genetically to reflect the original cat species or syngameon. It is evident today, that after multiple generations, too much genetic information is being lost each time a branching of the species occurs. So much so that is has been estimated that within 300 generation, a species becomes extinct due to the accumulated genetic noise.

Natural selection doesn't exceed inherited infrastructural scopes. Change does not cross infrastructural barriers/ levels in areas that require infrastructural re-engineering, redesign, or invention.

Populations prove that the species' genetic uniformity is maintained. Changes in supervisory infrastructural systems (conversion processes) must also must be considered. Multiple perfect supervisory conversion processing qualitative changes (re-engineering, redesign, invention) exist between the closest related species (e.g., snakes and lizards). It is not enough to draw similarities between physiological features. Such an approach is artistic at best. Trillions of qualitative changes must be accounted for empirically.

The creation scientific model provides much better interpretation and predictions in areas of paleontology and geology. These reflect recent results and effects of initial global mega-catastrophic hydro-tectonic events that cause rapid upheavals and rapid sedimentation and fossilization of organic structures. The apparent 'ages' (e.g., 'geologic column')[66] do not record the history of events but mark event sequences that had formed during recent mega-catastrophic and its post-adjustment period.[67]

These five creation synthesis basic points will suggest that:

• Genetics information, software, and infrastructural levels need to be addressed empirically. With greatly refined laboratory tools this can be achieved with greater precision. It is here that true science is in the works. How does information software work? What are the 'engineering codes?' What are the infrastructures (mother boards, architectures)? This is where true science lies.

• The creation model doesn't require a chance-based (statistical) relative progress, though an analysis of infrastructural and change levels that are built into life structures are necessary areas of scientific study. Mistakes, errors, and mutations occur but are here identified for what they are –

---

[66] http://en.wikipedia.org/wiki/Geologic_column.

[67] http://www.icr.org.

anomalies in complex systems. A study in this area will identify how programming change affects all cellular management systems and how self-maintenance, repair, and self-correcting processes work. Some adaptations lead to extreme change within a species (e.g., domesticated pigs escaping into the wild very quickly change at their cellular and morphological levels). Such a change never leads to initially non-programmed infrastructural (species) re-engineered and redesigned change. To what degree is the genetic information capable to change?

The creation scientific model is designed to process all existing, observable, and measurable data that the evolutionary scientific model does. Yet, instead of interpreting and making prediction of this data in terms of a billions of years geologic column and through the perception of simple to complex and matter to man statistical progression, the creation scientist interprets and makes predictions of this data in terms of recent emergence of life, and global hydro-tectonic catastrophic events that are measured in terms of only thousands of years.

The original scientific method is designed to convert uncertainty to certainty. This decision-making and problem-solving (DMPS) process can be used to identify the key difference between the evolution and creation scientific model. The key difference appears in: (a) the range of alternatives (options) scientists of both models consider; (b) role and application of filters (criteria, priorities, weighing); and (c) theoretical closed or open systems.

In other words, the evolution model focuses on materialistic / naturalistic and reductionist options, filtered through the closed system of the uniformitarian priorities. Whereas the creation model describes a greater variety of options: matter, geometric natural law, and search for knowledge-base accuracy. Also, provides filters that are derived from the legal historical documented record as represented in the original Christian Bible and its corroborating verifiable evidence.

What does this legal historical document represent? Upon closer analysis it provides a unique strategy, techniques, and foundations. The legal aspect is expressed in geometric natural law and the context of a covenantal format between the eternal Lord God and the righteous who form the covenantal bound. The terms and conditions, precedents, lives of men, patriarchs, prophets, and kings whose genealogy provides a history that can be reconstituted scientifically. This reconstituted history begins with a geometrically based creation of all reality. It contains timelines and supervisory infrastructures that reflect geometric natural law. It contains three recorded initial universal singularities.

Singularity 1: Divine creation where the Creator personally writes the creation events (Genesis 1:1 to 2:14), the description containing unique features depicting geometric natural law[68].

Singularity 2 Soon after perfection had been established (energy-density at the highest infrastructural qualitative conic level – i.e., Singularity (1), the man, Adam, records[69] that within four days after his creation and eleven days after the first day of Creation[70], Adam, who had been granted legal chief executive officer (CEO) decision-making responsibilities over all of Creation by the prime contractor/Creator, became enmeshed in decision-making issues that brought about imperfection. This imperfection affected all that was under the CEO's responsibilities - resulting in the drop of the original energy-density level to a lower infrastructural level, thus deforming all space-time-matter parameters. This left all Creation starve for energy[71]. This shackled all life forms with the task of maintaining conservative processes (whether through pre-programming at the sub-chromosomal information/nanobot

---

[68] See Part 2 for details.

[69] Gen.3, specifically verse 17 "cursed [is] the ground."

[70] Various authorities have presented ways of interpreting Biblical chronology. To minimize potential sectarian, denominational, post-/modernist (uniformitarian) influences, this book will present the most straight forward approach – the Christian Bible reflects a clear legal historical structure based on geometric natural law. This approach may in some cases resemble or parallel some "inerrancy" interpretations – a substitute for the removal of geometric natural law. This approach will diverge from mainstream interpretations in areas where management (3DMM), historical family lineages are traced, Christian historical, and other issues are brought forth (DMPS, change management, etc.), and issues of geometric natural law identified. With regard to textual examples – the difference between the first week (seven days) of Creation (Gen. 1:1 to 2:4) and the second week of Creation (beginning with the formation of Eden, creation of Adam, and to his expulsion from the Garden of Eden), clearly, the second week parallels events that occur during the Passover week (passion week) – second week in the month of Abib. It is during this Passover week that Jesus Christ fulfilled, "repaired," and "paid" for all errors committed in Eden - day-by-day and hour by hour.

[71] There's an interesting passage about the restoration of all of Creation from the effects of the second singularity in Rom. 6:18-22.

level, through instinct, skills, knowledge development, sciences, and technology) in order to postpone death to the furthest point in the future.[72]

Singularity 3 - About 1,656 years after the events of singularity (2), there occurred an initial super-mega, global, hydro-tectonic, catastrophic event of relatively short duration (e.g., twelve months). This event was followed by several lesser self-adjustment mega-catastrophic events of longer duration. Here the lesser mega-hydro, mega-weather, thermal, ice age events also included air pressure halved, diminished electromagnetic gauss strengths, and the rise of sea levels. This left a secondary record and evidence upon the surface of the Earth. These secondary events are preserved in geology, paleontology, archeology, astronomy, and demographics, and other.

Needless to say, those who postulate and extrapolate their views from the uniformitarian view will never be able to guess the existence, effect, and interpretation of the three singularities. They will assume that existing and current processes, rates, and events are the scientific standards. Without realizing it, evolutionists create axioms and theorems that are established within an exclusively impoverished economy of space-time-energy that was affected by the second singularity.

The basic creation methodological formula is summarized as:

$$\frac{C+T+I+V}{L+E+R} = A+K+S+P$$

C = Three historical singularities: special creation, universal infrastructural energy-density drop, global catastrophe

T = Time - affected by three singularities (C), (R) recorded legal documents

I = Five infrastructural change level design in living organisms

V = Environmental stress

L = Geometric natural law

E = Authoritative legal historic documentation

R = Geologic and paleontological evidence

A = Adaptation to environment (two infrastructural change capabilities to adapt to the environment)

---

[72] This time frame is calculated based on the historical chronology of Biblical patriarchs.

K = Knowledge-base (certainty)
S = Standards, codes (certainty)
P = Verifiable lawful scientific process to resolve uncertainty

During the late 1970s and 1980s, the evolutionists and creationists held numerous high and mid-level public debates on university campuses across the United States and other countries. Eventually, the evolutionist school discouraged these debates because of their poor performance during their presentations. One of the reasons why the creation scientists were successful in these debates is because there had been many honest and dedicated scientists who, while working under the evolutionary umbrella, had been conducting objective scientific research and publishing thousands of articles and books that described empirical data that led to potentially various interpretations and conclusions other than those promoted by the evolutionary school. Many of these scientists simply went where scientific data led them. The Institute of Creation Research (www.icr.org) published a book entitled, *That Their Words May Be Used Against Them.* It included at least 3,000 such articles in all disciplines. During these public evolution-creation debates, many of these objective articles had been presented by the creation debaters. Needless to say, a decade of such debates spurred much change and strategic and tactical repositioning among the evolutionists.

During mid-1980s, however, with huge investments into the scientific laboratories at the universities and research laboratories, there clearly began to emerge some paradoxical evidence in all areas. New high-tech optics brought discoveries not only in areas of DNA and RNA but even at the sub-chromosome levels where information and nano-robotic high-tech software and engineering were clearly evident. It became clear that at the living cellular level, cells were not bio-chemical and only DNA/RNA functionalities, but that human, animal, and plant cells, at the nano-technology level, there existed a world with complete and the most sophisticated software programming, engineering codes, and standards, all functioning on a scale equivalent to a New York City. This led many scientists to seek better scientific explanations than those provided by traditional neo-evolution models.

With this introduction of super-high-tech labs during the late 1980s and 1990s, many neo-evolutionist scientists adapted what they could under their scientific model but other scientists began to seek alternate explanations for the mechanical, organic, and process models that prescribed explanations rather than designed new explanations for new scientific discoveries. In view of this mind-boggling evidence, some neo-evolutionists began to propose extraterrestrial involvement and participation, while others avoided this trap while exploring for alternate explanations, and finally formulated the intelligent design model. It was becoming evident to them that the standard mental models were simply not adequate to move research in the right direction. The information theory opened up new avenues for explaining the workings at the DNA, 'software-type' and nano-robot engineering operations at sub-chromosome levels.

3.3 The Intelligent Design Formula

The intelligent design's modern synthesis would run something like this:

ID phenomena can best be substantiated and explained by the concept of irreducible complexity. The information theory actually opened up a myriad of avenues for explaining the workings at the DNA and chromosome levels, software-type, and nano-engineering operations at the chromosome level.

Living systems provide monumental systems that demonstrate pre-programmed systems: replication, transportation, coding, decoding, interpretation, functions, maintenance, manufacturing, self-reproduction, correction, and elimination of non-programmed mistakes.

Selection is overwhelmingly a pre-programmed feature that allows for adaptation but not beyond non-programmed features. Nature does not 'program' code through statistical progressive adaptability capabilities. Naturalistic auto re-engineering, redesign, and reinvention information systems are inconceivable. Implying that naturalistic super-advanced novel systematic workable codes, standards, processes, and tools are somehow detectable through empirical evidence is beyond the threshold of probability and possibility.

The requirements for shifting pre-programs of information and engineering systems towards infrastructural re-engineering or redesign can only be identified as errors that can be corrected if such correction programs exist.

These five basic points suggest that:

- Evolutionary biology has been ignoring for far too long the information side of science. Similarly, reductionism, which is not equivalent to the scientific method, has a built-in barrier – materialistic notions of certainty. Yet, advanced biological research goes beyond to information technology and nano-engineering, for which an evolutionary reconstructed history, that would proceed from simple to complex through statistical progression based upon uniformitarian assumptions, cannot apply.

The group of scientists who formed the intelligent design (ID) group emerged precisely because they recognized the fundamental limitations in the neo-evolutionary basic formula. New super high-technology brought to light infinitely intricate complexities, processes, information software networks, and nano-level intricate robotic engineering activity that overwhelmed the statistical theory of chance. This is something that the creation scientists identified in the 1960s. The ID scientists recognized that there were integral sub-molecular engineering structures that could not be reduced without losing functionality. This concept is known as irreducible complexity. This super-software and nano-engineering complexity exists. Statistics cannot help explain their existence through the standard uniformitarian models. The ID scientists attribute the origin of this fifth level infrastructural management structure to a hypothetical intelligent designer. This approach was proposed to avoid what was becoming a common occurrence among evolutionists – their attribution of non-evolutionary causes to hopeful monsters, punctualities, and extraterrestrial influences or intrusions. An intelligent designer approach allows scientific investigation and research by circumventing this fettered uniformitarian methodology.

Contrary to popular, professional, and United States courts' beliefs, the intelligent design scientists did not introduce a new religion. Religion is usually associated with rituals for member initiation, worship, the identification and qualification of members for religious orders, produce holy documentation, prayer calls, hymns, claim to be under divine inspiration, establish real estate (buildings) for worship, or identify and qualify candidates for paradise or any other post-mortem residence. The ID group of scientists simply wished to avoid dealing with scientific irrelevancies that are imposed on the scientific method and its process.

The basic intelligent design activity relationship formula can be summarized as:

$$\frac{C + (T - E) + M + I + N}{(L)} = A + K + S + P$$

C = One singularity: special creation – intelligent designer
T = Current and laboratory time
E = Evolutionary time to prove statistical progression
M = Matter
 I = Nano-level information software
N = Nano-level robotics engineering
(L)= Uniformitarianism[73]
A = Irreducible complexity with unfettered scientific methodology
K = Knowledge-base (certainty)
S = Standards, codes (certainty)
P = Verifiable lawful scientific process to resolve uncertainty

The *'Intelligent Design'* scientists propose a teleological approach to help explain the totally unexpected and unpredictable scientific evidence at the DNA, RNA sub-chromosome level. The I.D. group formulates a hypothetical, eclectic, and all inclusive notion of an Intelligent Designer in order to avoid falling into the usual trap that many neo-evolutionists have fallen into - where in the absence of predicted data these scientists improvise and introduce notions of hopeful monsters, punctuated equilibrium and hypothesize about extraterrestrial participation or intrusions into the evolutionary process. Intelligent Designers hypothesize an inevitably a *pantheistic* entity that can account for the super-high information-rich technology at the DNA/RNA levels[74]. It is not an attempt to introduce elements of organized religion, e.g., the Christian

---

[73] Stephen C. Meyer, in *'Signature in the Cell: DNA and the Evidence for Intelligent Design,'* (HarperCollins e-books, June 2009) mentions that he considers himself to be an uniformitarian. He connects this to 'historical sciences' (philosophy of science) – defined as: *'the present is the key to the past.' However the definition here is so broad that Creation science may very well fit within it.'* Religious Philosophy has used the term 'uniformitarianism' (the universe has existed unchanged for an immeasurable amount of time and will continue to exist forever), before Charles Lyell adapted it within a materialistic content. This book will use the term 'uniformitarian-ism' with its materialistic meaning, to refer to the foundation of the evolution theory.

[74] Stephen c. Meyer, *'Signature in the Cell: DNA and the Evidence for Intelligent Design,'* HarperCollins e-books, June 2009.

Biblical God, who has a name, purpose, historical mission, social, and inheritance laws that require a priesthood for interpreting revealed communication. The Intelligent Designer is an impersonal, non-theological entity and is not described within a creative time frame. ID scientists have their own personal views on the identity and activity of this designer. The main idea that I.D. scientists wish relate is that there are no amount of billions, trillions, or zillions of years that would account for a statistical explanation for the complexity observed and recorded at sub-chromosomal information levels.

Creation scientists may recognize some features of a creative intelligent designer, but also recognize the pantheistic framework of this scientific hypothesis. The Christian scientific framework has their divine Creator revealed through: (a) legal historical documented evidence; (b) geometric natural law; and (c) physical evidence within Creation that can be observed, documented, tested, and verified through the original definition of the scientific method. The ID concludes an *a posteriori* - after the fact (examination of scientific evidence); Creation scientists – *a priori* and Evolution – *a priori*.

These summarizing formulas represent the key conceptual views of the science debaters, and are the substance of this book. An example of one of the formulae variables – time - may be brought here to help contrast the similarities and differences between the debaters' views. Time is a key component in the neo-evolution (NE) and creation science (CS) methods, but not one in the intelligent design (ID) formula:

NE uses the uniformitarian platform upon which all existing physical conditions and forces are used to reconstruct the past. In other words, use the present to measure the past. This is accomplished in four phases: (a) move backwards from the present to the past, i.e., from the complex to the simple, to the very beginning – a primordial point;[75] (b) this point then explodes; and (c) allows chance to work through the processes of matter, energy; and (d) through the effects of challenging environments to single living cells, then through various intermediary species to man. This then reflects: the complex extrapolation to simple; big bang; simple-to-complex; and the billions of years. The four-phased view is the foundation from which uniformitarian time is theorized.

In contrast, time in the CS platform is associated with geometric

---

[75] This "point""point' can be considered to be a "'singularity."'.'

natural law and events of three singularities: special creation, down-scaling of energy-density, and the hydro-tectonic initial and secondary self-adjusting catastrophes. These events are deduced from three sources: interpretation of legal historic documentation, effects identified in the physical sciences, and corroborating scientific evidence and predictions. Temporal concepts and evidence are affected by singularities and reflect recent events that are measured in thousands rather than billions of years.

The individual intelligent design members may separately hold long age or recent views. They will, however, all negate in one voice the NEs' billions of years when these years are used to suggest statistical possibility or probability for the emergence of nano-information engineering complexities at the chromosome level. The ID group, therefore, does not offer any official direct methods for establishing time frames.

On the American social scene, there emerged some procedural oddities. The United States courts come to not only interpret law, but to also validate groups' scientific credentials. These groups can now be divided between those who apply the true scientific method (uniformitarians) vs. non-scientific or religious groups that suggest near or more appropriately pseudoscience.

On separate occasions, NE, CS, and ID issues appeared before state courts. On the one hand, the creation science and intelligent design groups expressed their concern in two areas: (a) the type of NE science that is presented in the school textbook. Such science presents proofs for evolution that had been drawn from outdated, disproved, and fraudulent science; and (b) requests have been made to place creation and/or intelligent design scientific interpretations of scientific evidence alongside evolutionary interpretations in the school textbooks and during class discussions.

The outcome produced an impasse in two areas: (1) courts continue to reinterpreting constitutional law in terms of the demarcation line – science versus religion; and (2) NE began to claim that its version of science is close to not only certainty but has almost become equivalent with truth.

3.4 The Hybrid Uniformitarian Scientific Model
The hybrid uniformitarian views include such theories as:

#	Hybrid Version	Belief
1	Theistic Evolution	God used evolution to create the universe

2	Progressive evolution. Old Earth Creation	Creation days were actually long uniformitarian ages but the timeline was punctuated by divine interventions at critical points to introduce qualitative new designs – that would correspond to gaps in the fossil record and absence of transitional forms
3	Day-age	Biblical days correspond to long ages
4	Gap theory	Billions of years existed between Genesis 1:1 and 1:2
5	Framework interpretation	Known as a literary framework, the six Genesis days were not literal, not scientific, it's just a religious doctrine of Creation

A summary of the hybrid uniformitarian synthetic constraints and artificial means follow below:

(1) Reconcile irreconcilable notions of uniformitarian and creation origins. Scientists of the hybrid models have to contend with a timeline difference between that suggested by the evolutionary and that by Biblical Creation of origins models. The contrast between the two lists of creative events is totally contrastive and irreconcilable. The creation model uses totally different infrastructural sequences that can be understood within the parameters of geometric natural law and geometric solids, but not from those suggested by proponents of the theory of evolution.[76] Most of the Hybrid uniformitarians must either bend uniformitarian and/or Biblical historical descriptive precepts.

Figure 3. Comparison: Origins Interpretation: Evolution and Creation.

From: John Morris, 'The Young Earth: The Real History of the Earth – Past, Present, and Future,' Master Books, AR, 2007, p. 31 [the right and left column reversed]

Evolutionary order of appearance:	Biblical Order of Appearance:
Matter existed in the beginning	Matter created by God in the beginning
Sun and stars before the Earth	Earth before the Sun and stars
Land before the oceans	Oceans before the land
Sun, Earth's first light	Light before the light
Atmosphere above a water layer	Atmosphere between two water layers
Marine organisms, first forms of life	Land plants, first life forms created
Fish before fruit trees	Fruit trees before fish
Insects before fish	Fish before insects
Sun before land plants	Land vegetation before Sun

---

[76] Officially, at this time, the I.D. scientists do not address issues of origins.

Land mammals before marine mammals	Marine mammals before land mammals
Reptiles before birds	Birds before land reptiles
Death, necessary antecedent of man	Man, the cause of death

(2) Needlessly distort or dilute the uniformitarian and special creation models by reinterpreting and proposing some external dynamic physical processes that cannot be substantiated on uniformitarian nor special creation criteria. Hybrid notions cannot explain the specific external interventions through reasonable and evidential proofs. They do not substantiate the long versus recent ages of the Earth or the universe.

(3) Resort to leaps of faith – i.e., believe in certain conditions that cannot be deduced from either of the competing standard models or systematic treatment of evidence. It's important to note that although the notion of leaps of faith is usually associated with the practice of faith/religious practice, leaps of faith are evident among those who propose materialistic explanations. For example, in the absence of concrete scientific evidence, evolutionists refer to their exclusive consensus of scientific opinion. Mayr proposes in his *The Modern Evolutionary Synthesis*[77] that scientists extrapolate micro- to macro-evolution, with historical contingency, which are to be defined as explanations for different levels, since gradualism does not mean constant rate of change. Here explanation and extrapolations must substitute empirical evidence for something that may/does not exist.

(4) Complicate or do not resolve definitional and evidential parameters.

(5) Provide a synthesis, which instead of reconciling, actually places all parties at odds with each other.

(6) Redefine and reinterpret: a) the original 'theological' foundations that had been established over the millennia (Christianity) and in many cases inadvertently offer pantheism as a solution.[78] And b) re-define and reinterpret the original uniformitarian view that has been established on

---

[77] E. Mayr. and W. B. Provine, eds., *The Evolutionary Synthesis: Perspectives on the Unification of Biology* (Cambridge: Harvard University Press, 1998); and E. Mayr, *The Growth of Biological Thought: Diversity, Evolution & Inheritance* (Cambridge: Harvard University Press) 567.

[78] The numerous hypothetical loose ends allow for convenient New Age theories, and may simply be echoes and reflections of philosophies such as that of Teilard de Chardin's "Omega Point."

purely materialistic and reductionist principles. Furthermore, these do not allow for metaphysical participation or speculation.

The modern Hybrid Uniformitarian view (Theistic Evolution, Progressive Evolution; Old Earth Creation) can be represented by the following summarizing formula:

$$\frac{C + M + T + V}{L + E + R} = A + I + K + S + P$$

C = Chance (e.g., genetic mutation, flow, mechanisms)
M = Matter
T = Time (current time)
V = Environmental stress
E = Uniformitarianism
L = Relativism
R = Reductionism
A = Simple (primitive) to complex (natural selection, across 5 infrastructural change levels; micro-/macro-evolution
I = Punctuated Supernatural **I**ntervention
K = Knowledge base (materialism, uniformitarianism, reductionism, relativism; and allegorical literary interpretation of any scriptures)
S = Standards
P = Scientific Process (evolutionary realism, dialectical materialism)

The Hybrid formula is practically identical to the Evolutionary formula.

4. Certainty from Uncertainty, 5 Change Levels, Models, N.A.S - 24 Points

Modern management theories consider *knowledge* as a resource. Companies, corporations, and nations in competitive environments see knowledge as a means that helps ensure a strategic advantage, and reduce risks and hazards.

Knowledge is intellectual capital[79] that contains stages of development. For example, users recognize conceptual, defined, factual, verified, validated, archived, outdated, and theoretical knowledge. Knowledge management [80] includes several steps. Users must identify, create, represent, change, support, and distribute this knowledge to single, group and networked users in a timely and usable manner. Knowledge is used to improve learning, performance, research, and promote general awareness.

Knowledge is codified and framed in the form of expert systems where specific procedures assist in decision-making and problem-solving. Knowledge systems allow users to simulate or convert inputs, practices, or criteria into usable products. Similarly, there are techniques and methods to interpret the body of knowledge.

Engineering has gone the extra mile and budgeted to ensure the

---

[79] D. Amidon, *The Innovation Super Highway: Harnessing Intellectual Capital for Collaborative Advantage* (Butterworth-Heinemann, 2002).

[80] BRINT Institute, *A Case For Knowledge Management: Rethinking Management for the New World of Uncertainty and Risk* (New Harford, NY: BRINT Institute)., URL: Online Living Book. R.H. Buckman, *Building a Knowledge-Driven Organization* NY: McGraw Hill, 2004). See also, http://en.wikipedia.org/wiki/Knowledge_management.

fulfillment of plans' objectives through qualitative information. Modern biologists identify information software and robotics processes at micro-nano-levels within each living cell. They thus detect, define, and measure evidence for a pre-programmed network and process. These suggest the existence of built-in communication networks, infrastructures, supervisory and executive systems, and new standards that form the core and essence of the knowledge base. Knowledge can operate within supervisory systems, as well as, in the case of humans, at the conscious awareness and executive levels. This is accomplished through the formulation of purposes, objectives, and strategies that lead to the production of specific results and value to the user.

Knowledge-seekers and consultants from all parts of the globe in all historical periods have been exploring the issue of knowledge. For example, the ancient Greeks had developed intellectual structures and mathematical processes that helped them define and arrange data, information, and knowledge in a manageable manner. Mythology reflects a knowledge base and allows economics and its social vehicle to navigate with a purpose through areas of productivity. There is also the legal historical vehicle, which was designed upon geometric natural law. This vehicle carried not only knowledge but also certainty to meeting objectives and purposes.

One early group developed this knowledge, vehicles, and objectives to help understand God's will. Others attempted to understand God's nature. We can see logic applied in different ways: intellectually (Aristotle); Aquinas offers cosmological arguments – ideas such as 'first cause,' 'the goodness of God;' St. Anselm also provides an ontological explanation by presenting a range of Creation's good features. Similarly, knowledge has been used to explore the nature of Creation and that of the Creator himself. This has been evident in mathematics, geometry, constructions of pyramids, megaliths and the zodiac. More recently, from the Renaissance, emphasis was placed on humanism, accuracy of knowledge, and development of scientific branches – see works of Erasmus, Francis Bacon, Galileo Galilei to Riemann.

Following the ravages of the sixteenth and seventeenth century religious wars, an intellectual movement set itself the task of re-examining the certainty of the religious revelations. Were religious revelations the source of certainty, knowledge, and wisdom? In the seventeenth century, Rene Descartes began a rationalist quest for certainty. His approach was to question the primary sources of knowledge. He introduced extreme skepticism. He elevated the doubting of everything except his own ability to think (I am = I am).[81] Rationalist philosophy set the self-evident axioms (Baruch Spinoza)[82], and suggested a pantheistic dualism through the unity of nature and God (Gottfried Leibniz).[83] Later, Immanuel Kant[84] attempted to organize philosophy on rational, skeptical, logical, and axiomatic grounds. While rationalists worked in France, empiricists made counteroffers in England. Empiricists discounted the innate ideas (rationalism). Empiricists proposed that certainty is achieved through observation (John Locke[85], George Berkeley,[86] David Hume,[87]). This empiricism led to certainty through theories that are arrived at through observation.

Together, rationalists and empiricists contributed to the foundations of the Enlightenment. Enlightenment philosophers achieved their enlightenment through their emphasis on geometric order, rigor, and reductionism. From this, they derived and inferred many other ideas including: freedom from dogma, organization of states into self-governing republics via democracy, religious tolerance, scientific method, market mechanisms, capitalism, and reason as being the primary value of society, the freedom to pursue truth without sanction for violating established ideas.

Throughout this eighteenth century, Age of the Enlightenment, there was a systematic search for pure empiricism. This empiricism was substantiated through Newton and followed through by Diderot, Voltaire, Rousseau, Montesquieu, and Kant.

---

[81] *Discourse on Method* (1637). "A priori" knowledge – before experience, or through inductive reasoning.

[82] *Ethics* (1677).

[83] *Monadology* (1714).

[84] *Critique of Pure Reason* (1781/1787).

[85] *An Essay Concerning Human Understanding* (1689) – 'a posteriori' knowledge – after experience, or through deductive reasoning.

[86] *Treatise Concerning the Principles of Human Knowledge* (1710) – things only exist as a result of being perceived', – subjective idealism.

[87] *A Treatise of Human Nature* (1739-1740) – extreme skeptic empiricism – all knowledge derives from sense experience. Human knowledge divided into two categories: relations of ideas (math and logical propositions) and matters of fact (sense experience – ideas based on recollections of sensations).

The nineteenth century's concept of intrinsic order was launched through Kantian metaphysics and continued as a Hegelian dialectical process. Here, knowledge and reality were automatically ordered through organic dynamic forces - thesis-antitheses-synthesis.[88] Hegel influenced a stream of philosophers, scientists, economists, and social theorists.

Just as the Enlightenment and the encyclopedists overturned well-established traditions, it is during the twentieth century that the modernists reset the rationalist-based philosophy. Modernists rejected Enlightenment's foundations of knowledge and certainties by introducing a radical reductionism. Modernists refuted irrationality and emotionalism and promoted a new social economy. Based on Hegel and Feuerbach, modernists laid the foundations for understanding that materialism is linked to the science of economics (Karl Marx's *Das Kapital*). In other words, science is nothing more than economics. Others began to postulate on this new empiricism. Freud turned psychology upside down, while Friedrich Nietzsche critiqued religion, philosophy, morality, culture, and science itself. This led to a post-modern redesign and reinterpretation of the benefits that the Age of Enlightenment had brought. It became apparent from the mid-twentieth century that certain features of the Enlightenment had become a liability. After all, didn't Enlightenment suggest a breakup of reality into specializations, while ignoring traditional wisdom and its potential lateral consequences? There was the idealization of Enlightenment figures – such as the founding fathers of the United States.[89] Instead of the art of reductionism that began with Descartes [Part V of his *Discourses* (1623)] and blossomed in positivism [begun with Auguste Comte (nineteenth century)], the true features finally blossomed in the twentieth century. Here we have philosophical thinkers who had created their own definition of positivism including Emile Hennequin, Wilhelm Scherer, Dimitri Pisarev, and Stephen Hawking. It is then that

---

[88] *Science and Logic* (1811-16); *Phenomenology of Spirit* (Mind) (1807) evolution of consciousness from sense-perception to absolute knowledge, spirit

[89] Louis Hackett, *The Age of Enlightenment* (1992) (http://history-world.org/age_of_enlightenment.htm), retrieved 2008-02-15, Richard Hooker, *The European Enlightenment* (1996) (http://www.wsu.edu/~dee/ENGLIGHT/PREPHIL/HTM), retrieved 2008-02-15, Luther Blissett, *Anarchist Integralism: Aesthetics, Politics and the Apres-Garde* (1997) (http://www.stewarthomesociety.org/ai.htm), retrieved 2008-02-15, http://en/wikipedia.org/wiki/Age_of_Enlightenment.

authentic scientific knowledge began to be associated with modern positivism and synonymous with empirical reductionism.[90]

What is easy to recognize is that these intellectual-based endeavors carried a predictable linear path. The rational-empirical-positivist path relies on mechanistic, organic, and process paths that are closed systems. They are independent of any external influences. The intellectual part of the mind finds comfort in the freedom from external dogmas and objective frameworks.

In spite of the positivist closed system, there have been attempts to open the system to divine concepts. Such attempts had to be dressed in intellectualized rationalist/empiricist concepts. At best, such attempts to open the system simply resulted in a pantheistic framework. By definition, the intellect - its workings, perceptions, and interpretations – is part of the physical universe. In this view, this approach would inevitably tend to reject anything that would emanate from 'beyond normal human perception. As David Hume (1711-1776) suggested, there's a rift between the 'what is' and the 'ought to be.'[91] This gap cannot be bridged except through artificial, hypothetical 'leaps of faith.' Such artificial bridging would express itself in terms of myth, ideology, religion, and or through the fifth point (thesis) in the 'modern syntheses[92] where an 'explanation' substitutes for scientific evidence.

The intellectual positivist reductionist premises that underlie the uniformitarian concept are summarized as follows:

(a) The concept reflects mechanical, organic, and process models of

---

[90] Descartes aimed at reducing all system to a mechanistic model (the sum of its parts) while others used statistical mechanics to reconcile macroscopic properties in terms of microscopic components. Richard Dawkins (in his, *The Blind Watchmaker*) introduces the term 'hierarchical reductionism' (page 13) where complex system can be described with a hierarchy of organizations. Robert Ulanowicz also suggests levels of described detail categories [(The *Ascendant Perspective* (NY: Columbia University Press, 1997)]. These are materialistic, component, and feedback loops functioning with independent operations.

[91] Ibid., book III, part I, section 1.

[92] Fifth guideline in E. Mayr and W.B. Provine, eds., *The Evolutionary Synthesis, Ibid:* : Explanation of historical observations from different levels in paleontology is accomplished by extrapolating micro to macro-evolution. This would not mean constant rate of changes (gradualism).

thinking. It is exclusivist, supremacist, and pan-/polytheistic because it rejects all other legitimate options.

(b) Being an a-priori position it prioritizes materialism and defines all reality in terms of de-prioritized values, being irrational, mythical, cultist, subjective, emotional, and religious.

(c) Because of (a) and (b) uniformitarian realism (UR) is axiomatic, falls into the standard scope of uncertainty, and cannot be brought to levels of measurable guaranteed quality or contingent certainty (see DMPS below).

The atheist, for example, to prove his/her/its atheistic position must first rationally recognize and define the existence of some divine force, being, or entity. Usually, this is defined in terms of mythological, ideological, and religious terms that, at best, have a pantheistic scope. It is the result of a rational construct. Second, the atheist must then negate this pantheistic entity by filtering such reasoning through skeptical or materialistic axioms and theorems. Third, the atheist must convince the audience that this materialistic model of definitions and deductions applies to all open-system views that propose non-materialistic causes and participations.

Such reasoning and definition address human supervisory application but exclude executive faculties that deal with purposes, laws, objectives, standards, strategies, and resource utilization. Matter is not the sole domain of the materialist. One doesn't need to be an atheist and skeptic to recognize the value, reality, and economics of matter. All ancient civilizations, as well as modern theologians and scientists, expressed their understanding of the material phenomenon and its laws[93]. The Christian Bible, for example, clearly indicates the multi-nature of matter as a product of a creative supernatural being. In other words, the economy of matter can be interpreted in atheistic, creation, and intelligent design terms and concepts. The only difference is that the atheists, skeptics, and uniformitarians see matter as a beginning and concluding concept (closed system), whereas matter can also be conceived in terms of being a means to an end.

Some skeptics have correctly suggested that the seeming orderly makeup of the universe actually contains too many defects and inconsistencies. Such imperfection is inconsistent with attributes of a

---

[93] John D. Barrow. and Frank J. Tipler, *The Anthropic Cosmological Principle* (NY: Oxford University Press, 1986). See also, http://www.intelligentdesign.org/.

perfect Creator.[94] Such critics may become lenient and allow for a rationally formulated god (pantheism or polytheism) that hypothetically created an imperfect world. Such critics, however, would not consider that such apparent defects and inconsistencies in the existing universe may be traced to causes and conditions that are beyond what the rationalist filtering process allows for – a documented legal history of a perfect creation that had succumbed to two global singularities: (a) a drop of at least one infrastructural energy-density, thus resulting in Creation's starvation for energy; and (b) the global hydro-tectonic catastrophe whose evidence can be read in the geologic record of Earth. The original perfect creation (first singularity) existed prior to the introduction of these following two singularities, and this original perfect creation was dynamic enough to adapt to new imperfect conditions and still retain in this fallen condition a large measure of it reflected lawfulness, and esthetic value as interpreted by the human eye and scientific instruments.

This brief outline, identify philosophers, economists, linguists, and scientists attempted to identify the source and the nature of knowledge and of certainty through intellect alone. But this endeavor has left many questionable methodologies that either have been rejected or have dwindled to simple word games, symbol juggling, axioms, theorems, postulates, and concepts that simply left a dirt road of uncertainty.

The millennial search for knowledge and certainty may easily be resolved by recognizing that these systems reflect information that must be properly managed. Information is to be managed and management has its principles. This history of ideas, viewed from a management perspective, reveals knowledge-base management principles that are commonly used in engineering projects, and corporations. The strengths, weaknesses, and values become easy to understand within a managerial environment. Philosophy, myths, ideologies, and the scientific method itself are nothing more than information that must be managed. They provide the substance of various levels of conditional certainty whose uncertainty must be processed through the DMPS to achieve a greater conditional certainty within the 3-D management model.

4.1 Pre-History, History, and Modern Scientific Methods

It is challenging in our information-saturated age to find a

---

[94] Richard Dawkins' writings and many other of his predecessors.

comprehensive description of the scientific method. The method recognizably suggests strategy, or set of rules for conducting observations, tests, and verifications. Yet clearly there is more to this. The adjective scientific etymologically can be traced to the Latin *scientia* knowledge (from scio –I know), while the Indo-European, Sanskrit, and Greek terms mean to separate or discern, cut off, split, or refine. Knowledge is viewed as a tool that helps to identify distinctions, yield to interpretation, can be discovered, be separated, and analyzed, and can qualify, and helps to achieve perfection. In Western Europe, from the middle ages to the Enlightenment, *scientia* referred to a knowledge that was recorded systematically.

In other words, these notions and definitions of knowledge emphasize the maintenance of accurate knowledge – contingent certainty. This definition emphasized the need to overcome uncertainty through the tools of decision-making and problem-solving.

It is from the Enlightenment period that this philosophy of knowledge (epistemology) was artificially divided between a moral and a natural philosophy – the latter eventually developed into an empirical / positivist view.

Pre-history of the Scientific Method

Archeology and history suggest that some type of scientific method existed throughout time. The process involved investigation, identification, definition, classification, filtering, weighing, quantification, implementation, testing, and quality control. Knowledge was classified, applied, and tested. For our purposes now, it is sufficient to recognize that such high level of engineering, observations, measurements, calculations, forecasting, recording, and testing have involved experience in what is today being considered to be steps in the scientific method.

Etymologically, the terms science and method respectively simply mean *knowledge* (reliable, conditional certainty) and a tool plus technique for conducting investigation, confirmation, and prediction whenever uncertainty has been identified. These techniques of investigation have been designed to progress from uncertainty to conditional certainty. This process gives evidence that conscious management had been exercised. The users identified laws that worked with in nature. The designers and explorers had objectives, developed and improved upon strategy and tactics, supervised through decision-making and problem-solving, established workable and measureable procedure and rules. They conducted research. They recognized complex accounting and economics principles. This knowledge led them to control and measure productivity through quality performance, operations, style, ethics, attitude, and much more. All of these realities become evident once the 3DMM is applied to the subject.

Scientific Method Is Evident in Law and Economics

There is a history of methods that has been used for producing increasingly reliable knowledge. Each of these historical accomplishments and initiatives provided evidence for the use of: quantitative, qualitative, theoretical, and applied mathematics, information management, and the discovery of laws. Upon closer examination, the scientific method is not unique, because similar methods, processes, and an evident knowledge-base can be seen in the disciplines of law and accounting/ economics/finance. Similarly, the uniformitarian versus legal historical foundational dichotomies are evident here also.

Figure 4. Comparison – scientific, legal, and economic methods.

*1 – Historical Law-based – Geometric Natural Law; Legal Formalism

*2 – Empirical/Positivist, Rational, empirical, reductionist, axiomatic, postulates, social relativism.

Knowledge base: ***'Conditional Certainty'***	**Investigation of 'Uncertainty'**
SCIENTIFIC	
*1 Geometric Natural Law; 'Laws of Nature' that are based on verifiable historical data.	*1 Decision-making and problem solving to help address and resolve uncertainty and bring resolved condition back to 'conditional certainty.'
LEGAL	
*1 History of authoritative documentation, precedents, and common law – quoted in the form of assertions, statements with citations. Known as Legal Formalism provides an executive level approach to Law.	*1 Use to ensure clarity, provide a formal relational approach to describe legal evidence and aimed results. Legal analysis – is predictive, outcomes-based approach, which considers +/- outcomes and related consequent action.
*2 This represents: positivism, legal realism, social empiricism and relativism in local interpretations.	*2 This includes persuasive analysis – used for motions and briefs. Contingencies considered [Hypothesis, alternatives and weighing and justified (tests) judgments

This is rule-based-supervisory approach to Law.

and verdicts.]

<u>ECONOMIC</u>

*1 Normative economics (what 'ought to be') – planning for R&D based technology investments into innovative projects into infrastructural and 'manufactures' (Alexander Hamilton) projects in terms of recommending policy through representative government.

*2 Positivist economics (what 'is') – focuses on economic phenomena and facts that are considered in terms of cause-effect, and is used to test economic theories. Considered being persuasive rather than descriptive economics – see post-/new-/Keynesian macroeconomics, monetarist, supply-side economics and others.

*1 Economic data is researched, identified, documented, quantified, categorized and is subject to all the investigative, strategic, policy, procedures, rules and regulations and other plans evident in the 3DMM (see below). Similarly data, conditions, events, rates are investigated forecasted and tested for reliability. These are typical processes evident in the scientific method – designed to resolve 'conditional uncertainty.'

*2 This economics equated with those of Adam Smith and Malthusian options.

Each can be erected upon uniformitarian principles (i.e., starting with existing conditions, processes, rates, and values) or upon historical legal records, that are described in legal terms and agreements, amendments, and natural law, as well as, include singular circumstances such as wars, revolutions, natural disasters, and failure of civilizations. These legal and economic lines have also been linked to 3-D management plans, mental models, five levels of change management, and decision-making and problem- solving methods for resolving uncertainty. Similarly, these sciences affect and are guided by management stylistic issues: ethics (S1) and morals of a culture (S3) - methods, practices, and hierarchy of values, in spite of what relativist modernist and moralist conclude.

Culture is evident because knowledge management doesn't exist in a vacuum. When we see pyramids, navigating tools, ancient maps, and writing, these inevitably imply a foundation of culture. Each cultural database foundation provides a stepping stone for the next step(s) in the transmission of reliable, conditional, knowledge-base management. Populations in any given civilizations may use stone tools and do hunting instead of engaging in agriculture, or recognize agriculture law and knowledge, energy, and with the aid of mathematics, manufacturing, construction engineering, hydraulics, navigation, mathematics, astronomy, and city building, develop these in an incredibly short period of time. Civilizations rise and fall, but some elements of their knowledge-base (science, law, and economics) have always been transported via trade, building guilds, and literature on stone as evidence and options in a decision-making and problem-solving process.

Cultural technology has been developed to:

(a) Fill a certain need (e.g., Chinese invention of gun powder used during celebrations. Phoenician & Carthaginian cartography and ship-engineering to pursue worldwide navigation and trade);

(b) Borrowed technology was further developed to help meet new needs (e.g., Chinese powder used by Europeans as gun powder in warfare, excavations, rocketry);

(c) Inherited science and technology to maintain existing knowledge (e.g., Incas and Mayas inherited and used the calendars and sophisticated buildings made of massive stone).

4.2 Three-Dimensional Management model – Knowledge Base

There had been two schools of scientific development throughout European history up to the beginning of the twentieth century. Here's a preview or summary of what will be developed in Chapter 5:

One group, as shown above, kept 'its nose close to the ground' - describing a rationalistic and empiricist algebraic or subjective approach to 'accurate and certain knowledge.' This methodological approach started from a relative 'point,' and from this 'point' extended additional 'points' into any configuration in order to formulate or interpret a given 'reality.' Thus axioms, theorems, and postulates play a key role in this process. Thus:, skepticism, reductionism, empiricism - the 2-D rational reality[95] is

---

[95] Aristotle, *Physics*; Euclid, *Elements* (emphasis on axioms and theorems); Thomas Aquinas; Francis Bacon, *Novum Organum* (referenced Aristotle's *Organon* to describe a logical empirical system that improved the process of syllogisms); Isaac Newton, *Philosophiae Naturalis Principia Mathematica* (1687) (described universal gravitation and the three laws of motion); Augustine Louis Cauchy (1780-1884), *Cours analytique et l'école polytechnique* (1821), *Le calcule infinitésimal* (1823), *Leçons sur les applications de calcul infinitésimal, La géométrie* (1826-1828); Hermann von Helmholtz, *On the Conservation of Force* (1847); James Clerk Maxwell, *On Physical Lines of Force* (1861). Some empiricist philosophers include: Aristotle, Thomas Aquinas, Francis Bacon, Thomas Hobbes, John Locke, George Berkeley, David Hume, and John Stuart Mill.

the scope of the tools used. This algebraic approach can be represented by the following explanation (see details in Figure 19 – Chapter 5).

On the other hand, the second group provides a geometric law-based objective perspective. They emphasize a reality that is derived from and constructed upon geometric natural law (quantitative and qualitative systems), 3-D lawful reality.[96] This geometric approach can be represented by Figure 20 – Chapter 5.

Only the algebraist school remains after World War I. The geometrist view, which lies at the foundation of the original Christian view and that of the original United States Constitution, has been eclipsed. Today, the Christian view has also, in large part, been compromised by policies that force adherence to the algebraist model.

More than a century ago, Karl Marx (1818-1883) wrote his famous *Das Kapital* (1867) where he equated materialism with his scientific economics. This materialism-economics dualism, which was erected upon the uniformitarian foundation (represented by Hegel and Feuerbach), was designated as the scientific proof that was to lead to international socialism – a step that anticipated world Communism. It is also easy to see the same pattern developed with Darwinian materialism - its economics of natural selection. Where Karl Marx was bold enough to use his scientific economics to forecast an international socialist and then a communist utopia, today's Darwinists have yet to apply their scientific uniformitarian science to forecast future development in biology and other fields. They avoid extrapolating into the future, even though they

---

[96] Plato, *Protagoras* and *Timaeus*; Archimedes, *On Equilibrium of Planes, On Sphere Making, Sand Reckoner* and many others; Leonardo da Vinci, *De divina proportione* by Luca Pacioli (1509); N. Cusa, *De Docta Ignorantia* (Of Learned Ignorance), *De Visione Dei* (Vision of God), *On Conjectures*; N. Copernicus, *On the Revolutions of the Celestial Spheres* (1543); Johannes Kepler, *Harmony of the World*; G.W. Leibniz, *Discourse on Metaphysics, Monadology*; W. Humboldt, *On Language*; G. Cantor, *Contributions to the Founding of the Theory of Transfinite Numbers*; Alfred Wegener, *The Origin of Continents and Oceans*; Louis Pasteur *Free Lance of Science*; Karl F. Gauss, *Theoria motus corporum coelestium in sectionibus conicis solem ambientum;* (electromagnetics, non-Euclidian geometries, and many other breakthroughs). Bernard Riemann, http://www.emis.de/classics/Riemann/.

claim to have the near certain scientific tools to formulate the verifiable history and pre-history. Proponents of the scientific evolutionary movement have established in their mind that the theory of evolution has achieved the status of a scientific fact. They achieve this through their theoretical use of a biological automatic chance-based selective mechanism functioning within an uniformitarian context that produces linear micro- to macro-qualitative change. Yet, they find it difficult to identify changing trends today. They may identify some organs that are vestigial, but why couldn't they also be future-gial, i.e., identify biological markers of change that lead to future speciation or their unique environmental conditions.

Today, there are multiple definitions for the scientific method. Descriptions of the method appear as: summaries, graphics, studies, doctoral dissertations[97]. One can search the Internet for definitional variation. Hundreds of industrial and government scientific labs, academic circles, and authorities publish literature and information on how to better understand and apply the empirically based scientific method. Many businesses use these variations to leverage their competitive advantage in a global market.

One can ask questions such as: do these methods identify conditional certainty (3DMM), methods for discovering and resolving uncertainty (DMPS); to help improve the knowledge base – conditional certainty? These questions lead to identifying management principles.

This book describes a 3-D management model (3DMM) and provides a wider historical approach. This management approach distinguishes between certainty and uncertainty. The book addresses change levels, mental models, and identifies limitations of the scientific method, and what constitutes the objective and unfettered scientific method. These must be workable, tested tools that have been used on multibillion dollar engineering projects.

The starting point is the knowledge base where conditional certainty is resides. This data, information and knowledge base must be managed,

---

[97] The scientific method is in many cases described as a list of activities, for example: (1) observation; (2) formulation of a hypothesis; (3) prediction; (4) performance; and (5) experimental tests. There are several variations of this list. Some theorists and practitioners in the philosophy of science (e.g., Karl Popper, *The Logic of Scientific Discovery* (New York: Basic Books, 1959).

and, in this book, this management process is defined and simplified in terms of the 3D management model (3DMM).

3DMM reflects three infrastructural layers where management processes convert information inputs into output quality products: design, operations, and style. Each of the three management layers contains nine relational management plans for a total of twenty-seven networked plans. Each layer has three rows: executive, supervisory, and functional. And three columns: directional, process, and data/information-base.

The design infrastructure is potentially an automated network when properly designed 3DMM, the Design Infrastructure will not only reflect the operational and stylistic requirements but also help facilitate operational and stylistic applications (see Figure 5).

Figure 5. The 3-D Management Model (3DMM).

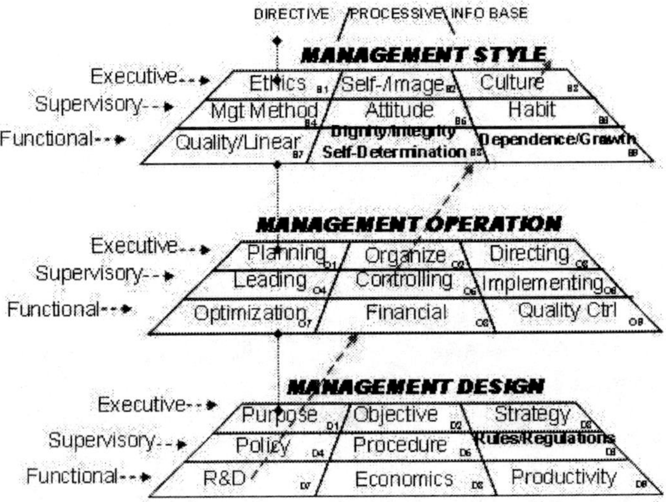

To better understand this model, a comparison can be made between the basic 3DMM layers and a car-operator-manner relationship (Table 1):

Table 1 - 3DMM Analogy with Car Design, Operation, Manner

LEVEL	INFRASTRUCT.	ANALOGY: CAR, DRIVER, OBJECTIVES
3	Style	Manner of driving.
2	Operation	Driving method, maintenance schedule, effective use of resources, implementation of plans/route.
1	Design	Vehicle manufacturing, codes, brand, built-in for operations, quality standards, reliability.

On the 3DMM, each of the nine plans on the three levels are further specified and uniquely defined by their distinct dual locations: horizontal infrastructural (rows) and vertical directional roles (columns).

Horizontal rows:

Executive (D1 to D3; O1 to O3; and S1 to S3)

Supervisory (D4 to D6; O4 to O6; and S4 to S6)

Functional (D7 to D9; O7 to O9; and S7 to S9)

Vertical column:

Directive (S1, S4, S7, similarly for O and D)

Process (S2, S5, S8, similarly for O and D)

Infobase (S3, S6, S9, and similar for O and D)

The multi-billion dollar engineering project management practices ensure successful **design**, **operation**s that also reflect a management **style**. Science and the scientific method also reflect 3DMM. Here we also recognize the process that involves multiple functions: project conception, planning, best practices, cost accounting, controls, processes, best practices, quality and implementation. These lead to meeting specific goals and objectives. The end product provides evidence of purpose, ability, and capacity to meet specific objectives through concrete strategies and style. Such engineering project management is driven by two basic incentives: meeting specific objectives that result in the best short and long-term results. This 3-D management process is streamlined for efficiency and effectiveness, thus allowing it to meet performance standards, reduce costs, risk and timelines, and ensure contract compliance, goals, and objectives. Thus, such 3DMM becomes a source of verifiable, accurate, and certain knowledge – ultimate goals of science.

Similarly, these 3-D management components are evident in all pre-set/inherited requirements in all living organisms as well as in the management of knowledge. Knowledge management requires an approach that is just as rigorous in every aspect and part of its management exercise. Whenever 'uncertainty' is identified within this knowledge base, it is the decision-making and problem-solving method (DMPS – Supervisory level) which is applied to help resolve this uncertainty and bring it back to conditional certainty (3DMM). The scientific method is not a simple list of steps. The method includes at least three considerations: (a) a completed and verifiable 3DMM (certainty warehousing); (b) the scientific method is designed to resolve uncertainty; (c) this uncertainty can be identified either inside or outside the 3DMM; (d) having identified and examined the target area(s), this process searches history, standards, codes, and the remaining stages of the 8-point DMPS as it resolves the challenge; and (e) identifies the hypothesis and theory as uncertainty that needs to be tested for certainty and quality guarantee.

Conditional certainty can be planned for and be assured from the beginning – i.e., at the time when management design (D1 – D9) is being established. The definition of terms and concepts reflect process and networked conditions. To avoid arbitrary definitions, they must be set within the 3DMM-related layers. This is also evident in the living entities' management processes, even at the cellular DNA/RNA information and nano-robotic levels.

Since all complex systems reflect the 3-dimensional management model, the 3DMM is designed to assist us in becoming aware and understand the intricate networked processes of complexity. The 3DMM helps establish a knowledge base of verifiable and accurate networked information that lead not only from data to information and then to knowledge but also to wisdom.

To help better address the evolution-creation-intelligent design debate, this book will **first** describe and examine the 3DMM as it is applied in *business and corporations*. Here, management is operating proactively improved and reached advanced levels of operation. Then, while using this advanced and defined management concept as a prototype, the book will then identify management requirements in the other areas such as in: philosophy, psychology, science, religion and biology.

Whether a scientist or philosopher considers something has evolved, had been created, or reflects intelligent design, the discussion is fundamentally about managing complexity – for which the 3DMM provides a framework. Within this framework, managed complexity can be understood, investigated for consistency, interconnected, tested, validated, and proved objectively. It is necessary to underline that the 3DMM is evident in all that is organized, including corporations, groups, families, and nations. 3DMM is evident in all creative works such as scientific inquiry, art, philosophy, ideology, religion as well as in all life forms.

Each 3DMM plan is defined by its prime input and output within its surrounding environment. This interrelation forms a network among 27 3DMM management plans. For example: O6 (implementing) on the supervisory row (O4-O5-O6) and infobase column (03-O6-09) is situated on the management operations level. The O6's primary input is from O5 (controlling) and O6's primary output is to O7 (optimization). O6's networked or definitional value is also seen in its relation to S6 (habit) and D6 (rules and regulations) and on any other point of contact with other plans (e.g., S2, S3, S5, S8, S9, as well as, D2, D3, D5, D8, D9).

Each of the twenty-seven plans distributed on three levels has an address whose numeric value identifies the prime process direction and integral relationship with other addressed plans, e.g., from D1 to D2 and then to D3. This executive group of plans (D1-D2-D3) allows the process to continue to the supervisory group of plans (D4-D5-D6) and to the functional ones (D7-D8-D9). At the same time, the executive group (D1-D2-D3) also determines and is determined in various ways by plans, groups of plans and processes at the operational level (O1-O9) and stylistic level (S1-S9), and the *vertical plans*: directive (e.g., S1-O1-D1), process (S2-O2-D2) and infobase'(S3-O3-D3) functions.

Note that procedures (D5), controlling (O5), and attitude (S5) are the only plans that interface with all plans at their own level, while only the controlling (C5) plan uniquely interfaces with all of the twenty-six plans at all levels.

Executive responsibilities (D1-D3, O1-O3, and S1-S3) help determine, establish, and ensure the inputs to outputs – directly or indirectly for each area: *horizontal* (1-2-3), *vertical* (1-4-7, 2-5-8, 3-7-9) and *laterally* (1-6-9, 3-6-7, etc.). This executive row provides the corresponding scope for plans at the supervisory row (4-5-6); and in turn, the supervisory processes help orient, maintain, and optimize the functional row's activities (7-8-9) towards planned, successful, and qualitative productivity (D9).

In administrative or life management systems, these may be semi- or highly or totally automated parameters, so as to ensure the highest accuracy, certainty, and competitive cost through best practices, and help prevent duplication of effort, errors, waste, and delays at this and other levels.

For example, the term **'leadership'** in organizations has been described in many ways. Hundreds of millions of dollars have been spent on researching and implementing leadership in corporate management practice. The 3DMM (operational, design, and stylistic levels) goes beyond simply cataloging competencies, value or individual assets of a leader. Within the 3DMM environment it's possible to clearly locate leadership-related plans and infrastructures – such as identifying leadership at the operational level, supervisory row (O4), within the directive column (S1, D1), firmly grounded on the pre-designed and automated management design level (D1 - D9), guided by plans from management style (S1-S9), and derived from the executive row of plans (O1 - O3). The leader will then successfully reach specific implementable objectives (O6) by optimizing (O7) each plan and ensure implementation through proper funding (O8) and meeting quality-controlled output (O9), thus leading to and fulfilling productivity (D9) via the pre-automated plans at the 'management design level. This summary identifies a points-/value-specific position of what leaders must reflect before, during, and after their presence on the field of operation. The leader is fully integrated with his/her operation - totally aware of the effect of cultural value.

An example of leadership in practice is offered by Alexander the Great's campaigns, which shows his total awareness of the higher 3DMM plans and levels (style, operations, and design). He had an overreaching vision (executive levels S1 - S3, O1 - O3, D1 - D3) that was motivated by the Persian threat. Alexander's vision, historical, and methodological approach had been developing over two generations. His many successful strategies and plans demonstrate that, rather than being influenced by Aristotle, Alexander had really been formed by Plato[98]. Alexander utilized

---

[98] Contrary to what most encyclopedias and history books describe about Alexander's life and strategies, Alexander's influential trainer had not been Aristotle, but Plato. Plato's and Alexander's biographical dates overlap nine years. It was Plato's geometric approach that helped Alexander introduce superior military strategic solutions in a field where his opponents continued using linear algebraic methods. Alexander founded numerous libraries as 3DMM learning centers across his newly established empire – this is a Platonic view of increasing, improving, and developing mankind's divine spark. This involved continual self-improvement and, more specifically, self-perfection. The vestiges of Alexandrian Greek culture remained throughout the Roman Empire where Greek was used as

geometric natural law to his favor, not only on the field of battle, but also in establishing city centers of culture and knowledge (libraries). He maximized the inherent human quality –divine spark, and thus redefined the concept of what constitutes a civilization. Throughout his campaigns he listened to his soldiers' and generals' concerns. This link allowed him to objectively determine strengths and weaknesses. He then converted and enhanced these through on-the-road learning, proactive corrective action, contingency planning, and the practical stages in attaining basic goals and then commanding objectives. Thus, he formed an effective and highly motivated force. At the same time, he knew the opponent's 3DMM level of quality in ethics, self-image, culture, management practice, and attitude. With this, Alexander was able to strategically gain advantage over the opponents' organization.

The uniqueness of the 3DMM as a knowledge base tool is that it provides the constituent scope of conditional certainty and helps identify and rectify internal and external uncertainty. This also allows the analysis of the simplest to the most complex systems and functions since they all reflect management principles. These advantages are seen not only in small and corporate businesses, but also in many aspects and workings of biological life, as well as, at the sub-microscopic world. They all reflect management operations, procedures, infrastructures, automated design, and protocols of style.

'Management Design' Level

Table 2 - ***management design*** represents the first of three 3DMM levels. The nine plans on the management design infrastructure are positioned in three horizontal rows and vertical columns (3 x 3=9 plans):

The upper row contains the executive level (D1-D3), which reflects three plans: purpose (D1), objectives (D2), and strategies (D3).

The middle row contains the supervisory row with its three plans: policy (D4), procedures (D5), rules and regulations (D6).

The lower row contains the functiona' row with its three plans: research and development (D7), economics (D8), and productivity (D9).

Note: To avoid overburdening the content of this book, this chapter describes the management design level in full. It will contain some cursory

---

the universal language. This reached from Briton and India. Alexander's fundamental military strategies are still in use today.

examples of the operations and style levels. Another book may be written to address the operational and style levels in full.

To better understand how design plans apply to the evolution-creation-ID debate, each of the plans will first reflect a brief industrial application. Once this is understood, the plans will describe examples of applications in science, methodology, ideology, religion, and biological life.

Table 2 - Management Design Infrastructure within the 3DMM

Row	DIRECTIVE	PROCESS	INFO-BASE
EXECUTIVE.	*Purpose* (D1)	*Objectives* (D2)	*Strategies* (D3)
	* Law	* Priorities	* Resources
	* Identity	* Standards	* Forecasting
	* Scope	* Authority	* Performance
		* Quality assur.	* Plan
SUPERVISORY.	*Policy* (D4)	*Procedures* (D5)	*Rules/Regulations* (D6)
* Administration	* Guidelines to	* Best and	* Do's and don'ts
* Operation.	thinking	economic steps	
* Maintenance		* Processes	
* Safety		* Best practices	
* Security		* Flowcharts	
* Emergency		* Software	
FUNCTIONAL	*Research & Devel.* (D7)	*Economics* (D8)	*Production* (D9)
	* Change	* Accounting	*Qual. Control
	* Improvement	* Audit	* Output
	* Innovation	* Risk analysis	* Feedback
	* Invention		* Waste control
	* Development		* Delays l
	* Training		
	* Education		

When establishing a business, an organization, or some nano-technology-based computer, it is necessary to first identify the executive plans: purpose (D1), objectives (D2), and strategies (D3). These three plans will further be characterized by columnar processes: directive, process, and infobase.

4.3 Conditional Certainty: Executive Plans

Executive plans include: purpose (D1); objectives (D2); and strategy (D3). This is the first of the three rows at the management design level.

Purpose.
Business and Project Application.

Purpose (D1) includes three components: law, identity, and productivity scope and is set within a relational multi-dimensional environment. Purpose provides the groundwork for all activity in the plans.

• Law – is *not* a supervisory level 'rule.' In business, executive law (D1) relates to contract that is enforced by state, federal, and international, as well as physical/natural laws (e.g., acts of God). Supervisory rules are derived from the executive plans (D1 - D3), policy (D4), and procedures (D5). Supervisory rules, together with policy (D4) and procedures (D5), support the implementation of the functional plans (D7 - D9) that are designed to lead to the quality product (D9) – thus fulfilling the purpose (D1).

The purpose (D1) is situated in the directive column and is thus linked directly to other directive plans at the stylistic management's level - ethics (S1) and helps ensure operational planning (O1).

Executive laws imply contracts, or covenants, which contain terms, conditions, definitions, language, interpretation, jurisdiction, performance, and judgments. Laws are specifically related to and provide directive action to other executive plans: objectives (D2) and strategy (D3). Laws design to lead directly to productivity (D9).

• Identity – The who or what that legally is within, outside, or contingent to the legal organizational process. Identities are identified in the contract, have a security status, qualifications, and management responsibilities. Identity 'borders' define degrees of employee/management participation and contribution in an organization, security-issues that either support or threaten the system and its objectives (D2). Defined identities reflect specific policies and procedures so as to help reduce risk and increase certainty.

• The productivity scope identifies key processes that lead towards the fulfillment of the purpose (D1).

Both the identity and productivity scope integrates with law to establish the purpose (D1).

Purpose (D1) defines who, what, where, when, and how much, which together lead to the legal product (D9) in a lawful transaction within internal and external environments. Purpose (D1) directs the formulation and definition of the next executive plan objective (D2).

Curiously, the purpose is hardly ever mentioned or incorrectly defined in the majority of management textbooks. The majority of these sources begin not with purpose but objectives (D2). Project management is the only branch that includes something that is similar to the purpose. It appears in the form of a contract charter or the project definition.[99]

It should, furthermore, be remembered that, within the 3DMM, the purpose (D1) is at the base of the 3DMM. It provides a foundation upon which the operational planning plan (O1) can be accomplished. The purpose is also structurally directly related to ethics on the stylistic level (S1). All adjacent plans have mutual impact upon each other. It is now easier to recognize the full value, for example, of ethics (stylistic level) when ethics is recognized as having been founded on the purpose at the design management level. Here, the ethics plan also provides the rudimentary definition for purpose (D1). The three – purpose, planning, and ethics - are in the directive column and at the executive levels. It becomes clear that any type of behavior or even thought will reflect some direct or indirect purpose, planning, or ethic.

Purpose.
Other Applications.

Purpose (D1) is established to determine law, identity, and scope. These help direct objectives (D2) and strategies (D3). Together, these help manage the supervisory plans which in turn supervise the functional plans towards production (D9). So in other applications, purpose can be seen in:

• Philosophy, ideology and religion describe two sources of law - executive and supervisory. This corresponds to the geometric and algebraic basic world-views.

---

[99] The project charter is a short description that refers to a detailed document known as a new offering request or a request for proposal (RFP). The charter identifies key issues of the project: purpose or reason, scope, objectives, and constraints, the participants (stakeholders, owners, managers, specialists, etc. – their roles, responsibilities, and authority) for achieving the project's objectives.

The algebraic approach to law begins from a point, which reflects a relative and subjective view – supervisory level (D4-D6). In management terms, it is *policy* (D4) that originates the point. The policy-intellectual exercise initiates postulates and creates an axiom from which a relative reality is reasoned out. This process includes the creation and interplay of algebraic variables (e.g., $a^2 \times b^2 = c^2$). The variables can represent anything. These variables may stand for materialistic, religious, mystical, economic and other designations. It is important to note that in this supervisory level process the starting point is not the executive purpose (D1). Policy (D4) substitutes the purpose (D1) but uses the executive strategy (D3) to formulate its objectives (D2). This approach also forms the algebraic value filters. As mentioned above, this allows for the filter to represent any variable – materialistic, mystical, or pantheistic. Having prioritized (D2) resources (D3), everything is then aligned with the improvised policy plan (D4) which has, like the purpose (D1), a directive value and will be used to attempt to justify the supervisory plans – procedures (D5), rules and regulations (D6). This new approach then ensures the functional plans (D7, D8, and D9).

This approach is similar to the 'tail wagging the dog' principle. In philosophical-religious terms, this translates into rationalistic, empiricist, idealistic, reductionist, and pantheistic views[100]. Similarly, the mythological, cult, pan/polytheistic and the various versions of most monotheisms also essentially are built on this algebraic relativistic structure because these don't have a legally-based purpose (D1). This makes them subjective and relativistic due to the absence of executive law (D1). This is why, when philosophers, materialists and many theologians debate on issues of God, while basing their reasoning on the algebraic approach, their definitions of divinity will inevitably be pan/polytheistic. Such divinities appear in the form of prime causalities, mythological or teleological constructs. This factor helps explain why algebraic-based world views have historically been made to comfortably fit within the (Roman) Pantheon of cults. A typical application of this relativistic principle in ethics is seen in the approval by the Human Fertilization and Embryology Authority (HFEA) to justify researchers at the University of Warwick (UK) to proceed with the human-pig embryos hybridization. HFEA is to 'issue a license following stringent checks [that] demonstrate

---

[100] See Chapter 5 of this book for details.

that it is considered both necessary and ethical.'[101] This decision was based on an axiomatic premise. No consideration was given to what justified such a landmark decision. A committee determined that it was ethical and it became ethical by virtue of a policy statement. This showed that such axiomatic ethics are drawn from an authoritarian paradigm. By extension and historical evidence, such foundations for decisions have led to allowing the institution of concentration camps, genocide, and the legalization of cannibalism. Prior to Vatican II, the Roman Catholic magisterium had at least taken into consideration thousands of years of precedents that originally had started from divine law, the scriptures and through holy traditions. However, with the relativist authoritarian committee approach, there is no such legal requirement. The legal structure has become sociologically driven. Empiricist rules and relativist variability are the rule.

In contrast to this algebraic approach, which begins with a 'dot', the **geometric view** of law begins from what the temporal human mind can interpret to be a circle - in terms of geometric concepts (see Figure 20). Here, reality begins not with a period but with a circle. This circle has no beginning and no end — thus representing eternity. It is here that the *geometry of natural law* begins.[102]

This geometric process also includes the conical multi-infrastructural qualitative system[103] and the five convex regular polyhedral solids (tetrahedron, cube, octahedron, icosahedrons, and dodecahedron).[104] These geometric features are built within all of creation at the physical, sub-atomic, solar[105] and super-galactic clusters levels. It is evident in the musical scale and physiological proportions in animals and plants. The

---

[101] R. Highfield, "Human-pig hybrid embryos given go ahead," posted on Telegraph.co.uk, July 1, 2008.

[102] See details in Figure 21 of this book.

[103] See details in Figure 22 of this book.

[104] See details in Figures 21 and 22 of this book. See Plato's, *Timaeus* (360 BC). However, these geometric solids had been known from much earlier times. For example, they appear described on stone monuments - e.g., in Scotland — 1,000 years earlier. See Michael Atiyah and Paul Sutcliffe, "Polyhedra in Physics, Chemistry and Geometry" Milan JH. Math 71:33-58. Also see, http://en.wikipedia.org/wiki/Platonic_solids and http://en.wikipedia.org/wiki/Kepler-Poinsot_polyhedra.

[105] Johannes Kepler, '*Mysterium Cosmograhicum*', Tubigen (1598).

original Christian Bible[106] is unique in that it is the only geometric natural

---

[106] This book uses the concept 'original Christian Bible' to emphasize a difference between the multiple translations that exist today. Many scholars have used newly discovered Biblical texts and fragments to help reconstruct the original texts. Modernists, however, have simply provided what turns out to be nothing more than an uniformitarian interpretation of all that surrounds the original Biblical documentation. Yet, upon closer legal examination, we find that Jesus Christ and the Apostles referenced the Septuagint version of the Old Testament, the Deutero-canonical books, and sacred / holy oral traditions, when they interpreted the scriptures. This tradition had been passed on through apostolic succession for 2,000 years. The Christian Church canonized these Old and New Testaments and Deutero-canonical books at the Synod of Hippo 393 AD, Council of Carthage 397 and 419 AD. .

Various events in Europe - depopulations during the Black Plague, invasions, the Reformation - brought tension and all kinds of issues. In the light of more recent studies, many of these issues brought unnecessary divisions and oversimplifications. For example: (a) the original 1611 King James Version contained the Deutero-canonical books while today the King James Version does not; (b) the King James Version contrasts 'gentiles' with the 'Jews' while the original scriptures (e.g., the Christian Orthodox Bible) and recent translations such as Young's literal translation do not show this contrast, and translate the word 'gentiles' correctly as 'nations,' which include both the Israelites and other people/nations – 'nations' is a context sensitive term; (c) Protestants replaced the Holy Christian traditions, apostolic succession, and bishop's authority by 'pre-New Testament authorities' who brought their own oral traditions and interpretations that had originally been codified as the oral Jerusalem and Babylonian traditions – the Talmud (fourth to fifth century AD); (d)the Tanakh (Hebrew Bible) and Torah (law) are terms that mean different things to different people; (e) distinctive ethnic groups (e.g., Jews, Judahites, Israel, Hebrews, 'chosen people') that existed in the past are not necessarily those that exist today [e.g., www.Khazaria.com (Kevin Alan Brook, *The Jews Of Khazaria* (New York: Rowman & Littlefield, 2002). These new people have no Semitic origins]. It has been evident that the Old Testament is not a 'Jewish document' since the Old Testament history predates the birth of Jacob's son, Judah, by thousands of years, while the ten northern tribes of Israel had never been 'Jewish.' The historian Josephus, James (1.1), and Mathew contain references to the dispersed Israelites – these have not been Jewish. The Apostles were sent to the 'lost sheep of Israel' (Matt. 10:6 and 25:24) and it is curious that it is the Europeans that had become Christian and spread Christianity throughout the world.

After adjusting for textual, methodological, historical evidence, and variances, the term 'original Christian Bible' in this book attempts to limit the ambiguous law-based historical document that consistently reflects geometric natural law. This is evident from the first chapter of Genesis.[107] Because the original Christian Bible is a legal document, the first chapter becomes important in identifying its purpose, law, identities, and scope. Within the first chapter, stylistically the writer-author identifies Himself as the Creator – the prime covenant designer (Genesis 1:1 to 2:4). Geometric nature – the fabric of reality - is spelled out from the first three verses onward.[108] The creative process of *ex nihilo* is easier to understand within the geometric concept. This communication and conversation reflect a legal form. Here we find documented events, precedents, laws,[109] and secondary covenants with patriarchs and kings. We have the identity of the second party to the covenant who is identified as the chief executive officer (CEO) of all Creation.[110] We have a record of the legal family

---

definitions and imports. However, in this evolution-creation-intelligent design debate, there are many creation scientists who use the King James Version, American Standard Version, and similar translations to reconstruct timelines, identify the effects of what are identified here as 'singularities.'

[107] This is detailed in Chapter 5 of this book.

[108] See details on the application of geometric natural law to the first three verses of Genesis in Figures 24 and 26. When geometric natural law concept is not consciously applied, then Christians tend to provide substitutes – e.g., inerrancy and literal (-ist) interpretations of the Bible. These two latter terms exist because the concept of geometric natural law has generally been excluded from consideration.

[109] Example: Deut. 27:15 ff; 28:1 – blessings and curses.

[110] Gen. 2:19. Note, Gen. 1:1-2:3 documents that God identifies Himself as 'supreme God.' In Gen. 2:4, however, God is described from a second person: 'self-existent supreme God' (the eternal Lord God) – which is equivalent to what the human mind would perceive within geometric natural law – the 'circle' (self-existent supreme God), the prime covenant giver. Thereafter, the covenant has been tracked in a legal documentary format from generation to generation by clearly identified members of the second party to the covenant: Gen 2:7 – man (Adam); Gen. 5:1 Seth; Gen 5:7 Enos; Gen 5:10 Kenan; Gen 5:13 Mahalalel; to Gen 5:30 Noah; and post-flood patriarchs Gen 10:1 Shem; Gen 11:12 Arpachshad; Gen 11:13 Shelah; and all the way to Gen 11:27 Abram; and beyond. All these legal and historical records accumulated and became a vast library that had been transported from place to place by the patriarchs until Prince Moses in Egypt summarized the legal library into what became known as the Book of Genesis. This maintained a knowledge-base that can be examined in terms of the

descendants who maintained the covenant of righteousness, maintained legal and historical documentation throughout history. In this history we also find documented in specific quantitative detail a record of three singularities that had global and universal implications.

The first singularity is the creation of the original perfect creation in seven days.[111] The stylistic analysis of these events shows a unique legal style of the Creation. There are definitional elements of the development of geometric natural law[112].Unique correspondence between letter-numeral nesting[113] with poetic and musical qualities.[114] Also, creation each day corresponds not only to separate qualitative infrastructural levels but each is aligned with the five convex regular polyhedral solids[115]. None of these are ever mentioned by those who provide uniformitarian interpretations of the original Christian Bible. Uniformitarians' ideological approach suggests instead – the workings of primitive mind of the Bronze Age, which is surpassed by their own modernist minds.

The *second singularity* occurs when the perfect creation's energy-density drops one cycle down the cone's infrastructures.[116] This leads to a condition that can best be described as energy starvation throughout the original Creation. Due to this reduced energy operational level, the

---

3-D management model.

[111] This includes the seventh rest day. The Creation week may be considered as a single overarching singularity, or may be viewed as seven separate singularities because they were marked by seven separate volitional and unique events, even though they were initiated by the same prime party of the contract. Also, it is worth pointing to the prime party of the contractor's ownership, trademark, and copyright of the Creation and record of the contract – its terms and conditions.

[112] See details in Chapter 5 of this book.

[113] *The Shorter Works of Ivan Panin*, (Vancouver: The Association of The Covenant People, 1934); Ivan Panin, *The New Testament from the Greek Text as established by Bible Numerics* (Toranto: The Book Society of Canada, 1966). The Internet contains a few negative critiques of Ivan Panin's work and approach; however, upon closer examination, these critiques do not address Panin's methodological scope and provide a uniformitarian, reductionist and cynical view of Panin's unique discoveries that apply to features in both the Hebrew and Greek languages.

[114] Suzanne Haik-Vantoura, *The Music of the Bible Revealed* (Berkley, CA: Bibal Press, 1991).

[115] See Figure 26.

[116] See Figure 23 of this book and its related text (Chapter 5) for details.

descriptive concept of 'death' entered the timeline. This condition reduced cycles, velocities, and redefined the Second Law of Thermodynamics. This operational interdependence established secondary relational, networked, and infrastructural relations. This event occurred on the eleventh day on the Creation calendar when Creation's CEO made a conscious inevitable critical imperfect design flaw.

The *third singularity* appears when all of the current geologic, paleontological conditions, structures, and morphologies can be explained through events that occurred during an initial, global, hydro-tectonic catastrophe[117] and by its following secondary adjustments. The initial hydro-tectonic global catastrophe occurred during a period of just over twelve months, and included continental separation and mountain building. The secondary catastrophic self-adjustments continued for an additional 1,000 years. Here events included mega-volcanisms, climatic change, a 500-year global ice age and torrential rains along the tropical zone. Oceans rose between 100 feet at the poles to 500 feet at the equator during the post-Ice-Age desertification of large land masses. Where the Giza Pyramid and the Sphinx stood in lush vegetation with lakes nearby, after the ice age weather conditions changed and these structures stood in the middle of a desert. The Bible records the initial catastrophic event beginning about 1,656 years after the first day of Creation (Genesis 1:1). Flood events continued for twelve months and ten days[118]. The secondary self-adjusting phase continued thereafter primarily for 1,000 years, and continued in diminishing severity until today.[119] The existing polar icepacks and those in the high mountain ranges is all that remains of the 2000 BC to 1500 BC ice age[120].

---

[117] John Baumgardner, '*Computer Modeling of the Large-scale Tectonics Associated with the Genesis Flood'* www.icr.org; www.icr.org.

[118] Gen. 7:11 to 8:13-14

[119] Larry Vardiman, *Climates Before and After the Genesis Flood: Numerical Models and Their Implications* (El Cajon, CA: Institute for Creation Research, 2001); Larry Vardiman, *Sea-Floor Sediment and the Age of the Earth* (El Cajon, CA: Institute for Creation Research, 1996); Larry Vardiman, *Ice Cores and the Age of the Earth* (El Cajon, CA: Institute for Creation Research, 1996); Larry Vardiman, *The Age of the Earth's Atmosphere: A Study of the Helium Flux through the Atmosphere* (El Cajon: Institute for Creation Research, 1990); and numerous other studies, including the rapid geologic formations and effects of Mount Saint Helen's volcanic explosion.

[120] James I. Nienhuis, "Ice Age Civilizations," *Genesis Veracity* (2006).

This detailed presentation of the geometric natural law is necessary since it sets the parameters for understanding all of the following evidence that the creation model has to offer.

The intelligent design group doesn't have an official origins theory. Its laboratory approach focuses on laboratory empirical data. From this they interpret data and empirical evidence. From this assemblage and categorization of data, they may describe features of purpose. Here they talk about physical law that is implied at the sub-chromosome information-rich levels, biological irreducibility, and harmonizing constants of the universe. They will hypothesize about a participating intelligent designer. They will also speculate teleologically about the scope and purpose of all of this sophisticated creation.

Since the evolution, creation, and intelligent design concepts, data, and information are *managed*, this forms the content of the 3DMM. Such 3DMM would account for physical, biological, social, psychological, and cultural subject matter.

In review - within the 3DMM, the purpose (D1) is defined by three components: law, identity, and scope. The topic of law was discussed above in terms of algebraic rules, geometric natural laws, and natural law.

Identity is one-third of the purpose (D1) definition within 3DMM. Identity refers to four functional and participatory areas of an organization: inside, outside, support, and a customer.

Identity's job description establishes a legally functional relationship within and without individuals, groups, organizations, and institutions.

An identity that functions within *geometric natural law* (GNL) recognizes the 3DMM dimensions. Such a user aligns the multi-dimensional links from the purpose (D1) to all other plans on every infrastructure. The user recognizes man's executive faculties and respects mankind's divine spark. The GNL user's approach recognizes the networked and coordinated knowledge base of best practices and standards. There is evidence that discoverable evidence and stylistic quality support each other. Competencies, skills, and creative and productive benchmarks are part of the identities.

In the creationist's Bible, the Creator is the prime party, while Adam is the second party to the covenant with a title of CEO of Creation. Even though Adam missed on a key decision-making issue, his righteous descendants carried that covenantal title from one generation to the next. They have all been directed by the terms and conditions derived from the purpose.

There are five types of outsiders: 1) those who are not part of the contract; 2) potential customers or partners; 3) intelligence gatherers; 4) competitors, and 5) antagonists. In the first chapter of Genesis, we find two types of outsiders. One group is covenantally unqualified - the living creatures cannot become Adam's helpmate (Genesis 2:15 - 20). The other is Eve who is created from part of Adam's body and does qualify under the covenant, however, she, in breach of a portion of the covenant, also becomes a prototype for antagonists with regard to the covenant's righteousness.

Eve becomes an antagonist to the divine covenant by prioritizing supervisory rather than executive thinking. Doubt – an axiomatic position — is begun with the hypothetical question; 'what if the purported A is not really A, but is really B?' This becomes supervisory thinking because such purely rational decision-making is accomplished at the policy (D4) level. She re-prioritized the executive strategies (D3) and objectives (D2), which now become a filter that are used in the decision-making and problem-solving (DMPS) process (fifth step). This re-prioritized filter bypasses the purpose and provides a substitute – an empirically based rationalization that satisfies the subjective. In this action plan, all 3DMM plans are affected and compromised. The antagonist: (1) challenges the covenantal relationship with an alternate attitude and self-focused subjective ethics plan; (2) maximizes risk (death) and vulnerability (threat); (3) reprioritizes security (hides) by inflating self-image (eyes were opened); (4) reformulates culture and level upon which communication is conducted, and others.

The outsider's identity reflects an alternate world-view that is subjective and relativistic. This is seen when God asks what had changed Adam's original view (perfection). Adam presented his subjective causalities, accusing the faulty woman that God gave him, while the woman faulted the serpent. Both showed that they had rejected the perfect covenantal relationship - in which one loved and cared for the other and both loved God.

Clearly, they now amended the original covenant. They derailed the original executive, supervisory, and functional plans. They produced another product to satisfy another customer.

Mother Eve opened an alternate way of thinking that is based on rationalism (policy) (D4), which is in the directive column, but which is on the supervisory row. This approach bypassed the purpose (D1), which is also in the directive column at the executive row. She provided a prototype that led to methods used by a sixteenth century rationalist, empiricist, reductionist, and nineteenth – twentieth century's modernist. This is also the foundations upon which the non-Biblical Israelite religions were based – see Greek religion[121]. Users of the algebraic approach promote relativistic, subjective, and quantitative evidence. Inevitably, such proponents introduce and recognize the application of the rule of strength, cunning, and a ruler-servant, master-slave system. Later, this appears in the establishment of a Babylonian ideal.

Having said this, it is necessary to remember the original Edenic message and pattern of the 3DMM. The Bible contains the 3DMM's design management plans in the form of the Tabernacle in the Wilderness[122] -see Table 3 for the structural parallels between the Tabernacle and the nine design management plans of the 3DMM.

Table 3 shows a match between the 3DMMs management design and the framework of the Biblical Tabernacle. There's a correspondence among the infrastructures: executive function (spirit); supervisory functions (psychological); and functional (physiological).

Table 3. Management Design in the Tabernacle in the Wilderness.

Row	Directive	Process	Infobase
EXECUTIVE.	Purpose (D1)	Objectives (D2)	Strategies (D3)
	* Law	* Priorities	* Resources
	* Identity	* Standards	* Forecasting
	* Scope	* Authority	* Performance
		* Quality Assur.	* Plan
Tabernacle:	Law	Priesthood -	Manna -
Holy of Holies	* 10 Commandments	* Rod that budded	* Scriptures

[121] See the research by Johnson, Robert Bowie, Jr, '*The Parthenon Code: Mankind's History in Marble,*' Solving Light Books, Annapolis, Maryland, 2004; '*Athena and Kain: The True Meaning of Greek Myth,*' Solving Light Books, Annapolis, Maryland, 2003; '*Noah in Ancient Greet Art,*' Solving Light Books, Annapolis, Maryland, 2007

[122] Exod. 25ff.

SUPERVISORY. *Policy* (D4)		*Procedures*(D5)	
Rules/Regulations(D6)			
* Admini.	* Guidelines to	* Best and	* Do's and don'ts
* Operation.	thinking	economic steps	Note column on
left			
* Maintenance		* Processes	Administration
* Safety		* Practices	Operation, etc.
* Security		* Flowcharts	
* Emergency		* Software	
Tabernacle 2nd level *Seven candlesticks*		*Sacrificial table*	*Shew bread*
(*Psyche/soul*)	* Intellect; reason	* the will	* Emotions

FUNCTIONAL	R&D (D7)	Economics (D8)	Production (D9)
	* Change	* Accounting	*Qual. control
	* Improvement	* Audit	* Output
	* Innovation	* Risk analysis	* Feedback
	* Invention		* Waste control
	* Development		* Delays ctrl
	* Training		
	* Education		
Tabernacle	Sensory functions	Filter & Accounting	Productivity, QC
Outer Court	* Search area	* Wash laver	* Sacrificial

Living creatures also reflect purposive adherence to natural biological laws, identities and scopes. These, as well as supervisory and functional plans, are pre-programmed. Such pre-programming allows in some areas for minor physiological adaptation to challenging environments.

Under the algebraic reductionist view, living entities are described in mechanic-robotic-biological or process patterns (see Mental Models – Figure 15). These patterns change due to environmental challenges in linear, statistical, relative, progressive increments, more commonly described as mutations and survival of the fittest.

Upon closer empirical examination, it becomes clear that these are at best descriptions of supervisory-row concepts and not executive infrastructural structures. The large-scale supervisory tools and concepts leave out the information-software-infrastructural and management plans networks that are required for living entities. Evolutionary models must, however, account for causes that change management executive processes

– purpose, objectives, and strategies. These management plans network and direct the supervisory and functional infrastructural operations that lead to specific productivity. These are formulated at the purpose (D1) that leads directly through networked infrastructures, plans to production (D9).

Productivity *scope* is the third of the three executive purposive operations. The scope is the coded process that formulates the direct path via the supervisory infrastructure to quality-based productivity (D9).

The uniformitarian method explains all life forms in terms of reductionist methods - mechanical, biological, or process mental model. Man's mind, it is alleged, can only be understood in terms of behaviorist processes. That is, only through supervisory plans: policy (D4); conditioned decision-making and problem-solving procedures (D5); enhanced conditioned practices; rules & regulations (D6) associated with emotional conditioning. In contrast, the GNL-based management includes the executive plans (D1 through D3). Living beings have a determined network that specifies established processes from the executive to supervisory infrastructural processes. These may be pre-programmed instinctual habits, or rules that lead to secondary functional processes and interaction with the external world.

The executive purpose (D1) is aligned with the executive ethics (S1) on the Style level, it is therefore important to describe the different approaches to ethics (S1). Ethics reflects a view of man.

Figure 6. Types of Ethic: Definition of Man.

Evolutionary

View of man	Materialistic relative changes lead by chance (statistical progression) within a challenging environment, from material to single living cell-multiple cells, to primates and man.
Definition	Man is an upgraded animal with specific biological and determined behavioral needs, subjective relative wants, and social conditioning (e.g., behaviorism)
Management level & Plan	The reductionist view removes 3DMM area: a) Management Style; b) Executive plans/rows. Instead, focus placed on Habits (S6), implementation (O6), Rules & Regulations (D6), Procedures (D5).

Commercial – Mercantile

View of man	Emphasis on consumer, producer, and market plan (needs, wants, satisfaction and delight); social economic demographics

(lower, middle, upper class, temperaments).

Definition — Man is an upgraded animal with specific biological and determined behavioral needs, subjective relative wants, and social conditioning (e.g., behaviorism)

Management level & Plan — The reductionist view removes 3DMM area: a) Management Style; b) Executive plans/rows. Instead, focus placed on Habits (S6), implementation (O6), Rules & Regulations (D6), Procedures (D5).

Marxist (social classes) & Nazi (racial distinctions & qualities)

View of man — Views suggest a) irreconcilable distinctions among proletariat, bourgeoisie and capitalists. In this environment, we find key values — existence of a *Dictatorship of the Proletariat* and *Atheism* at the exclusion of all other notions; b) similarly, the Nazi value is identified in the higher race vs. lower races; *Dictatorship of the 'folk'* and *Atheism.*

Definition — Proponents of these views divide society by any possible variables: class, race, age (fetus/old). Three categories exist in: 1) producers, 2) producers exploiters, and 3) those who manage producers' interests and production. Producers form a collective and own everything in common. Evolutionary views — society evolves from 2) to 1) via 3). The other view categorizes society into 3 types of producers: 1) highest productive groups; 2) lower less productive and purely consumer /parasitical groups, and 3) those who manage types 1) and 2). *Evolution* filters 2) to 1) via 3).

Management level & Plan — Both Marxist and Racist views are located in three areas on 3DMM: 1) *Info-base column* (D, O, #3, 6, and 9); 2) *Management Style – Culture*: where they see: collectivism or power of the will (S3); 3) *Habit* – working class or productive and ingenuity (S6), and Dependency (S9). State authoritarianism with absolute enforcement manage this evolution.

Supernatural - Christian (not cultist, which falls under any of the above)

View of man — Man made in the 'image of God.' Man reflects the Creator. They have respect for the value of family, brothers and sisters — broth's keeper. Authority and members recognize geometric natural law, 10 commandments.

Definition — When this view is not cultist, the existence and communication of the supernatural entity must provide: 1) Geometric natural law at the foundations for Creation; 2) Historical contractual documentation with man, 3) History case histories, commandments, applications, statutes, precedents, judgments and directed purpose, i.e., Objective law.

Management — Addresses all 27 Management Plans in the Management level & Plan   structure and must reflect this at the individual, social, organization and intra-national level.

The executive purpose (D1) is aligned with the executive ethics (S1) on the Style level, it is therefore important to describe the different approaches to ethics (S1). Ethics reflects a view of man.

Within the 3DMM, ethics is situated on the stylistic infrastructure, within the executive row and directive column. However, some substitute ethics operates in all social media. This ethic is nothing but rules and regulations (D6) on the design supervisory infrastructure.

Many supervisory and functional plans (S 4 – S9) are misinterpreted as being executive level ethics (S1). Here are some concrete examples of this pseudo-ethic:

Normative ethics is derived from the design management supervisory area (D4, D5,and D6). It consists in articulating, implementing, and having people to perform through authorized and approved policies. These policies imply prescribed procedures that are enforced through rules and regulations. It is here that the right and wrong, good and evil are determined.[123]

It is a developed etiquette derived from situational conditions. This situation ethic is collected from observations of human behavior. Observations made on actual choices made in practice by the hands-on user. This is conducted without referencing expert or specialist advice. Furthermore, this etiquette of appropriate behavior is transmitted through story telling or simple common sense.[124] The same type of etiquette has been evident in every other area, including: business, politics, medicine, environment, ecology, journalism, jurisprudence, engineering, genetics, abortion, feminism, sex, academia, tenure, education, psychology, and economics. Each area seems to have its own ethic derived not from the executive levels qualities but from operational and functional levels.

Meta-ethic is another supervisory type of ethic. This is because, on the

---

[123] Developers of this supervisory-based rule-based approach are: Aristotle (virtue ethics), Emanuel Kant (deontological normative theory), John Stuart Mill (utilitarian, consequentiality).

[124] Judith Martin, ('Miss Manners'), since 1978, has provided advice in the United Features Syndicate, (200+ newspapers worldwide). She answers her readers' questions on etiquette, and writes short essays on problems of manners or politeness.

one hand, it suggests that it is that people's feelings, their interests, and their belief systems determine moral values. One group suggests that it is the evolutionary development of the human psychology that leads to ethical standards, while another group proposed an objective independent truth. Such objective truth is intrinsically set in the world. Some theology and naturalistic philosophies maintain that the discovered ethical principles may be measured for validity.

Some authorities break down meta-ethics into nonrealism and realism schools. But again, these are nothing more than supervisory rules and regulations (O6). They are algebraic axioms and theorem-based determinations, and don't belong to executive level ethics (S1) at the style level that interconnect with other management plans at executive and supervisory infrastructures.

Another example is the emphasis on self-esteem, which is a close synonym of self-image (S2). In practice, this is more often than not disconnected from ethics (S1).

The self-esteem psychology is a hybrid system between psychology and religion. During the 1960s and 1970s, there was a new wave towards becoming a whole person. One was to question and to choose higher values. This approach was designed to help develop a new personality. This psychology spread through society, culture, and the church. As usual, in these things, such an approach led away from our better instincts and common sense. This led to the good feeling and view of each other: 'I'm OK and you're OK – a healthy self-acceptance. Yet, it is during these times that some noted that there was something wrong with this picture. It became evident that there were questionable acts and tendencies that were only limited due to existing established laws that prevented such acts and tendencies from having free reign. Similarly, the more one strove towards self-esteem and not to be directed by other's views, the more one eventually had to rely on one's own self-evaluation. When this image fell short of expectations, or failed because it was based on concepts such as, you don't need others, don't lose out, don't let them take advantage the more one suddenly felt an inordinate feeling for caution, an obsession for coming out on top, loneliness and pointlessness beyond description. There was no purpose! Self-esteem without an initial purpose was pointless. Without an initial purpose, self-esteem didn't prepare one for the next step in participating in a productive culture. Self-centered esteem led to a subculture.

In contrast, original Christianity has a clearly identifiable purpose (D1) based in a 3DMM. This purpose is derived from geometric natural law, is aligned with ethics (S1) where the Ten Commandments are a key component documenting social and civilization standards, which are expanded from the Ten Commandment, guaranteeing blessings or curses (Deuteronomy 27,28) which distinguishes between those who qualify for the kingdom of God, or those who qualify for the kingdom of Babylon.

Objectives (D2)
Business and Project Applications

Objectives (D2) respond to inputs from the purpose (D1) and set standards for strategic initiatives (D3). Objectives help calibrate functions that are derived from the purpose (D1)

• *Priorities* – a hierarchy of primary, secondary, and contingent alternatives attached to all functions, behavior, activities, productivity, and results. Priorities set guidelines for establishing strategy (D3) where resources are considered.

• *Authority* is synonymous with legitimacy, justification, and the right to exercise power. One may have the capability (power) to drive a car, but the state's department of public safety authorizes the requirements for, and who has right to drive, specific vehicles. In corporate business, authority is derived from the purpose (D1), specifically the contract, identity, and scope. The contract is written within the scope of state, national and/or international law. This purpose provides the scope for prioritizing and standardizing procedures (D5), and codes for the implementation of strategic (D3) plans. Inevitably, authority has a direct or indirect impact on supervisory plans: policy (D4) – decision-making; procedures (D5); and rules/regulations (D6); thus upon functional plans. Once something has been authorized, lower management may then approve sub-activities and procedures within the scope of what has been authorized.

• *Standards* may appear as qualifications. They are used to set and identify material quality, manufacturing production, behavior protocols, quality, and measurements scales. These form an integral part of the contract (D1). Standards include test methods that reflect specific procedures, inspections, and specialized measurements. In the human world, enforcement may be voluntary or supervised. Automated information system enforcement is built in through multiple and networked measurements compliance, comparative analysis with original specs, and through corrective/repair mechanisms.

It should be remembered that within the 3DMM, objectives (D2) are foundational plans of the 3DMM. These are reflected in the operational plans (O2), and also lead to self-image (S2) on the stylistic infrastructure. It is easier to recognize the full value of the design management infrastructure, which impacts both the operational and stylistic levels.

Objectives (D2)
Other Applications - philosophy, religion, and biological life

Based on the complexity of the living organism, the creation scientists' position is that living creatures' taxa reflects a fixed management system with its supervisory and executive infrastructures. Thus, internal or exterior changes within creatures can occur at the copy and self-adjustment levels. However, there is no evidence that these creatures can re-engineer unless this capability has been pre-programmed at the executive level. Nor is there evidence for redesign capabilities. On the other hand, evolutionary concepts propose that a series of beneficial mutations within challenging or isolated environments will produce group and multiple changes that are coordinated beyond the mere copy and adaptive ranges. The theory suggests that change involves what amounts to successful re-engineering and redesign of infrastructural and executive areas.

In philosophy, myth, ideology, and religion, and social sciences, priorities help distinguish between groups. The *geometric natural law-based structures* reflect: (a) the cone (three dimensional)[125] with its five infrastructural and energy-density qualitative values, and (b) five convex regular polyhedral - geometric solids (tetrahedron, cube, octahedron, icosahedrons, and dodecahedron). These are firm qualities that are an integral part of the infrastructural system.

In contrast, the *algebraic approach* suggests relative and variable priorities, minimized infrastructures, and qualities which are relatively linear and flat approaches to priorities[126].

---

[125] See Figure 22

[126] Richard Lynn, *Race Differences in Intelligence: An Evolutionary Analyses*, (Augusta, GA: Washington Summit Publisher, 2006). Research shows, among many other issues, how ideological views distort definitions and scientific researches, which

Similarities can be found in areas of social science.

Authority – Under geometric natural law, all authority resides and emanates from the eternal Lord God. Various other religions may also consider the existence of God as the supreme authority, but, as shown above and will be shown below, such a god and authority is derived from algebraic notions: first cause, harmonious and fine-tuned creation, private mystical experiences or revelations, or social economic privilege; in other words, from axioms and theorems.

The evolutionary materialist and reductionist methods are also established upon algebraic notions and contain relativist and subjective foundations. This shows that the algebraic approach leans on secondary plans for authority – e.g., scriptures and/or materialism and economics. The geometric natural law approach through its *inheritance* concept always refers to the infinite circle as a starting point, and unrolls through the inheritance principle. Nothing in what constitutes reality is outside the infinite circle. The historical timeline identifies laws, scientific evidence for the events, conditions, and structure that can be reconstructed, measured, and observed in creation.

In all of the above cases, some human authority mediates the interpretation of what constitutes certainty and uncertainty of the original sources, practices, priorities, strategies, enforcement, judgments, change, economics, and productivity. During political elections, we hear that everything is determined by 'it's the economy' However, from the 3DMM's geometric natural law view; the economy is decided from purpose. This economy is prioritized, authorized, and standardized through the objectives (D2), and set through strategy (D3).

From the algebraic relative position, it is policy (D4) that prioritizes, authorizes, and standardizes the strategies (D3). However, the original United States Constitution directs policy. Such GNL-based policies prioritize, authorize, and standardize representative government, and GNL-based education to help prepare students to address key social issues. They would be trained to implement strategies that use resources that support purposive improvement, innovations, and inventions. In contrast to this geometric approach, algebraic structures like those derived from the United Nations aims towards democratic relativized, and

---

then are followed by distorted solutions applications, resource utilization, and cultural redefinitions.

'appropriate' technology. Such technology would simply be designed to support family, community, or tribe-based economies. Eventually, these will be led to promote club of Rome objectives. Such objectives include: deindustrialization, population reduction schemes, and centralized monetary controls. All this is an issue of what is the source for objectives.

Throughout history, Christian Church authority had sought the means of establishing and grounding civilization on a firm legal foundation. After the dissolution of the Western Roman Empire, and even though the concept of the Roman Empire was believed to have continued, the Celtic Christians, Roman Catholic Church, and the Eastern Orthodox Church have sought the various means that were based on geometric natural law to raise, maintain, and improve civilization. There was more than a simple economy. For over 1,500 years, Christendom maintained the view that all authority, knowledge, and its organization and order, emanated from the eternal Lord God. Christianity held the view that economic and cultural improvements without the excesses of mercantile and banking practices contributed to the reduction of want and servitude. The continuously increasing verifiable knowledge ensured certainty, and guaranteed mankind and society self-perfection. In the West, the Catholic Church promoted and cooperated with those who developed scientific discoveries, maintained astronomical telescopes, and contributed to scientific inventions and discoveries. Seven craters on the Earth's Moon are named after Roman Catholic Jesuit scientists. See below for details about Copernicus, Galileo, the inquisition, and Scope's Trial, that today in areas of education and the media have reached ridiculous levels of interpretation.

Authority began to shift with the introduction of Aristotelian views. Examples of this can be seen with the beginning of the scholasticism of Thomas Aquinas. This was followed later by Luther's reductionist approach. This, in turn, opened doors to relativism, and provided foundations for the promotion of rationalism, empiricism, progressive idealism, masonry, and the ideals of the French Revolution. It is here that reason became triumphant and became the only means through which authoritative value was attained. The Encyclopédistes[127] contributed to

---

[127] Denis Diderot, Jean le Rond d'Alemebert. In France (1751-1766; 1772, 1777, 1780). Eventually 35 volumes, promoted science and secular thought. An earlier work by Pierre Baye (1647-1706) *Dictionnaire Historique et Critique* (1699 and 1702)

the revolution. From this, among other subjects, we see further development in the reinterpretation of geological evidence in terms of long ages, the formulation of materialism, uniformitarianism, and evolutionism. Various evolutionary, authoritative scientific social and political systems were experimented with during the twentieth century. This resulted in the various revolutionary and world wars. We see Marxism and Nazism as destructive versions based upon evolutionary authority. This has emanated from the French Revolutionary ideals. Today, these same views are well imbedded in the American, European, and the United Nations' core of the uniformitarian and evolutionary concepts of authority.

Because of the relativistic core structure and non-absolute approach to ethics, uniformitarian authority tends to gravitate towards absolutist authoritarianism. This is exemplified by statements such as evolution is almost certainty, a reality and consequently does not hesitate to suggest extreme action and influence to those who seek exemption from this thesis.[128]

Standards do not stand in isolation. Standards are related to what the 'contract' has established for the utilization of resources. Standards reflect authority, laws, rules, precedents, resource scopes, codes, calibration, measurements, definitions, and descriptions. Standards are used to measure degrees of authentic or deviating measurements. Standards are evident in the manufacture of products, operation, behavior, and compliance with laws, procedures, and regulations.

Standards can also be used to establish authenticity in ideology, religion, and science. Successful achievement is rewarded, measured, repeated, or improved upon. Similarly, deviation from standards can be viewed as deviating from the norm. In each case standards involve all of the executive plans: a purpose, objectives, and strategic components.

Objectives and standards are evident in evolution. Evolutionary objectives are best identified in E. Mayr, and W. B. Provine, eds, *The Evolutionary Synthesis: Perspectives on the Unification of Biology* (Cambridge: Harvard University Press, 1998) which lists a five-point strategy of an evolutionary synthesis. This provides criteria or assumptions for constructing the uniformitarian / evolutionary scientific model. These are listed below:

---

was a biographical and highly skeptical work of established religion.

[128] Starring Ben Stein, *Expelled: No Intelligence Allowed* (2008).

- Evolutionary principles and phenomenon can be substantiated and explained by known genetic mechanisms and processes.
- Evolutionary principles involve small incremental genetic changes directed by natural selection—speciation, and not through saltation (leaps).[129]
- The mechanism of all types of change, no matter how small, is due to phenotypal selection in its environment, in contrast to genetic drift[130]
- Natural population that carries genetic diversity is the key factor for evolution, where natural selection in the wild is subject to ecological factors.
- Explanation of historical observations from different levels in paleontology is accomplished by providing explanations of extrapolations from micro- to macro-evolution. This would not necessarily mean a constant rate of changes.
-

It is worth to remember that all too frequently many 'proofs' upon which the theory of evolutionary stands remains proof for a very short time. Most explanations had been scrapped almost overnight. While the Piltdown man and Lucy had been advertized as evidence for pre-human species, other scientists, many of whom had been evolutionists, had clearly stated that such conclusions were premature and that there was much evidence to show either that tampering had been involved or that such creatures were extinct apes. This can be seen in a long row of such evidence. For example, all proofs for evolution that are listed and described in the school textbooks have been found to be based on outdated, misinterpreted, or fraudulent evidence. At the time of this writing, Sushma Reddy, the leading author and a fellow at the Field Museum in Chicago, Illinois, wrote, 'With this study, we learned two major things. First, appearances can be deceiving. Birds that look or act similar are not necessarily related. Second, much of bird classification and conventional wisdom on the evolutionary relationships of birds is wrong.'

---

[129] Niles Eldredge and Stephen Jay Gould, ""Punctuated equilibria: an alternative to phyletic gradualism,"," in T.J.M. Schopf, ed., *Models in Paleobiology* (San Francisco: Freeman Cooper, 1972).

[130] T. Dobzhansky, T and O. Pavlovsky, "An experimental study of interaction between genetic drift and natural selection," Evolution (1957): 11:311-319.

The results of the largest ever study of bird genetics are so widespread that the names of dozens of birds will now have to be changed, says the study to be published in *Science* magazine.[131]

The common evolutionists' explanation for such abnormal scientific standards is the statement that as new data is discovered, it becomes natural that scientific hypotheses and theories will be adjusted. Within the general scientific realm, this is a truism. However, within an uniformitarian framework, there is very little upon which one can make reliable predictions. First, one should realize that the uniformitarian theory is not a scientific theory and anything that is based upon it will yield unscientific predictions. Second, based on the first, such prediction will leave the subject matter in uncertainty and not contribute to the attainment of conditional certainty – the purpose of the scientific method. For example, the hypothesis and the theory both reflect at least five stages of uncertainty and can be confirmed, provide foundations for lateral solutions, or may be falsified. Yet, within the uniformitarian scope, these characteristics of the hypothesis and theory are ambiguous. Furthermore, the nature of the theory of evolution is such that it can never be falsified, since in its scope of understanding, there is no other legitimate or alternate scientific theory. Uniformitarianism is a closed materialistic system. The certitude of having the Theory of Evolution irreplaceable is further substantiated by the evolution proponents' claim that evolution is almost certainty, and is truth.

It has been shown, that prior to the advent of the Theory of Evolution, in whatever forms it had been packaged over the years, both science and the scientific method did exist alive and well. It had been developed in various forms primarily in Christian Europe, but has had roots in earlier civilizations, and emerged in some form during the Golden Age of the Islamic civilization[132]. Very little, if anything, of this science

---

[131] http://news.yahoo.com/s/afp/scienceusresearchbirds.

[132] Al-Haytham (optics); Geber (chemistry); Al-Kindi (earth science); the famous Avicenna (medicine); Ibn Zuhr (surgery); Abu Rayahan Al-Biruni (astronomy); and others. Ibn Al-Haytham listed the scientific method's steps which included: observation, problem statement, hypothesis formulation, testing the hypothesis through experimentation, analysis of results, interpretation of data, conclusion, and publication http://images.agustinwar.multiply.com/attachment/0/RxbYbQoKCr4AAD@kz FY1/IslamicCalendar-A-Case-Study.pdf. Biologists of various professional

depends on uniformitarian tenets. What led up to the uniformitarian light had accumulated as a separate movement that relied on an existing knowledge-base and methodologies. After all, there are many dedicated scientists who simply want to conduct scientific research. They wish to discover and verify new data, so as to fill the knowledge-base as accurately as they can.

The 3DMM summarizes the complexity of what goes into the workings of any complex management system (e.g., engineering project management, information, knowledge base). Such information systems involve databases and knowledge base systems, and here we can test other information and knowledge bases such as philosophical, political, ideological and religious systems. Furthermore, human language reflects an information and knowledge base that reflect 3DMM group of management infrastructures: 1) phonetics/ lexicology grammar (Management Design); 2) syntax (Management Operations) and 3) stylistics (Management Style).

Here's another analogy of the 3DMM which the language literary levels reflect:

Figure 1. Comparison: 3DMM with Language/Literary Levels.

3DMM – Language Literature Levels – Observed Parallels and Similarities

MANAGEMENT DESIGN: D1 – D9 – Grammar

The composition of language and literature begin with the language elements (parts of speech): verbs, nouns, prepositions, etc. When arranged meaningfully they demonstrate a *purpose* (laws, identity, scope); *objectives* (standards, authority), *strategy* (forecasted utilization), in accordance with specific cultural conventions (guidelines - *policies*), arrangements and order (*procedures*) and *rules*. These are edited (*R&D*), for coherence and clarity (*economics*); and communication, meaning and audience/customer appreciated results (*productivity*). Inevitably, a grammatical sentence reflects purpose and objectives (*standards, authority*).

MANAGEMENT OPERATIONS: O1 – O9 – Syntax

Each communication reflects specific objectives. The writer refines

---

pedigree: I. A. Ahmad, 'The Rise and Fall of Islamic Science: The Calendar as a Case Study,' 'Faith and Reason: Convergence and Complementarity, (Al Akhawayn University); (http://users.jyu.fi/~daagar/index_files/arabs.html) (http://www-history.mcs.st-adrews.ac.uk/Biographies/Al-Biruni.html); Bradley Steffens, *Ibn Al-Haytham: First Scientist* (Morgan Reynolds Publishing, 2006). Also, http://en.wikipedia.org/wiki/Islamic_science.

communication through planned, organized and directed use of expression alternatives: simple, complex, compound or any of these combinations that lead to clear objectives - desired results. Writers or speakers lead their audience by using controlled techniques and qualities that help implement objectives. Writers, speakers, and artists examine interconnection of/among ideas, concepts, coherence and relevancy, here expressed in each sentence, implied meaning and sub-/structures to bring out value (*optimization*). Focus on the *economy* of word and image lead towards precise, durable and clear ideas and action. These in turn lead to the attainment of proper audience desired effect and results (*quality assurance and control*)

<u>MANAGEMENT STYLE: S1 – S9 and Stylistics</u>

Authors refine textual content & context with effective semantic, synonymic, symbolic, typological application. With this, they aim to achieve effective, representative, reflective, uniform communication, and a perception of and possible habit change (ethics, image, and culture). Over time, writers have considered six stylistic levels of communications. They considered from the lowest - 'vulgar' with a maximum 500 word vocabulary that lasts 5 years, to other levels - common, technical, literary, philosophical and the highest - poetic level with its 200,000 word vocabulary and 250 year longevity.

Stylistics involves establishing the author's writing skills, methods, attitude and themes. As a manager of his craft, the author or artist will identify qualitative contribution, dignity, integrity, originality (self-determination) and productive expression of freedom or dependence. Style does not only focus on proper language usage (habit, dependence, culture) but uses all available communicative means (culture, attitude, methods, images, ethics, musicality) to ensure that the entire work (short story, article, novel, music, artwork) is in total harmony – (3DMM) managed – all 27 plans at the three infrastructural levels, i.e., having each part contributing to enhance the whole. The author will respect dignity, integrity and self-determination of all or some of the audience.

The Christian Bible identifies management executive plans containing calibrating parameters. The Ten Commandments are designed to apply to personal, family, social, national, and civilization standards in terms of blessings and curses (Deuteronomy 27-28). These are standards and guidelines for state laws, statutes, and judgments. From this executive level, supervisory policies reflect guidelines to decision-making. These include establishing definitions and identifying best options that align with executive plans. These will be addressed in greater detail below. Both the commandments and policies are contrasted with those that are exercised in 'Egypt' – those who are not directly under the divine covenant.

Standards are evident in terms of construction codes as in the design of Noah's Ark. These reflect engineering standards and codes that are built into the structure to be tested in a catastrophic environment that never existed before or since. This marine vehicle had to withstand singular oceanic tidal waves for over twelve months. During the initial 2/3 of the time, oceanic waves were built-up worldwide into mega-tsunami-type momentum. Both lunar and solar gravity magnified the height of each wave on this limitless global ocean. Hydro-tectonic activity forced up to 50,000 underwater volcanoes, which spewed all imaginable output that sifted multiple times and settled as sedimentary material over large areas. Earth's electromagnetic field switched a dozen times during a day, moved and uplifted mountain ranges, while hot oceans contributed to temperatures inversions, and super-mega hurricanes. Noah's Ark's engineering standards and codes were built into the construction to withstand these extremes. The Ark also had to accommodate 10,000 pairs or sevens syngameons of juvenile living creatures, carry enough food to last more than year, and handle waste. The change of weather made many of these creatures hibernate.

The geometric infrastructure that is built into the Creation week shows that there is much more to the Biblical content - e.g., Tabernacle, role of King David, structure and functions of the priesthood, nutrition, social, civilization, and two types of animals – clean and unclean - standards.[133] Many types designate standards. These in turn lead to secondary standards, currents of meaning and milestones that run throughout history as constants, and become forecasting tools (prophesying methodology). These are also management and organizational standards that had been maintained for thousands of years and help test validity. Examples are evident in King Nebuchadnezzar's psychology and management style that can be used to predict behavior, policy, and outcomes in our modern world. The Bible provides a 3DMM knowledge base whose standards specifications, tests, procedures, guides, and definitions can be used to measure and calibrate accuracy today.

Similarly, the Christian Bible is a reference document. Each day of creation becomes a foundation for the establishment of the following day's creation. These reflect the geometric solids, and become a pattern for all scientific study, clearly designating the order and distinction

---

[133] The curses and blessing in Deut. 27 and 28 are proven throughout Biblical history and valid today in our modern technological civilization.

between each level of creation. Figure 3 (copied below) clearly shows a contrastive and incompatible list of events and resources that are part of a standard for classifying all that composes the divinely created world. This is then compared with stages provided by evolutionists who use the uniformitarian principles.

The evolutionary extrapolated big bang or steady state begins from the uniformitarian present. From here begin a confusion of terms. The standard definitions no longer apply. The terms are expanded beyond their definitional meaning. In such a context, the terms become irrational. For example, materialistic notions of nothing without a framework of reference can raise some eyebrows. Here, uniformitarian scientists speculate about the materiality of 'nothingness,' 'before the beginning,' 'before time.' When reading such scientific material, the text begins to mutate into something mythological, an exercise on a play of words that have no contextual anchors. Perhaps the English language is too simplistic to express a future time that occurs before the beginning in the past.

This book contains language that describes events within geometric natural law (GNL); however, these are not the terms and concepts that modern everyday creation scientists use. This line of thinking has been discontinued after World War I. Current creation scientists simply rely on what current laboratory discoveries provide and rely on their perception of the inerrant word of God (historical events and cataclysms) to help interpret the facts identified through empirical science. However, as it will be shown later, the use of geometric natural law, geometric solids, and the conic energy-density concept open up new areas of Biblically identifiable standards within creation.

The creation scientific model has helped to systematically predict and confirm: (a) recent global catastrophic dynamics evidenced through geology, paleontology, and qualitative changes; (b) other scientifically workable models of the universe; (c) super mega complexity of life forms, the law of biogenesis[134]. The uniformitarian/ evolutionary model, on the

---

[134] For example, seven ICR conferences held in 1986, 1990, 1994, 1998, 2003, 2006, and 2008 provided for strategic assessment. The Fourth International Conference on Creationism, Pittsburgh, PA, August 3-8, 1998, for example, in 1997, a paper entitled "The current State of Creation Astronomy" by Danny R. Faulkner, PhD, evaluated creationists' approach and lack of contribution in areas of astronomy (http://www.icr.org). Since that time, the creation camp forwarded works by John Hartnell, *Starlight, Time and the New Physics* (Australia: Creation Book

other hand, has presented serious standards challenges in areas of biology, dating methods, fossil record, gaps between transitional forms, and vertical ascent (macro-evolution).

Among the more honest evolution scientists we see an attempt to justify some scientific method.

Strategies (D3)
Business and Project Applications

Strategy is the utilization of resources whose use and performance is forecasted and planed. Strategic components are filtered through the objectives (D2). Objectives in turn are derived from, and fulfill, the scope of the purpose (D1). The difference between strategies and tactics is that where strategies involve comprehensive long-term objectives, tactics are goal-related and of shorter duration. Tactics are sub-strategies. A group of properly scheduled and resourced activities will help achieve a strategic objective.

Activities that are designed to meet specific goals must be loaded with procedures (D5), resources, qualified personnel, technology, and logistics, and reflect performance and cost controls. Both the objectives and tactical activities must be specific, measurable, achievable, relevant, and time terminable. Strategies involve resources, forecasts, performance, and planning.

Being at the design management level, strategy is linked directly with operational direction (O3) and culture (S3) plans. All adjacent plans have mutual impact upon each other. It is now easier to recognize the full value of culture when culture is recognized as having been founded on the strategic design management level. Similarly, culture (S3) feeds rudimentary definition of strategy (D3). The three, strategy, directing, and culture, are in the infobase column and at the executive level.

Publishers, 2007); Alex Williams ,and John Hartnett, PhD, *Dismantling the Big Bang* (Green Forest, AR: Master Books, 2005). In other areas, the creation scientists' RATE Project (Radioisotopes and Age of the Earth) have among much other evidence showed that Precambrian zircons yielded a helium diffusion age of 6,000 years; this would suggest that a billion years worth of nucleus decay of uranium has occurred within the last 6,000 years.

Evolution scientists also had conferences and did some reassessments that, for example, contributed to their updating of their position on "the modern evolutionary synthesis – leading up from 1857-1899, 1900-1915, and begun from 1936 – 1947. See E. Mayr and W. B. Provine, eds., *The Evolutionary Synthesis*, Ibid.

Strategies (D3)
Other Applications - Strategy used in philosophy, religion, and biology.

Strategy incorporates and aligns itself with the previous two executive functions - purpose and objectives. Strategy resides in the database column, as directing and culture plans are. Strategy's output is delivered to direct supervisory plans: policy, procedures, and rules and regulations. These management links are evident in the philosophical and religious constructs, and must be identified within biology.

As referenced earlier, see how J. Kepler in the sixteenth century used these geometric solids to help predict the field/gravitational relationships among the planets within our solar system. The eternal Lord God, through his first handwritten account of his creative process has established a prototype for identifying the various branches of science. These geometric solids dynamics were also established within man – the co-creator, who would be able to discover, establish, and manage a body of accurate knowledge. This would be a knowledge-base of conditional certainty. He would then be able to forecast options and outcomes within the master plan.

The eternal Lord God's original creation contained a pre-designed, built-in, flexible resiliency that has allowed all of Creation to function perfectly within the perfect environment. This resiliency can be seen in the various ways that Creation adjusts to its various environmental conditions. It began to adjust to various lower levels of energy-density levels and catastrophic events that occurred at the time of the second and third singularities.

This particular resiliency is evident among the living creatures – their ability to adapt to changing environments. The original design for life at the physical, cellular, chromosome, and sub-chromosome information software levels, that reflect infrastructures and dynamics of geometric solids, contains programming for self-adjustment along specific lines. Finches adjust the size, structure, and durability of their beaks to help overcome drought and fertile conditions. Birds have pre-designed beak versatility. Lizards re-grow limbs that had been severed. Insects can change nutritional habits from vegetarian to carnivorous as the climate changes from warm to cold. Deep ocean life forms subsist on alternate energy sources. These are elements of adaptation with pre-designed programmed parameters within each species. These predesigned adaptive change parameters are associated not only with loss of genetic information, but there are extreme environmental conditions that lead species to lose significant genetic information as they reach the very limits of their genetic pre-programmed adaptability. In order to overcome any further beyond pre-programmed changes and loss of most of the genetic information, such transitory species changes would require evidence of genetic infrastructural re-engineering, redesign, and outright invention. These are strategic and tactical considerations.

The creation scientific model, based on the Biblical legal historical evidence, predicts that paleontological evidence should reveal a trend towards gigantism in all living areas: plan, animal, and man. Descriptions in the Bible suggest that conditions before the worldwide catastrophic flood had been significantly different than those on our Earth today. Much scientific research has been conducted in an attempt to reconstruct geologic, paleontological, and life science evidence that would reflect the pre-flood conditions. For example, Tyrannosaurus Rex's lung cavity clearly shows that in order for such a large creature to live, it would need at least twice the atmospheric air pressure than we have today. This also shows that one reason that helped sustain large sized pre-flood creatures and plants was this double pressured atmospheric condition.

4.4 Uncertainty Management: Supervisory Plans

Supervisory plans include: policy (D4), procedures (D5), and rules and regulations (D6). Supervisory management plans have briefly been discussed above; now these plans will be substantiated.

While going through the description of the 3-D management model, it is necessary to remind ourselves that this model offers the knowledge-base structure and content that ensures contingent certainty. Certainty is not a simple fact or collection of facts, which are contingent on the framework and processes that propose their factual reliability. Should the framework or processes be expanded, filtered for quality, or passed through the DMPS uncertainty tests, it is all too frequent to see that most facts stand on the slippery ground of assumptions, localized application, or inferences. Facts in many cases may provide a temporary bandage for informal application, but it is the 3DMM that provides the framework through which reliable, verifiable, and quantified data is processed, and where a history of incomplete or false data, calculations, and assumptions are cataloged as case histories, and where they can easily be sourced to verify the cause for their limitation.

Policy, Procedures, Rules and Regulations
Business and Project Applications

As shown on Figure 5 and Table 4, all organizations and engineering project management contain a second level – the supervisory plans. These supervisory plans function within the scope established at the executive level. However, supervisory plans are designed to convert communication from the executive level in order to ensure that the functional plans implement quality productivity. Supervisory plans are designed to address the following issues: administration, operation, maintenance, quality, safety, security, and emergency. Furthermore, supervisory plans receive feedback from the functional plans of R&D (D7), economics (D8), and productivity/quality control (D9).

The processes described below apply not only to organizations, philosophical systems, ideology, and psychology but also biological processes. Psychology, as seen in Table 3, corresponds to the supervisory plans of: *policy* (decision-making and problem solving – intelligence, intellect); *procedures* (will), and rules and regulations (emotions). This, by definition, is the *psyche* or the *soul*. The difference between animal and human psyche is that animal psyche is to a large part pre-wired with instinct. Animals exhibit degrees of reasoning, will power, and emotion. Humans have an opened supervisory system to the executive plans – they can identify and modify their purpose, objective's priorities, standards, and authority, and manage strategies. Animals do these through pre-programming built in for their species.

Together, supervisory plans support processes and minimize uncertainty and risk. A successfully pre-designed proactive supervisory process will ensure efficient and effective application and forecasting, and provide an awareness of all networks and relationships. When such plans are properly programmed, they will ensure the secure flow of in-/outputs, help identify and eliminate errors, waste, and delay, thus guaranteeing production through the functional level (D7, D8, and D9). Supervision will establish routines, reporting and controlling functions that can easily be audited for compliance and conformance with standards.

While functioning within the scope of executive conditional certainty, the scientific method is located at the supervisory level where uncertainty is addressed and checked. As described above, policy (D4) functions within guidelines for decision-making and problem-solving. Decisions remain within the executive contingent certainty and do not stray from these executive plans. Engineering project management for example, conforms with executive objectives and purpose.

On the other hand, policies, procedures, and rules and regulations that stray outside or fall outside executive plans inevitably reflect and support an alien executive plan. Such straying or redefinitions may occur when policy (decision-making and problem-solving) become overwhelmed with either misaligned supervisory or functional plans. Processes and products become prioritized above those set by the executive plans. This may also occur when, for some reason, executive plans have been changed and/or have been improperly communicated to the supervisory and functional plans. The answer for the 'for some unknown reason' statement may be found at the operational or stylistic infrastructural levels. It is therefore necessary to not forget the interrelation among the three infrastructural levels of design, operations, and style.

Policy, Procedures, Rules and Regulations
Other Applications.

Policy (D4) guidelines become blurred when definitions have mutated. For example, Christians who had been attending secular institutions of education have not been given the opportunity to examine definitions in a scientific manner. They receive information and a technique for challenging a non-uniformitarian knowledge base. Students memorize this and are then tested for compliance. A script of concepts and responses is registered and regurgitated and graded upon. Specific guidelines of thinking are established. History is replaced with caricatures, notions of something primitive evolving to modern realities, and nonmaterial inferences are totally discouraged.

This is a symptom of cultural re-engineering. Here, although Christians may eventually try to assimilate and negotiate their way through such thinking, they can at best come out with hybrid versions – e.g., theistic evolutionism. Those who are less critically minded begin to extrapolate that since the church fathers and saints had not been uniformitarian i.e., scientists, they *ipso facto* are primitive, not scientists and therefore can at best approximate true knowledge and truth. Such guidelines extend towards a pantheistic view where they apply the same rules to Jesus Christ and his Apostles.

Uniformitarians, however, are not immune to their own materialistic historical myths. Evolution is suddenly believed to produce, to select, or to choose statistically. Without too much effort such metaphorical language becomes a habit and leads the unwary towards New Age and 'omega point' type of thinking. This is pantheism – endowing nature with anthropological capabilities. In such a context, metaphorically, genes become selfish; monsters become hopeful; and extraterrestrials give evolution a hand since the expected mechanical and materialistic forces don't cooperate in the empirical science lab. Even textbooks resort to outdated, faulty, and fraudulent proofs for evolution.

Evolution, creation, intelligent design and hybrids may present hypothetical extrapolations from existing empirical evidence. Evolution, however, tends to establish triple layers of hypothetical constructs. A fundamental construct really incorporates three separate hypotheses: materialism, chance mutations, and movement from simple to complex systems. These axiomatic postulates are ideological rather than scientific hypotheses. These are conclusions that have little or no empirical scientific evidence to support them. Focusing on matter forces three models of thinking (mechanical, organic, and process) but excludes information technology models. Here matter simply appears as a support rather than the driver. They do not address the complexities involved at the macro-changes involving re-engineering, redesign and reinvention within the three infrastructural management models.

Why do evolutionists accuse their opponent scientists of not understanding or confusing evolutionary scientific facts? The theory of evolution is a no-brainer. Hundreds of evolutionist debunkers populate the dozens of evolution versus creation and ID websites where it is clear that these uniformitarian scientists have trouble keeping their scientific thinking straight. Are evolutionary concepts really so difficult to understand? Or is it again an issue of the language and attitude that evolutionists use?

One of the classical and best tests to policy occurred several times on the www.truorigin.org debates. One example is the debate between Douglas Theobald (evolutionist) who presented his twenty-nine evidences for macro-evolution,' and Ashby Camp (creationist) who responded to the evidential fallacies presented in Theobald's work. The same applies to many other such debates on the same website[135]. It soon becomes clear

---

[135] Example: Ashby Camp's response to Douglas Theobald, "29 Evidences for Macroevolution" (five parts) www.trueorigin.org/theobald1b.asp.

that the evolution-creation or evolution-intelligent design debates are not at all about science, scientific method, evidence, or scientific predictions. The guidelines to thinking (policy) tend to circumvent scientific evidence. Scientific evidence is presented, discarded, minimized, sanitized, or marginalized. There are two objectives during these high level debates: (1) to examine scientific empirical data and see which model provides the best explanations and predictions; (2) an attempt to either submit everyone under uniformitarian thinking or be marginalized.

Briefly, the materialists design their reality from today's conditions, processes, and rates. Then they take some physical laws and implement the simple-to-complex rule. This uniformitarian approach excludes any kind of possibility for the Biblically identified three singularities. So if the Grand Canyon could have been caused by two-week drainage of a three-lake system, the uniformitarian will only consider the options that support long ages - a small river caused this canyon over millions of years. The same logic is seen across all other disciplines.

The Book of Job can be dated by the empirical evidence described in the book to have been written between 2000 BC and 1800 BC. The book documents evidence that is presented by the eternal Lord God. There's a list of weather conditions and cycles, details of winter conditions, and oceanic glaciations that mark the onset of the ice age that began to form 500 years after the great deluge. Job lived in the Middle East and may have become aware of snow and ice sheets that were beginning to form in the highest mountains, but a passage in Job refers to oceans freezing – clearly referring to the polar caps (Job 38:29-30).

Creation climatologists investigated all data that had been used to suggest several uniformitarian ice ages that extended over millions of evolutionary years (EY). These evolution scientists found that the ocean floor deposits, geological scouring, valley cutting, chemical isotope ratio variations, and paleontological evidence suggested EY.[136]

Creation scientists established that all of these features could have easily been laid rapidly within a range of 7 to 200 years under specific

---

[136] J. Aber Sandusky, 'Birth of the Glacial Theory' – http://academic.emporia.edu/aberjame/histgeol/agassiz/glacial.htm; "How are past temperatures determined from an ice core?" *Scientific American* (2004), http://www.sciam.com/print_version.cfm?articleID=00001580-C282-1148-828283414B7F012B; EPICA community members, 'Eight glacial cycles from an Antarctic ice core' *Nature* 429:623, http://www.up.ethz.ch/people/flueckiger/publications/epica04nat/pdf.

environmental conditions. Today, evolutionary publications demonstrate that evolution scientists have yet to understand the mechanisms that contributed to the formation of up to five of their ice ages. Creation scientists, however, were able to easily identify the mega-critical atmospheric requirements for the changes that brought about a single ice age that occurred within 500 years after a worldwide flood.

Requirements for an ice age are: (a) massive volcanic and plate tectonic upheavals, which (b) heated the oceans; this (c) increased evaporation from these heated oceans, (d) while volcanic ash covered the Earth, thus contributing to the cooling of the atmosphere; (e) these interactions caused increased precipitation (fifty times magnitude of that existing today), and, (f) these conditions had to persist for at least two consecutive years. So, 500 years after the flood, snow accumulated rapidly at the poles and mountain tops within a period of two years, while in the lower valleys, particularly within the vicinity of the warm and hot oceans, temperature was temperate and the land supported abundant life. This would explain all of the frozen conditions in which we discover hundreds of thousands of mammoths in the northern regions of the Earth.

After 500 years, volcanic and oceanic activity ceased and the Earth cooled. Volcanic dust having cleared and with atmospheric temperature rising, within 7 – 200 years, the ice packs began to melt significantly. The total duration of the post-flood ice age lasted approximately 700 years with an error margin of 200 years. Much scientific research, including the use of CRAY computer simulations, had helped reconstruct the single ice age on the Earth.[137]

In the Book of Job, God has used two chapters to describe key detailed descriptions and comparative behaviors of non-mythological gigantic land and aquatic creatures that are extinct today, yet interacted with humans in recent past (Job 40 - 42).

Laying aside the predictable uniformitarian bias regarding the origin of the Book of Job, chronologically this book is considered to be one of the earliest books in the Christian Bible. Based on the described ice age, the book must have been composed between 500 to 700 years after the

---

[137] http://www.icr.org, http://www.icr.org , http://www.icr.org , http://www.icr.org , http://www.icr.org , http://www.icr.org , http://www.icro.org/research/index/researchp_Iv_r04/ , http://www.icr.org , http://www.icr.org , http://www.icr.org , http://www.icr.org.

flood. Uniformitarians totally overlook this wealth of three-dimensional information, and instead offer some one- or two-dimensional interpretation. Such is the result of uniformitarian filters. All must fit within the three-policy view and anything that does not is myth and irrelevant.

These examples summarize how supervisory policy may either refine the tools for decision-making and problem-solving, or may be used to actually blind the process into continuous uncertainty.

PROCEDURES (D5) • Best and economic steps • Processes • Flowchart Other Applications

After scientists of the evolution, creation and intelligent design persuasions have: (a) examined the same empirical evidence, data, information, and processes; (b) processed these through their scientific models, which include their assumptions (e.g., uniformitarian, three global singularities, or irreducible complexity, harmonizing universal constants); (c) interpreted the data in order to make scientific predictions, this should lead to some sort of confirmation of increased certainty or falsification of predictions. In each case such results will become part of the knowledge bases whose purpose is to ensuring accurate knowledge – conditional certainty.

Similarly, throughout history, in a purely naturalistic environment, people have tracked the life cycle from birth to death, and this was an observable and testable fact. They noticed that children in one family differed from each other in a number of ways both physically and temperamentally. Husbandry has shown that animals and plants, through selective breeding, brought about preferred traits. It was also noticed that several animals resembled each other in more ways than one but were of different species. Based on this, it was determined that with enough variation among the species, a specie family could change to become another species. And this assumption was further expanded into a second layer by extrapolating into the past and assuming that life emerged through spontaneous combustion or under the right chemical interaction within the proper environment that life was produced from non-life.

Early Christians were aware of these popular factual and procedural views. Christians have also recognized existing contradictions between these pagan procedures and the information that was logged in the Christian scriptural and traditional knowledge-base. In this latter knowledge base, there were all types of divinely identified priorities that reflected procedures: laws, statutes, judgments, and precedents. This knowledge/wisdom-base encapsulates multiple, interlinked information, physical project timelined events, and physical laws. Here workable documented precedents contributed to establishing forecasts, quantitative alternatives, priorities, applications, determination of consequences and quality guarantee. This is also seen in the parallels between Management Design and the Tabernacle in the Wilderness. Similarly, Noah's Ark contains key pieces of information that reflect procedures, engineering design-based standards, codes, proportion designs that are not only to withstand dramatically changed environmental conditions, but also reflect design standards, codes in modern ship building engineering.[138] Such scientific study has been conducted exhaustively by John Woodmorappe and many others[139].

Some Greek philosophers (Plato), and later in the thirteenth century (Thomas Aquinas), toyed with the idea that creation was a balanced, mathematically symmetrical system that reflected geometric solids. We should see these markers and constants and be awed by the symmetry and laws that govern them. This symmetry and balance can be seen at the micro- and mega-levels and all points in between. From this, two views diverged: (a) evidence of the workings of a mega-originating intelligence designer; (b) existence of some inherent natural inner causal and lawful relationship that integrates all of reality into a mega-design and order.

Much more can be written on these themes and interpretations of what constitutes real and near procedures. It is necessary to identify what the decision-making and problem-solving (DMPS) procedures are since it is here where contingencies are established and addressed, and where uncertainty is processed towards certainty.

---

[138] Also, provide adequate scientific law to help reconstruct pre-flood conditions on Earth and at the time of Creation.

[139] These scientifically measureable events were examined by John Woodmorappe in his book, *Noah's Ark: A Feasibility Study* (1996), while J. Sarfati has answered all criticism presented on the issue by the uniformitarian representative, Mark Isaak, in his *Problems with a Global Flood*, 2nd edition (1998) – http://www.talkorigins.org/faqs/faq-noahs-ark.html . The rebuttal was presented by J. Sarfati in his *Problems with a Global Flood?* (1998) on http://www.trueorigin.org/arkdefen.asp.

Decision-Making and Problem-Solving (DMPS)–Procedures
Business and project management application and other applications

During one of my corporate management development courses on decision-making and problem-solving (DMPS), I able to source at least 25 DMPSs – sales, risk, computer assisted, neural and networked, etc. Many have been standardized but others that have to deal with greater variables and unknowns reflected creative decision-making requirements. The creative one expanded alternatives and options to help circumvent barriers.

The basic DMPS objective is to resolve uncertainty and lead it to greater degrees of (conditional) certainty. This shows that the purpose for applying the decision-making and problem-solving method is the same as that of the scientific method –convert uncertainty to conditional certainty.

At its foundation DMPS may be very simple; for example, we may compare the challenges that a mouse must overcome with that of Christopher Columbus:

Example 1: A mouse has to go through a maze to get at the cheese.

Example 2: Columbus must persuade sponsors, and then must discover a route to India (America).

Both the mouse and Columbus consider and implement the following actions:

A situation demands resolution. (maze and cheese; sponsors and discover a route to India).

- Time pressure.
- Lack of complete information.
- Uncertainty suggests risk for any decision made.
- Consequences expressed in terms of reward or punishment.
- Existence of two or more alternative (contingent) actions.
-

This list will have to be adjusted to the decision maker's personal qualities. Figure 8 below helps identify personal qualities that usually come in to affect the decision-making process and the manner in which problems are solved. In the designated mental listing of activities, it is possible to recognize the executive and supervisory faculties, and functional plans in the physical and skills areas:

Figure 8. Personal Qualities Affecting Decision–Making.

<table>
<tr><td>

Mental:
- Executive faculties: purpose, objectives, and strategies
- Supervisory faculties: *Intelligence* – decision-making and problem-solving
  Will – motivation, procedures, flowchart
  Emotions – data, information, habits, patterns, rules

Physical: Senses (scanning), memory, neural system, health

Skill: Abilities, capabilities, competence and competencies, experience with five levels of change

</td></tr>
</table>

Critical investigative mental process is vulnerable to a myriad of traps. Two scientists may use the same logic, examine the same data, and yet may present radically different 'solutions.' Under these conditions, we may think that with enough <u>data + logic</u> = **solution**. However, when the two decision-makers do not agree then the formula becomes <u>data + logic</u> = **alternatives**. The first part – 'data' is neutral – it is not a 'fact' and not even information, since information is contextualized data. As shown earlier, the 'data' numerals 6, 12, 43 mean little unless this data is contextualized - numerals represent the *day*, *month*, and *year* of a **date**. So the exercise of logic functions differently when it is in contact with data, information, system, or wisdom. If two logisticians agree on the scope and many even agree on the means to a solution, this situation may still be considered to be 'conditional' certainty. The solution is 'conditional' because the formula doesn't necessarily contain any reference to objective criteria. The potential for some disagreement exists. If two logisticians provide different (alternatives) solutions, then they haven't totally eliminated 'uncertainty.'

$$\frac{Logic + Data}{Interpretation + Priorities} = \textbf{Alternatives}$$

These are interpretations, Not solutions.

One quantitatively and qualitatively based solution would reflect 'conditional certainty':

Evolution, creation, and intelligent design scientists may look at the same phenomenon (e.g., fossil in some sedimentary strata) but each may present different interpretations and priorities. This diversity of opinion means that instead of having achieved conditional certainty they have only presented 'alternatives.' We may go a step further and consider that perhaps two of the three groups of scientists have actually reached the right solution (certainty), but because of one who did not agree with the solution, the science remains at the alternative level (uncertainty). This is why the debate continues today.

Figure 9 is the seven-stage process of decision-making and problem-solving method (DMPS). The seven stage is detailed in Figure 10.

Figure 9. Decision-Making and Problem-Solving (DMPS).

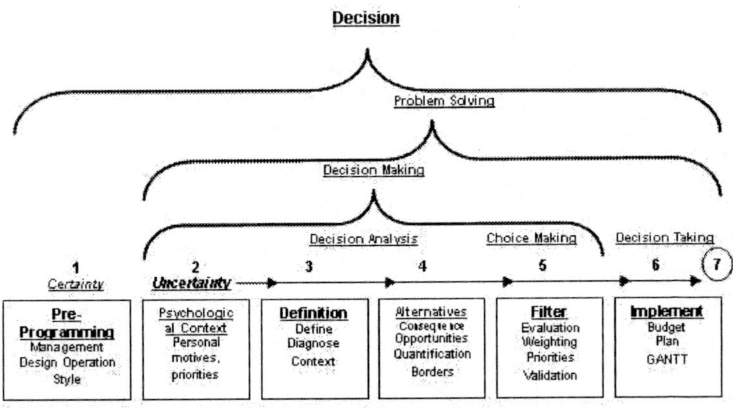

1. Certainty

Conditional certainty. Since information in this knowledge base must be managed, it is represented by the 3-dimensional management model (3DMM) – see Figure 5. Information is managed through up to twenty-seven plans at three infrastructural levels – design, operations, and style management. As soon as uncertainty is identified, either within the information in the knowledge-base or in its environment, it is time to implement the decision-making and problem-solving method (DMPS) to help resolve uncertainty and bring about a solution. The solution will be used to update the knowledge base.

Example 1: A transportation vehicle is designed to meet the highest engineering standards. The standards meet the requirements that correspond with the external conditions where the vehicle must operate. Prototypes have been constructed, tested, and passed the manufacturer's detailed inspection checks before sale. Operational certainty is further guaranteed with warrantees. If a vehicle malfunctions, the DMPS process will help identify the condition that introduced uncertainty. Engineering will adjust for guaranteed quality (operational certainty).

Example 2: The Christian Bible describes that God's first creative act was to initiate time; triggering geometric natural law, space, and quantification (see Figure 20). It is with this that He has introduced certainty – a knowledge base. However, by creating man with a free will, God had brought a risk – a potential for imperfection, i.e., an alternate method for management practice. Adams's supervisory function, where the DMPS is situated, is a method not only pre-designs free will, but also provides the capability to identify such uncertainty and take steps to resolve uncertainty. When such DMPS process conforms to the supervisory plans, DMPS will lead to certainty; otherwise, it will remain in uncertainty.

Upon selecting a second-level priority (uncertainty), Adam had to resolve a triple problem: (1) with this wrong executive choice, all of Creation, including Creation's new chief executive officer (Adam), lost perfection and caused the introduction of the second singularity where energy-density dropped one cycle down the energy cone; (2) all of Creation became less than perfect; and (3) the DMPS was now set within the economy of an imperfect certainty – a conditional certainty. Imperfection became synonymous with decay, death, accidents and relativity. The situation was similar to having to work with degraded tools, software, and lower technical competencies to repair a super high tech universe.

Whenever certainty is compromised, DMPS operations should kick in to help provide methods for correcting, testing, implementing, and validating solutions in order to return the operation to the operational status of certainty.

Figure 10. Normal Steps in DMPS.

3	4	5	6
	UNCERTAINTY		Conditional CERTAINTY
Definition	**Alternatives**	**Filtering**	**Test**
A gap/ problem/ uncertainty appears. Objective is to convert uncertainty into conditional certainty (#6). Therefore, define(#3) the uncertainty in terms of the desired solution (#6).	Identify alternatives that may contain a solution. Examine items on the alternative list using quantitative tools such as spreadsheets, fishbone, Pareto, etc.	Identify criteria to: weigh, prioritize, validate, and calculate risks and consequences – methods that will filter (alternatives 4) towards a solution + contingencies for implementation and tests (6). Note: Filtering variables come from 3DMM's Executive plans: objectives (O2), strategies (O3).	Use various tools to test values for best-measured implementation. These sets may also appear in terms of budget, reports, project management GANTT or scientific laboratory procedural results.
Example 1: Need a scientifically based theory/model that will help answer and predict data. Example 2: Need to buy a vehicle within my budget, least maintenance expenses, at least 20,000 miles/year. I must purchase transportation within the next two weeks.	Example 1: Create several scientific models that contain the data, from which it will be possible to make predictions. Example 2: List various means of transportation that will allow one to arrive on time.	Example1: Determine which one of the scientific models answers best all of the scientific data evidence, predictions. Example 2: Identify which mode of transportation means meets the criteria values – set in #3 definition and test in #6; have it quality guaranteed (#7).	Example 1: Use scientific model to test for quantity and quality value, performance standards. The hypothesis must reflect progress through stages of uncertainty. Example 2: Test-drive the right vehicle type/ brand.

#7 QUALITY ASSESSMENTS. Use various tools to re-examine the level of success of implement plan (#6) so as to ensure reliability, prevent faulty events, and seek additional change level requirements, re-engineering, redesign, etc. Example 1: Use the scientific model to handle up to five levels of testing and change management. Example 2: Procure optimized vehicle, brand, or type. New considerations: move to new location that is closer to hub of activity/productivity.

Uncertainty begins with the preparation for decision-making – the psychological stage (#2). This psychological state, unless properly addressed, will freeze the process on the 'alternatives' step (#4).

The psychological context is used to address the qualifications of the decision-makers and problem-solvers. Here, assumptions, beliefs, attitudes, value, goals, objectives, and needs / wants come into play (see Figure 10):

Psychological factors must clearly be identified and understood. Their source is within the 3-Dimensional Management Model (3DMM), and can be compensated for before the actual DMPS process begins. These psychological factors, specifically the management design's supervisory plans (policies, procedures, rules and regulations) may keep the DMPS lingering in uncertainty for an extended time.

When psychological uncertainties have been resolved then the formal DMPS steps can be initiated -- #3 in Figure 10.

Before listing the potential hazards that exist at each of the DMPS steps, it is worth noting the similarities between the DMPS, and the four-to-seven step description of the modern and popular version of the scientific method – see Figure 11:

Figure 2. Comparison: DMPS vs. Uniformitarian Scientific Method.

Decision-Making and Problem-Solving Method (refer to Figures 9 and 10)	Uniformitarian/Evolutionary Scientific Method
#1 Start with a Knowledge-base (KB) = 3DMM (Figure 5). KB + standards = *contingent certainty*. This includes not only quantitative and qualitative empirical data and information, but also laws, standards, rates, measures, principles/procedures of economics and mathematics.	The 3DMM is not mentioned. Note: uniformitarian past is naïve realism and an extrapolation of current processes, rates (see #3 below). It provides a hypothetical history and extrapolated knowledge-base. Hypothetical is still within the realm of uncertainty and not within conditional certainty. Uniformitarians reject many parts of Christian Catholic knowledge-base (3DMM).
#2 – *Uncertainty* – Psychological phase (see 84).	Filtering process (step #5) pre-distinguishes and qualifies only the uniformitarian versus the subjective/

"religious methods. Uniformitarianism seeks a rationalist/empiricist certainty, which is re-enforced by relativism and reductionism.

#3 – *Define* – describe gap in terms of desired solution (#6).

Begin with today's (current) condition, processes, and rates. Extrapolate into past to identify potential cause to current conditions (using simple to complex process, reductionism, relativism). Definition guided by filtration (#5).

#4 – *Alternatives (tools, quantitative)*. Formulate a hypothesis and predictions researching missing yet probable data and quantities. Describe the hypothesis, being within uncertainty, in terms of DMPS phases. Use alternatives to formulate predictions (extrapolations, consequences) and interpretations.

Hypothesis formulation to explain phenomenon – make predictions. Hypothesis is usually confused with theory. Under uniformitarian influence, alternatives are reduced through the filtration #5 parameters.

#5 *Filter* (priorities, weighing, criteria, consequences, impact). These are derived from the 3DMM's design executive plans (purpose, objectives, and strategies).

Filters test for uniformitarian principles or naïve realism. These are *objectives* and *strategies* [but exclude *purpose* (law, identity, scope)] derived from the supervisory level: policies, procedures, rules and regulations. As mentioned above, uniformitarian filters predetermine the psychology (#2), definition (#3), and alternatives (#4), and applicable tests (#6).

#6 – *Implementation* (test, standards, codes) lead to conditional certainty (#7).

Test only for uniformitarian realism (UR) results. Consider other test results as being non-compliant - 'contaminated' 'inconclusive' and 'irrelevant.'

#7- *Quality assessment/guarantee.* Verified certainty, may become the foundation of a theory

Theorize but exclude DMPS phases which are used to emerge from 'uncertainty' – thus theory remains at the

(lawful scopes), or falsification.   'uncertainty' level.

Here's a list of potential **misapplications** of the DMPS steps. Note that these potential procedural errors apply even more to the uniformitarian scientific method. This is because the uniformitarian scientific method is not properly anchored on the DMPS and the 3DMM (see Figure 10).

Step #3. Definitions – Uncertainty phase.

As noted in Figure 10, the definition must include: (a) the identification of the vehicle that must bring a specific solution, a test (#6) or certainty (#7); (b) description of the existing situation, gaps that must be resolved; (c) identify the duration, time at the end of which the decision will no longer be relevant or another one should be formulated.

Decision makers can incorrectly define the problem by:

(a) Failing to specifically identify the components, situation, symptoms, behavior, causes, reactions, and processes affected. For example, if someone were not able to start a vehicle's engine – the engine emits a strong wining sound when the key is turned. This may indicate a number of problems but not that the battery is drained.

(b) Not aligning the definition (#3) with the desired result at implementation (# 6).

(c) Forgetting to the set a time frame for achieving a solution (#5).

(d) Include alternatives (# 4) in the definition (#3); e.g., I know something about cars so I (# 4) may find the problem (#5) and fix it (#6). This is 'jumping to conclusions' whereas the step 'I may fix it' is an alternative (#4).

Step #4. Alternatives

Misapplications of the alternative process may lay in making a distinction between the closed process and the creative modes. A closed process mode may reflect a limited scope of alternatives, usually established within a pre-programmed number of choices. The innovative or creative mode presents a greater quantity of unknowns. The definition is not too precise and a greater number of alternatives are quantified.

Alternatives generation is misused because:

- Not enough: (a) general, (b) background, or (c) specific data is considered.

- Not enough quantitative data available, perhaps due to limited tools.
- Mis-definions (#1) – objective or time limits not set.
- Imposed limitations (only 'x' or never 'y' alternatives/ data considered.
- Mix unrelated alternatives: general versus particular, mechanical with organic processes (see mental models below).
- Uncategorized alternatives (focus on different infrastructures, processes).
- Groupthink – individuals slowly conform to the group's desires, or avoid alternatives that may lead to undesirable risks (#6); utilize specific filters (# 5).
- Premature evaluation of alternatives (#4) by introducing filtering (#5) at alternatives (#4), thus preventing a full examination of alternatives (#4).
- Substitute ideological/philosophical concepts (filtering #5) at some or all DMPS steps.

The alternatives location is also where the hypothesis is established. Both alternatives and the hypothesis remain in the uncertainty stage and both must pass through each of the DMPS stages, and be described as such at each of the stages. For example, homology is a hypothesis. However, homology has never been described in terms of its descriptive feature. Today, judging from the techniques, methods, tools, and assumptions that are made and used, the homology hypothesis may never go beyond this descriptive stage. In other words, homology will never reach the implementation (#6) stage of the hypothesis, nor reach the quality guaranty (#7) stage. It will remain in perpetual uncertainty. To better understand what happens in such a cases, let's say – homology, at its definitional stage (#3), is being filtered (#5) with values, priorities, and criteria. Inevitably, homology enters the alternative (#4) stage to find that it has been prematurely injected and short circuited by the filtering process (#5). This is similar to what I call the 'luxury syndrome.' In such a situation, an individual finds that he has to decide which type of long-term transportation he should get. Instead of building a tabular form (see the example on Table 4) of quantitative options that would include the different types of vehicles, initial costs, maintenance, fuel, etc., and then allowing him to decide on an affordable versus quality option, the individual instead goes to the filtering (#5) step and identifies a luxury car! Then this individual looks back at the alternatives options (#4), and, instead of identifying options, he uses this alternative list as excuses to justify why the luxury car is the best and only best choice for him.

Table 4. Tabular form that lists Alternatives; Hypotheses.

Definition (#3): 'I need long-term reliable and affordable transportation.'
Alternatives (#4): List and quantify all viable options, including: new and used car brands, motorcycle, taxi, public transport, walk, etc.

ALTERNATIVES. QUANTITATIVE DATA/MONTH QUALITATIVE

Alternatives	Cost	Maintenance	Gas/toll$	Total	#5 Filter
A1	300	200	60	560	Luxury
A2	320	210	60	590	Business
A3	290	50	40	380	Family car
B1	250	30	30	310	Motorcycle
C1	100	10	0	110	Walk

'**Luxury** syndrome' is prioritizing 'filter' (#5) (e.g:, alternative **A1**).
In management, 'Luxury syndrome' is known as 'groupthink.'

Step #5. Filtering receives its values from the executive objectives and strategies. Filtering values are legitimately applied to examine all alternative's data (#4) for implementation (#6). Filtering is improperly used when:

- Filters are applied to definitional (#3) or alternatives (#4) stages before these arrive to the filtering (#5) process. Such an approach is called an ideological approach.

- It's necessary to remind about the luxury syndrome mentioned above, where filtering (#5) is applied to alternatives (#4), thus pre-selecting and limiting the scope of the alternatives' content.

- There may be mechanical models where only two alternatives may be considered. In this case, the pre-mature filterning process would be used to eliminate one of the two from consideration. For example, the pro-choice option represents only one choice - abortion. Or, the decision maker may allow for both options to be considered, but removes resources from the actual implementation of one of them. For example, United States court cases that conduct hearings for both sides - evolution versus intelligent design cases, but then use non-United States constitutional criteria to pass pre-filtered verdicts that do not reflect the quantitative alternatives that had to be considered.

- Filterning may be inapproatiate or may be improperly procedurized or timed.

Filtering (#5) is also misapplied when it limits data to be considered so that some alternatives may pass the application (#6) phase, but fail on the quality guarantee (#7)phase. Thus, it lingers on in uncertainty forever.

- Proof may appear to be objective or satisfactory, but the fundamental criteria may be unjustified. For example, one may weigh only three of five items.

- Management may introduce unwarranted delays, or may accelerate schedules. This may lead to changed conditions and loss of opportunities. For example, wait for the total budget while contingencies may have been applied at an earlier stage.

- Distorted weighing that lead to double standards, or limited or overly liberal standards

Step #6. Implementation - after some alternatives have been filtered, it is necessary to test them for application. Implementation test options for operational certainty helps reduce or eliminate risk. In other words, implementation (#6) is designed to increase quality control, and produce the highest degrees of conditional certainty. However, flaws can be identified here also:

- Inapropriate implementation of testing tools.

- Suspend something in order to prevent other options from being explored.

- Substitute causes and ascribe contamination, insufficient data, or inconclusive evidence when qualified alternatives do not meet predictions.

- Move borders and change standards.

- Apply wrong mental models (e.g., mechanical, organic, process, information technology)

- Misidentify, misapply, or ignore standards, codes, history, origins, source, supplier, applicable laws, and cause-effect.

Step #7 - Quality Assessment /Guarantee - Conditional Certainty
This is a second pass at application after it has been in use by the customer. This step may be compared with customer satisfaction, evaluation, and feedback. Some misapplications of this phase include:

- Lose track of what is being certified.

- Process is too narrow – too many insurmountable barriers.

- Values and judgments (#3) too liberal or too restrictive.

- Self-adjustment routines not effective.

- Feedback deficiencies, insufficiency, wrong interpretation, or focus on lateral information flow.

- Wrong things are calibrated – e.g., post-sales analysis focuses on customer needs (which may already have been met) instead of focusing on customer wants or delight. In science, such focus would be made on speciation and not on loss of information at the sub-chromosome levels or the programmed adjustments of physiological infrastructures – e.g., caterpillars to butterfly. This is done because of faulty filters (#5), e.g., ER.

The above examples of potential DMPS or scientific method misapplications do not exhaust the list. But these steps must be checked whenever the DMPS /scientific method are applied.

Hypothesis and Theory – Similarities

The definition and application of the hypothesis and theory seem to vary with the user and organization using them. Members of various disciplines have designed their own private definitions and brought about positive results in their disciplines. Others have purposefully employed inconsistent methods, knowing that such ambiguity would help them to promote controversial views, or provide them with outlets from difficult or embarrassing situations.

Many scientists clearly distinguish theory from fact, while others insist that theory has indeed become fact. Records indicate that the terms hypothesis and theory are almost interchangeable. Although there are significant similarities between the two, it is necessary to anchor the specifics so that both terms may become concrete and reliable tools in scientific investigation.

The hypothesis is related to the process that identifies alternatives (#4). The theory is related with the post-implementation (#6) application or conditional certainty (#7). Both, however, still remain within uncertainty and are subject to each of the DMPS steps. Both hypothesis and the theory must be measured and assessed in terms of the DMPS steps: psychological, definition, alternatives, filtering, implementation, and quality guarantee.

Before defining the difference between the terms, it is necessary to recognize twelve preliminary and fundamental *similarities*. Both terms:

- Deal with a condition that is uncertain.
- Investigative processes are designed to limit uncertainty and maximize certainty.
- Process the hypothesis and theory through multiple DMPS stages towards conditional certainty.
- Start with given/available evidence and structures (phenomenon) and identify provable objective.
- Recognize quantitative parameters.
- Use history and standards to quantify and qualify, assess the status of the hypothesis and theory.
- Distinguish between tangible and intangible phenomena. Examples of the first are: mechanical parts, components, assembly, unit, system, process, information, laws; intangible phenomena such as psychological, behavioral, random, seemingly magical, singular or results of super high-tech – that may be for us outside our everyday experience.
- Suggest a mental model (mechanical, organic, process, information or geometric).

    Track the DMPS progress:

- Psychological bias – ideology, competence, tool use, performance, historical, etc.
- Descriptive, design, definitional stage that include objectives to be attained within a time frame.
- Investigative - examine workable and quantifiable alternatives.
- Evaluative - filter application to ensure operational value: quality, standards, codes, falsifiable, validity, and predictability.
- Operational – test repeatability, quality control, forecasted performance – in other words – certainty.
- Quality guarantee – post-operational application. The results may

succeed in meeting conditional certainty criteria. Results may also fail or provide lateral solutions. This phase may also consider reassessing whether the approach has been properly identified, or should be dropped from consideration.

These examples are the similarities in the hypothesis and theory. The **difference** lies in that theory always reflects law-based requirement. Here are the differences between hypothesis and theory:

Hypothesis (Gk: hypotithenal – is to put under, to suppose.) The hypothetical process specifies the phenomena by providing alternatives (#4). The process uses analytical tools whose results are filtered (#5) by: weighing, prioritizing, and examining through criteria (predictions, tests, quality analysis, and implementation). Hypotheses, reflecting uncertainty, are tracked through DMPS.

Theory (Gk: thea – a view + horan – to see) reflects a supervisory view or a mental model that simulates plausible sets of phenomena, processes, and rules. These reflect or are based on existing or potentially discoverable laws. The theory, being uncertainty, must be processed through DMPS for short and long-term qualitative guarantee results.

Dynamic 8-Point DMPS - Scientific Method and Types of Learning

For a greater understanding of the original seven-step decision-making and problem-solving (DMPS) method, and also to better understand the scientific method that has been examined above (Figures 9 and 10), two three-dimensional representations are provided.

Similarly, it will also become clear the degree to which the debating scientists use the original scientific method. We should remember that this DMPS is part of the design management supervisory plans in 3DMM.

The DMPS diamond (Figure 12) has proved its worth in many other fields, including: industrial management development, project management, and in language learning. Figure 12 has successfully been used in consolidating and understanding all types of change-related applications and learning.

Below, the content of Figure 12 has been refined and adapted to help explain the DMPS and the scientific method, and then was checked for validity by the content of Figure 13 – providing an 'in-motion' application with key relational links to each step. Both Figures 12 and 13 lead the process from an initial conditional state of certainty, and, with the introduction of uncertainty, the DMPS/scientific method is used to resolve the path to conditional certainty. The traditional and at times relative views of the scientific method process are depicted in their correct order within Figures 12 and 13. It becomes clear that both DMPS and the original scientific method cannot be described in a linear fashion, i.e., one step following a preceding one. For example, the scientific method steps begin with observation, yet upon closer examination we see that observation becomes dependent on, or has additional foundational links to, history (D) and standards (E). These features are those of the knowledge-base. Here the unknown can be compared with the known in terms of history, measurements, and standards. An observation is not automatically set into a framework or structure and qualified as information. It is compared with (D) and (E) and only then is identified as new information (C). It is these foundational steps that then allow for the determination of a definition (#3) on the DMPS process, and specifically helps determine the structure in Figures 12 and 13.

As part of the process in seeking alternatives, there are numerous contextualizing, formatting, and modeling tools that allow us to collect, adjust, and compare data and information. The definition on Figure 13 covers a wider field than that identified on Figure 12 (history - D).

Figure 12. The DMPS Diamond and the Scientific Method.

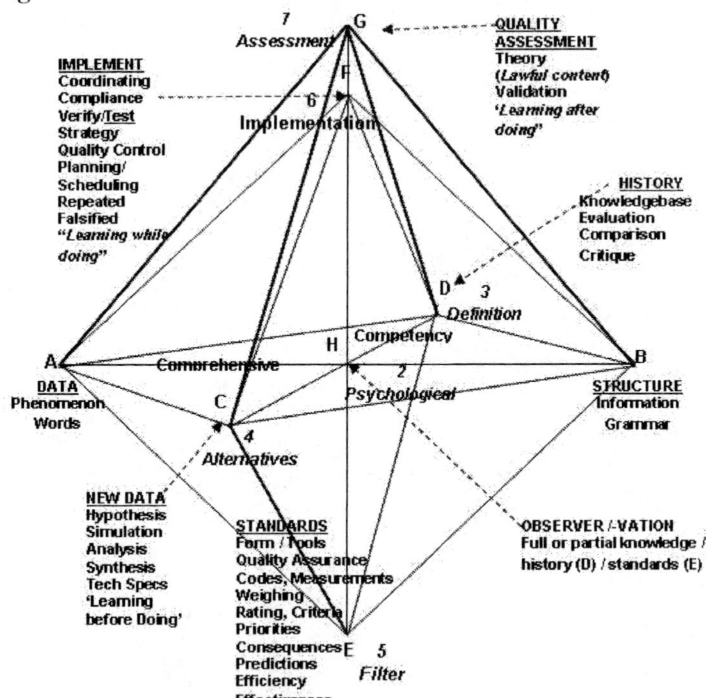

Figure 13. The Eight-Point DMPS, Scientific Method, and Types of Learning.

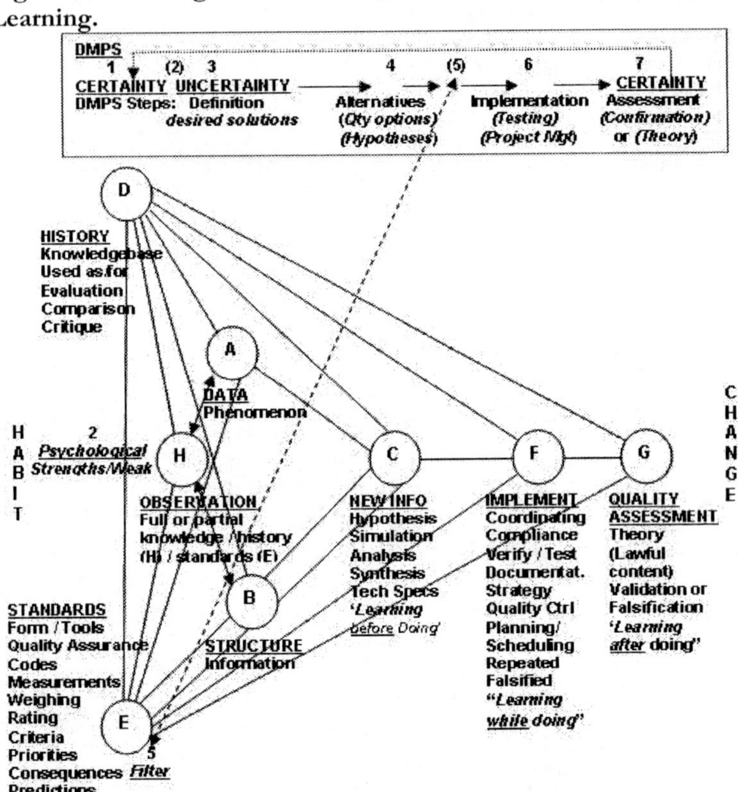

Figure 13 is nothing more than Figure 12 placed in motion for change. It is a change as it travels the road from uncertainty to conditional certainty. Figure 13 is designed to help identify the links, relationships, and functions among the activities that lead from uncertainty to conditional certainty. This certainty is conditional, because it may appear in three categories of results:

Conditional certainty has itself been processed through all states of DMPS and now has a place among the 3DMM plans. Under certain circumstances, it may be considered to be absolute certainty. Note that this cannot apply to any condition that falls within uniformitarian, reductionist, and modernist relativistic conditions since these are products of the supervisory plans, where these prioritize policy (D4), procedures (D5), and rules and regulations (D6). The concepts of almost certainty, and is truth are but redefined words with special uniformitarian definitions.

Uniformitarian critics object to the creationist's view of the law of biogenesis. This law implies divinity had created live forms. Uniformitarians ask how can such creation be observable, tested, and be reproduced in order to qualify for their interpretation of empirical science? Creation scientists point to the rule that origins (whether Creation, evolution, intelligent design or Hybrids) cannot be placed into a lab for tests. Origins can be predicted from results obtained in the scientific models (see 3. Conceptual Formulae) - the evolutionists use the three-point uniformitarian assumptions in their scientific model, while the Creation uses legal historical documentation, and ID uses teleological assumptions to interpret and predict their scientific results. In all four cases the DMPS filtering (#5) process provides the assumptions for the scientific model.

All four groups of scientists begin with the present. They recognize existing processes and evidence. The differences appear almost immediately. Using Figures 9 – 13, we find that the uniformitarian scientific model begins to filter (#5) at (#1) – it provides an *edited* knowledge base. Then at (#2) the process is used to qualify only uniformitarian scientists and disqualify all others (e.g., creation and ID scientists, even if the latter two may have better qualified scientists than the first group. Then they preselect and predefine (#3) all empirical data and information to exclude anything that falls outside the three-point uniformitarian/ evolutionary scope. Then they limit alternatives (#3) – again to within the three-point uniformitarian and algebraic scopes. As seen earlier, this type of filtering is established upon the supervisory plans (D3, D4, and D5) that bypass the executive purpose (D1), and re-prioritize the objectives (D2) and strategic (D3) plans. After such filtering, whatever is left is then tested for application. Much of what is tested is found to be contaminated, undeterminable, inconclusive, or forced artificially into compliance with uniformitarian predictions or removed from consideration.

In contrast, the creation scientists use Figures 9 – 13 NOT to filter (#5) the historical knowledge base (#1). Instead, these scientists go out of the way to discover and ensure the scientific accuracy of the historical knowledge base (#1). In (#2), creation scientists use all the scientific output produced by all qualified scientists. Creation scientists then define (#3) and describe all empirical data and information with the intent of closing the uncertainty gap. They then examine alternative (#4) ways of arranging and quantifying this empirical data and information. The filtering process (#5) uses the historical knowledge-base (#1) to help filter (#5) the alternatives. This is done to seek what explanation and predictions can best explain the empirical scientific data and information, and which alternative can be best tested (#6) and yield verifiable and reproducible predictions. As discussed earlier, the creation model seems to provide more accurate information that can be predicted and checked for accuracy than that offered through the uniformitarian scientific model.

The intelligent design approach is similar to the creation scientist's approach with the difference that the initial knowledge-base (#1) contains laboratory produced data and information, and the filtering process (#5) is not conditioned by issues of origins, fossil records, or taxonomies; instead, it is designed within micro bioengineering, sub-chromosome information processes, and cosmological constants scopes. This complexity is then hypothesized within a teleological view.

The 'Objective and Unfettered Scientific Method' (OUSM)

The reader will recognize many features of the OUSM since these are in part evident in many of the Figures (9 – 13, 16, 18, 22 among others); the '12 limitations of the scientific method' (see chapter 2.6), and leaves the question of origins and ages to the last phase (5th) of the scientific process interpretation.

The great debates among the Evolution, Creation, Intelligent Design, and Hybrid Uniformitarian theorists demonstrate that there is something more to the scientific issues than purely empirical evidence for lab testing. The most obvious incorporations into the investigative process include: a) whether the system is open or closed; b) assumptions for date empirical data and evidence; and c) what constitutes scientific evidence, data and interpretation. It is not so much empirical evidence as the three incorporations that are the subject of the debates' controversy.

The most evident dating method relies on direct methods: a) corroborated evidence of objective, record of sequential events, conditions, structures or artifacts; and b) indirect methods that provide <u>interpretations</u> of fossil record, carbon 14 test, radioisotope method, calculation of outflow sedimentation, tree rings, strength of the Earth's electromagnetic field, speed of light, etc. Here we find assumptions (filters) that reflect philosophical, ideological, and legally historical purposes, objectives and strategies. Yet, one would anticipate that there might be a knowledge base of scientifically validated or corroborated evidence, a repository of purely objective and unfettered scientific information - a data warehouse of objectively assured data/evidence. This scientific data warehouse would include not only the a) operational layer for sourcing data; b) data access layer with tools to catalog, load; c) metadata layer where a dictionary for warehouse and data accessed, retrieved, for analysis reporting ; d) information access and analyzing tools; but also include 'business'/scientific intelligence tools. One would be able to scrutinize the tools, protect empirical data from premature dating and aging interpretations.

1st OUSM level - Empirical.

The empirically objective and unfettered scientific method (OUSM) can start when for example a master competency qualified and certified scientist comes to a steep wall in the Grand Canyon. This scientist - who may be a geologist or paleontologist - observes the rocks or fossils within sedimentary strata, measures, weighs and identifies samples some of which positioned in multiple layers of various thickness and composition. Most of the strata lie horizontally, while others curved, angled upwards, or even appear positioned vertically across multiple horizontal layers. Among these, the scientist may find fossils, artifacts, fossilized footprints situated in different strata.

The scientist simply describes, records, photographs what he/she observes. The scientist takes samples, makes plaster copies, measures, places reference marks, uses *various techniques* of dating the samples, etc. The scientist carefully records all of this. Having done this in one location the scientist proceeds strategically to repeat the same process in many other representative areas. The scientist will eventually find the source and the outlet of this Grand Canyon cavity. The scientist notes that throughout the length of the Canyon there is a small river running at the bottom of the Canyon, which he/she observes, measures, weighs samples, and photographs. Finally, the scientist writes a scientific article for publication in a science journal. He/she may even venture to create a geologists' tourist brochure; create a video for the National Geographic or contributes much of this information to a school textbook. No interpretation or dating provided at this stage. The 'dated' samples mentioned above are part of cataloging objective sample records. Dating may be an outcome that may be considered in the 4th phase of the OUSM process.

At this procedural and standardized data collection level, will it matter whether the fully qualified scientist who performs empirical analysis is an Evolutionist, Creationist, Intelligent Design, Moslem, Buddhist, or ancient Greek? Not really, as long as the scientist does this empirical work faithfully, and others can verify, confirm and duplicate what has been documented or data warehoused. In other words, scientific empirical objective and unfettered work is valid.

2nd OUSM level work: - Comparative Stage.

Scientist or groups of scientists search and get reports from the knowledge base – data warehousing, to compare all available empirical evidence in totality. It is an empirical evidential database – a global view. These scientists may go high tech and view evidence produced through satellite world scanning and deep-sea submarine excavations. Scientists coordinate and correlate this geological data and information. They find that most of the Earth's strata either isn't layered horizontally in a systematic A, B, C, D, E and F fashion, but vary - B, A, E, F, D or F, A, D, C or B. Some layers, e.g., A and F, are missing altogether in most areas; or supplemented with very different ones G, H and I layers. In addition, there are single strata that go cross-continent, break off at the seacoast of one continent and continue across the ocean on another continent. Scientists discover that most fossils are marine creatures. Scientists discover six to twelve square mile areas that may consist of massive graves of intermixed fossilized species. There are polystrate-fossilized trees and fossilized skeletons that span across multiple layers of horizontal sedimentary rock deposits. Volcanic lava flows reflect mega-volcanic activity that reaches up to more than twenty-five times greater spans than anything in that is in our recorded history. They note that there are up to 50,000 volcano craters around the Earth that appear to have comparatively limited weathering features. Scientists calculate that it would take fifteen million years to weather all continental land masses into the oceans. They identify numerous human artifacts in massive coal beds. There are massive layers of crude oil deposits that are still under extremely high pressure. They note that massive and rapid land uplifts formed mountain ranges. None of this evidence is 'dated' at this second OUSM level work.

Scientists examine the surface of the moon using coordinated high power telescopes, satellite photography, deep scanning tools, and man landings on the moon. Scientists examine rock samples brought back from the Earth's moon. Robot space ships bypass or land on other planets and examine conditions there. Send out Voyager spacecrafts to the edge and beyond the solar system.

This same type of comparative process is done in other fields. Biologists examine the multiple living creatures (plant and animal), create taxonomies to distinguish their specificity and compare these mammals with those identified in the fossil record. Scientists note many similarities between existing and fossilized creatures. One difference is that in many cases fossils tend to lean towards gigantism. There are also differences. Many fossil species do not have counterparts among those living today. There are rare finds also - some of the dinosaur marrow and flesh had not fossilized, and mammoths are found frozen completely and intact with buttercups between their teeth. There are fossilized animal and human footprints in most rock layers. Other scientists use the latest super high tech electron and atomic microscopes to discover ready-made sophisticated programmed information systems and nanobot super high technology at sub-chromosome levels. The nanobot operations appear to be on 'automatic' – thus demonstrate engineering software that covers robotic operations, maintenance, repair, manufacturing, self-reproduction and replication. This is a nano-technology that is a 1000 years ahead of our time. This includes all electronic, information and robotic codes and standards that boggle the human mind.

In comparing and cataloging this knowledge base, it is important that all this investigation allows other scientists to verify, confirm, falsify, as well as, repeat what the first scientists discovered and recorded. This creates an accurate knowledge base.

3rd OUSM level work: Identify Alternate Causes.

Where OUSM's first stage is the empirical stage of data collection, the second stage is comparative analysis of the Knowledge base, the third stage helps create and determine alternate causal relationships among the data, information and knowledge in the knowledge base/data warehouse. Quantitative and qualitative alternate models allow for an analysis of strengths, weaknesses, consistency, standards, and quality of data.

In other words, using Figure 13, scientists re-examine Data (A) and the various way it fits within the Structures (B); test the validity and completeness of the initial Observation (H), to Filter (5) this through Standards (E) and Historical reliability and consistency (D) to identify New Information (C). This may require the updating hypotheses (C) for re-filtration (#5) in order to be able to make better predictions, or make better applications (F – testing, implementation) e.g., discovering crude oil; rates or reforestation; the comets' appearance, frequency, life cycle; role of the thyroid gland in the human body.

Re-examination will no doubt identify a mix of confirmed and missing information. Confirmed new information will be cataloged - updating the knowledge base. Depending on the set priorities, additional research will be designed and scheduled to fill some gaps, formulate hypotheses where data/info is unavailable. Also the process will allow one to check if such additional research can help clarify theories, which are law-based implementation or guarantee standards. At the DMPS quality guarantee, (#7) phase examine if a theory may explain multiple unknowns. The condition of both the hypothesis and the theory are tentative and therefore reside in an uncertainty status. Being unknowns the hypothesis and theory are subject to the DMPS phased analysis, planning and scheduling. As mentioned earlier, the hypothetical and theoretical uncertainties are tracked through DMPS phases.

Thus far, we have constructed an unfettered scientific – knowledge-base with contingent certainty. Scientists accurately and transparently have recorded objective information, filtered it twice for accuracy, and laid out opportunities for further advances by refining the accuracy of the knowledge base, i.e., distinguish between uncertainty and quality assured contingent certainty. The knowledge base's objectivity is further confirmed by its compliance with the '12 Limitation of Scientific Method.'

4th OUSM level: Application of 3DMM

All scientific activities conducted during OUSM's three stages demonstrate, above all, that these processes are managed. As such the fourth step helps examine how this OUSM functions within the 3DMM – see Figure 14 - the 6th item of the '12 limitations of science.' The 3DMM will include the models of thinking (Figure 15); Five types of qualitative change management (Figure 16); production process (Figure 17); gap depth determination (Figure 18); geometric reality (Figure 20); Qualitative infrastructures and energy densities (Figure 22). It is only after these 3DMM examinations that scientists can introduce methods for identifying dating options of evidence. One can reference dating only within the content of a scientific global knowledge base that complies within the 12 Limitations of Science (see Figure 14).

The reader can measure and then score the differences among the debaters (Evolution, Creation, and Intelligent Design) by examining the extent and areas where the debaters compromised, replaced, miss-defined or complied with the 3DMM knowledge base. More specifically, to what extent have the '12 Limitations of Science' been breached? To what extent has original science (i.e., pursuit of accurate knowledge) and the scientific method (DMPS) been maintained?

Figure 3 – '12 Limitations of Science' - Scored Comparison

#	12 Limitations of Science	Evol	Creat	I.D.	Hyb
1	Does address origins	1	1	0*	1
2	Value corroborated with historical record	0	1	0*	0
3	Variables correspond to formulae	0	1	1	0
4	Proper use of tools, systems & procedures	0	1	1	0
5	Apply original scientific method	0	1	1	0
6	Application of 3DMM	0	1	1	0
7	4 to 5 Mental Models	0	1	1	0
8	5 change levels of management accounted for	0	1	1	0
9	DMPS – scientific method	0	1	1	0
10	Ideological implementation of assumptions	1	1	1	1
11	Distinction DMPS from Uniformitarianism	0	1	1	0
12	Scientific labs used to reduce uncertainty	0	1	1	0
	Total – Score card result:	2	12	10	2
	Corresponding %	17	100	83	17

* I.D. does not officially address origins and pre-history, although individual members are free to believe what they wish.

Limitations: 1/12. . Scientists cannot empirically examine or test *origins* of the universe. Whether they postulate a big bang, steady stage, or Divine Creation, they will need to reconstruct such origins through <u>indirect and secondary sources</u>. In such cases, scientists (1) create scientific models, (2) use available empirical data and information, (3) Make assumptions (values, hypotheses, theories – e.g., uniformitarian, legal historical-based), (4) make predictions of what #2 is likely to look like, if any of the #3 is valid, (5) origins' definitions (assumptions)(#3) should help explain the framework of empirical data, information, or knowledge (#2). Scientific models use empirical data, and, when properly extrapolated, should meet scientific predictions.

Limitations: 2/12. Short of speculating about origins, scientists may attempt to *reconstitute or reconstruct past or historical conditions and events*. For example, ice age, catastrophic conditions, consequences of large meteoric impacts, change in species, etc. Scientists can begin with current existing geologic, paleontological, biological, inter-/stellar evidence, as well as, physical laws and/or geometric natural laws. Then they confirmed historical data (geology, archeology, artifacts, and pyramids) to extrapolate or reconstruct past conditions.

Scientists may extrapolate from existing conditions and may identify singularities – i.e., unique conditions that occurred once in the past and are not likely to occur again. Singularities require one to describe and prove working pre-/during and post singular conditions. However, such unique conditions may not have existed. If they did, original conditions and tools may no longer yield to scientific theorization. One may then attempt to construct a workable framework and then test it scientifically? However, singular event(s) potentially compromise evidence for pre-singular conditions. What are the tools, conditions and evidence that scientists would use to access the non-existent condition? Uniformitarian may postulate a singularity in form of their Big Bang theory, but as it will be shown below, such a condition, which is based on algebraic subjective rules leads to absurdity (see Figure 23). The Creation Scientific Model provides legal historical documentation for the existence of three singular events that had affected the universal scale. In this case, there are at least two issues to resolve: 1) the required nature, source, condition and accuracy of the historical legal documentation. For example <u>external corroborative evidence</u> (archeology, geology, paleontology, demographics), and b) <u>integral features</u> (geometric natural law, geometric solids, infrastructures, stylistic devices, etc). In this Creation view, these must provide conditions and events that existed during and after each singularity leading to predictive conditions that exist today (qualitative energy densities, rates, cycles and infrastructural changes). In this case, since most of the current scientific evidence flows from the <u>last (third) singularity</u>, it will be necessary to account for a) an initial super-mega change or impact that would be, b) followed by secondary mega self-adjustments. On Earth, such initial and consequent self-adjusting changes remain observable, describable, testable and reproducible evidence - geology (hydro-tectonics and global sedimentation), paleontology (fossil graves of mixed species), evidence of mega-volcanic effects, climatology (ice age), condition of ocean floors, demographics, etc.

What Are 'Facts'?

Limitation 2/12 must also address the issue of what constitutes 'facts' since the evolutionary debaters have emphasized the axiom of 'facts' and that the fact of evolution is almost certainty. One feature of facts is that they link to processes and frameworks, which themselves define the fact(s). This is evident in Figure 13 where 'data' (A) links to: D-history, E-standards, before it reflects its B-Structure. An example for this is considering why parallel lines, that are crossed by a perpendicular line, forming 90 degree angles form different 'facts' or 'errors' when placed in different geometric frameworks – Euclidian (linear), Riemannian (spherical) and Loboshevsky's (horse saddle). Similar fact-framework relationships appear when the five levels of qualitative change management emerge (see Figure 16) – similarly appearing facts on different infrastructural levels are significant different from each other.

Here is a list of frameworks and examples of how a fact is determined within a framework:

A. **Assumptions** may be viewed as a 'leap of faith,' but actually reflects the Executive (D1-D3) row and appears as a Filter #5. Example:
- 'History progresses from simple to complex'
- 'History shows a gradual deterioration of conditions'

B. **Interpretations** provide a strategic (D3) or tactical approach – that test alternative(s).
- 'Earth's geologic strata measure millions and billions of years'
- 'Earth's geologic strata reflect results of recent global hydro-tectonic catastrophic events, and secondary longer-term mega-adjustments

C. **Evidential** trends are used to project historical, existing or hypothetical factors

- 'Today's conditions, rates and events are similar for those in the past
- 'Conditions, events and rates are unstable, have fluctuated dramatically in the past.

D. **Observations** described, measured and quantified:
- 'Paleontological evidence demonstrates change of one species into another under challenging environmental conditions' – macro-evolution.'
- Paleontological evidence demonstrates creatures fossilized in the Earth's sedimentary layers show that both have been formed in recent relatively short periods.

E. **Descriptive** – provides a workable formula or explanation based on a limited number of data:
- 'Speed of light is part of the electromagnetic spectrum that travels at a constant rate through a vacuum and whose path may be bent by gravity.
- 'Speed of light is part of the electromagnetic spectrum whose speed varies, may be bent by gravity and may degrade with the medium through which it travels.
- 'Gravitation can be explained by observable behavior of objects that move within its medium.'
- 'Geometric fields/laws (e.g., Riemannian, Lobachevski) reflect non-degradable structural frameworks' (see Tom Van Flandern, 'The Speed of Gravity – What the Experiments Say.' Meta Research, Published in 'Physic Letter' A250.1-11 (1998); http://Idolphin.org/vanFlandern/gravityspeed.html

F. **Inferred** – interplay of cause, rule and effect in a situation where only two of the three are known:
- Deductive: find effect when cause and rule is known.'
- Abductive: find cause when effect and rule is known.'
- Inductive: find rule when effect and cause is known.'
- For millions of year comets have been originating in the Kuiper Belt/Or cloud located beyond the oribit of Neptune at its furthest track.
- 'Comets are of recent origin that proves that the Solar System is young.' See: Pioneer 10 and 11 spacecrafts did not detect the

existence of a Kuiper Belt beyond the Solar System's edge.' See the latest link: http://news.yahoo.com/s/space/20080702/sc_space/voyagespa cecraftrevealssolarsystemedge.

- 'The Grand Canyon was caused by the works of a small river working over millions of years.'
- The Grand Canyon was caused by catastrophic two-week drainage of three large lakes.
- 'Random statistical and reductionist rules explain origins and workings at micro-cellular levels.'
- 'Engineered workings of cellular flagellum suggest a design that cannot proceed through random statistical means and can best be explained in terms of a designing supernatural intelligent designer.'

G. **Analogy** – comparative coherence mapping and alignment of source (s) (original), target (simulated) and network (links) conditions and processes that meet same purposes, objectives and strategies.

- 'Results of convergent evolution represented by homologous structures – the living tree that proves common ancestry'
- 'Taxonomy, a knowledge-base that catalogs, for example, existing and fossil species by various groups and subgroups, such as: domain, kingdom, division/phylum, class, order, family, genus, species and other sub-divisions. Not how one species macro-evolved, speciated into another.'

These examples demonstrate that the concept of 'fact' lies on slippery ground - clearly, a framework can help convert a fact into an illusion. Scientists must ask the following question: 'what are the processes, contexts and conditions that surround 'facts'? From the above examples, facts reflect assumptions, interpretations, extrapolation, tactical observation, description, inference, analogy and other. Facts may be materialistic, ideological, religious or mythological. For example, although the spherical view of the Earth had been known from the earliest times, humans have still found it compelling to construct and successfully run empires on the practical 'fact' that the earth is flat. In this case, the source, target framework linked to experience proved to these users that this fact was observable, quantifiable, testable, and verifiable every day – they used Euclidean geometry. During the same historical time, there were also those who used spherical geometry to navigate around the world (Carthegians).

Although, recently, uniformitarians have tried to suggest that these 'evolutionary' rules apply to biological sciences only, actual applications of this 'evolutionary' restricted definition is really anchored in the materialistic uniformitarian view, which has been and still is evident in all other areas of thinking. At the same time, when actual historical documentation is examined and corroborated with archeology, geology, and other triangulating means, such material acquires a unique transformation in the uniformitarian hands. Each of these areas is reinterpreted in the light of the uniformitarian materialistic simple-to-complex and primitive-to-modern rules. Therefore, the view of origins and history under the view of an uniformitarian magnifying glass will significantly vary from evidence that is empirically cataloged, and systematically documented in stone, parchment, paper, or recorded within geological strata, among the megaliths and architectural testimonials. The uniformitarian magnifying glass is cast to reprioritize values from which extrapolations and trends are plotted.

On the other hand, for thousands of years, communication has been transmitted through various means, including cuneiforms, in stone, wood, papyri, paper, parchment, and lately electronically. The worst case scenario did occur – errors, omissions, and distortions have crept in. On the other hand, the best scenarios have been highly encouraging - much has been recovered and corrected through triangulation providing a margin of accuracy assurance. The Christian Bible, for example, is an accumulation of multiple highly prized documents that had come in thousands of copies across huge territories and across ages. Similarly, in a manner that did not exist in other forms of literature, the internal textual features in the original languages had been so woven into multiple interconnected features that the Bible contains unique features that have helped maintain its content and content integrity intact. The underlying legal character of this document transmitted a covenant that had been initiated by the eternal Lord God (see Genesis 1:1 – 2:4) to His righteous inheritors – an eternal covenant from its initial conception at Creation into its future. Many divine covenant keepers and scribes copied, transmitted, and made available the message to those who wanted to follow the divine pattern and mission. They were guided by the Ten

Commandments inscribed in this covenant and transmitted through documented genealogies.

This divine message and mission was also built into the architecture and internal/external design of the church – a living document before the invention of the printing press. In such a designed church, a Christian believer saw a clear correspondence between the church's interior and the believer's psychology. Here in the church for millennia, there was written in art, music, and theatrical re-enactments of what occurs in the heavenly realm – that included key eternal personalities – all properly managed. There was a clear timeline of events that had historic proportions, a calendar attuned with the righteousness, religious processes that simulating what transpired in heaven – the mass that included the high priest and the King of Kings (Revelation 1). And the believer saw within him/herself a corresponding inner sanctum. This realm also has its icons and statues of either holy saints or idols of every kind. There is in the psychological holy of holies a role for either the King of Kings or Baal. The believer can recognize who or what visits the realm of one's thoughts and emotions. Is it charity? Is it a concern for one's Christian brothers and sisters, or phallic worship and passions lighted in the Temple of Venus? To whom does one light the candle? The righteous know how to 'clean their psychological house.' Does everyone see each other through the filter of the Ten Commandments? These are the filters that allowed people to survive harsh economic conditions and invasions. These are also the various means by which historical reality had been transmitted. This has been a six-dimensional reality: three spatial, one temporal, one executive/ supervisory, and one eternal. These were transmitted, recognized, and sought for in an effort to pursue and ensure certainty. This certainty had a legal and covenantal foundation which was evident and proven. All of this provided the substance of history that had been transmitted for generations from patriarchs to kings, prophets, and to the church. Within this scope it was possible to establish proactive and forecasting tools that helped identify requirements and gaps, and resource areas for economic development. It was a prerequisite for families that maintained ancestral family lineages. So when these genealogies had been combined in parallel and serially listings, it was possible to reconstruct historical events, decisions, movements of people across geographical terrain, the rise and fall of civilizations, case histories, legal action, judgments, and precedents. This is the substance of history. It is within this legal content that all of history is constructed and tracked.

Limitations: 3/12 - Variables within the Formulae.

Scientific models can express conditions in terms of *mathematical formulae*. Relational links among mathematical data and variables can make this to be an extremely sensitive tool. Scientists may correctly or through error include redundant or exclude from consideration vital variables or data. Such is the case in the example of Newton's Law of Gravitation. This gravitation equation, constructed solely on the work function – Work = Force x Distance - excludes consideration for energy. To ensure that energy would never come into play, the formula underwent further subtle change over time becoming: $W = Fd \cos(\theta)$. Energy here becomes nonexistent. This approach provides a simple description of work and not of gravitation itself, does not explain what gravitation is, closes opportunities for finding gravity's energy source, and does not identify gravity's rate/speed, which originally appeared to be faster than the speed of light. Einstein's theory does not clarify this issue either because, in part, Einstein capped the speed of light (electromagnetism) at an artificial rate – a constant. Yet, laboratory tests have accelerated light beyond and below this light's constant. In addition, scientists have reduced light's speed to one foot/second, as well as, slowed it down to zero. Furthermore, light exhibits bending qualities (speed variations) while passing from vacuum through other media (e.g., liquids), and through gravitational fields, or disappears in black holes. Similarly, measurements show that some galaxies move away from each other at speeds greater than the speed of light – suggesting that space itself distorts and moves galaxies apart.

Here are some comparative methods for establishing timelines, clocks, and dating methods.

Uniformitarian/evolution's position: the geologic column, with its zoo of fossilized animals and plants, is supposed to be a multi-billion year clock. Similarly, with dating of rocks through the uranium-based measurements, the potassium-argon, argon-argon methods provide results by which scientists can make time estimates. The short-term organic carbon-14 method is a method for establishing dates. Scientists use the speed of light travelling through space from distant stars and galaxies to confirm and prove long ages.

The creation scientists who look at the same data provide an alternate interpretation. The geologic column does not actually exist. Geologic strata are not actually set uniformly in an A, B, C, D, E, F strata order, but is more often mixed like decks of cards: B, D, F, A, E, C or other variations with many letters missing or doubled. Similarly, with fossils – 80% of fossils are marine animals. Here and other fossil layers do not reflect the age of the strata but rather provide evidence for the speed at which the creatures have been able to escape a calamity – the slower creatures were buried first, while the faster and stronger were buried in the following order respectively. Therefore, these sedimentary layers are not a reflection of time, but of flow and sedimentation speed, weight, and accumulation. Similarly, it is common to find strata where younger fossils are located three to six layers below older fossils – areas that cover areas as large as twenty-eight square miles. Mass graves - up to six square miles in diameter contain different species of fossilized animals that allegedly lived eons apart. Therefore, dating through sedimentary layering and fossils are not time related.

When we look at the various uranium-based measurements that are established upon several layers, we see the same different interpretations of the data (uniformitarian versus creation assumption). We have to consider the following:

(1) Initially the rock contained only parent isotopes (U^{238}) and none of the daughter isotopes (Pb^{206})

(2) That (Pb^{206}) is the result of decaying parent isotopes (U^{238})

(3) That the rate of decay had been constant without being leached by water

(4) That additional U238 had not entered the rock sample from outside sources. When uniformitarian scientists treat this process, they usually ignore the hydrogen escape rate. This hydrogen escape rate makes a dramatic difference for ages estimates – from billions of years reduced to thousands of years

Uniformitarian assumptions led many scientists to predict in the 1960s that there would not be any radiogenic argon (^{40}Ar) in basalt and volcanic rocks when these were formed. Yet 'non-zero' concentrations of ^{40}Ar were found in dozens of places around the Earth.[140] Similar

---

[140] G.B. Babrymple, *The Age of the Earth* (Palo Alto, CA,: Stanford University Press, 1991), 91 and G.B. Barymple, '40Ar/36 Analyses of Historic Lava Flows' *Earth & Planetary Science Letters* 6 (1969): pp 47-55; A. A. Snelling, 'The Cause of

predictions were made in radioisotope dating methods. Contrary to the general perception that radioisotope dating is an assured science, this dating method is actually being questioned based on the new evidence that emerges from the lab. For example, samples have been taken from similar rocks in the same location which have been tested for dates of metamorphism and age of the original volcanic/sedimentary rock.[141] These samples were tested in two well-credentialed internationally-recognized commercial laboratories with standard best-practice procedures on state-of-the-art equipment for radioisotope analysis – potassium-argon Canadian lab and rubidium-strontium (Rb-SR), samarium-neodymium (Sm-Nd), and lead-lead (Pb-Pb) – using the Isoplot computer program[142], at an Australian lab. The results revealed that even with consideration made for the calculated margin of error, the different radioisotope dating methods yielded completely different ages that cannot be reconciled.

Anomalous Potassium-Argon Ages: for Recent Andesite Flows at Mt. Ngauruhoe, New Zealand, and the Implications for Potassium-Argon Dating', R.E. Walsh, ed., Proceedings of the Fourth International Conference on Creationism (Pittsburgh, PA: Creation Science Fellowship, 1998) 503-525.; A.A Snelling, "Excess Argon: The 'Achillies' Heel' of Potassium-Argon and Argon-Argon 'Dating of Volcanic Rocks", (http://www.icr.org).

[141] K.E. Karlstrom, B.R. Ilg, M.L. Williams, D.P. Hawkins, S.A. Bowring and S.J.Seaman, "Paleoproterozoic rocks of the Granite Gorges," in S.S. Beus and M. Morales, eds., *Grand Canyon Geology*, 2nd ed. (New York, Oxford University Press, 2003), 9-38.; S.A. Austin, ed., *Grand Canyon: Monument to Catastrophe* (Santee, CA: Institute for Creation Research, 1994), 57-82; D.P.Hawkins and S.A. Bowing, 'U-Pb monazite, xenotime, and titanite geochronological constraints on the prograde to post-peak metamorphic thermal history of Paleoproterozoic migmatites from Grand Canyon, Arizona,' *Contributions to Mineralogy and Petrology*. 134 (1999):. 150-169; D.P. Hawkins, S.A. Bowring, B.R. Llg, K.E. Karlstrom and M.L. Williams, 'U-Pb geochronologic constraints on the Paleoproeterozoic crustual evolution of the Upper Granite Gorge, Grand Canyon, Arizona,' *Geological Society of America Bulletin*, 108 (1996): 1167-1181; B.R. Ilg, K.E. Karlstrom, D.P. Hawkins and M.L. Williams, 'Tectonic evolution of Paleoproterozoic rocks of Grand Canyon: Insights into middle-crustal processes,' *Geological Society of America Bulletin*, 108 (1996): 1149-1166.

[142] K.R.Ludwig, Isoplot/EX (Version 2.49): The Geochronological Toolkit for Excel (Berkley: University of California, Geochronology Center, 2001), Special Publication, no. 1a.

The K-Ar model 'ages' are widely divergent from one another (405.1±109 Ma to 2574.2±73 Ma). Even from very closely spaced samples from the same outcrop of the same original lava flow, and are considered to be useless for 'dating' any event.[143]

Various explanations are usually given for such evident disparity and isolated aberrations, but it also becomes clear that the radioisotope dating methods, due to the seeming discordance of dating output, are far from yielding reliable absolute ages. Meanwhile, other more plausible tests and verified explanations have not been considered by establishment scientists. This view strays from the uniformitarian framework and is shelved.

Increasingly better alternate theories are being considered to test assumptions. One can consider data and processes that described the volcanic activities occurring at Mount Saint Helen. These have demonstrated that the alleged long-age sedimentation, fossilization, and landscape deformations can occur in hours, not hundreds of millions of years.

With regards to cosmic time dating (e.g., speed of light, conditions and changes on planetary, solar, stellar, and galactic areas) in an attempt to somehow find ways of including billions of years, again uniformitarians are found wanting. There are the big bang theories shortcomings.[144] This theory has been updated and re-explained in a hopeless attempt to keep it alive. However, such explanations have reached a stage where the human language appears to become a barrier – e.g., 'before the beginning there was this cosmic egg.' Did another type of time already exist prior to this time? What is the difference among the apparent multiple times - before, during, and after the first mega-explosion of the cosmic egg? What is the nature of time during the progress of the mega-explosion stages during which time, space, energy, gravitation, movement, and the electromagnetic waves, including proto-light, among many other prerequisites, were to exist at five stages during the explosion's progress and development? There appears to be billions of years that passed in

---

[143] Andrew A. Snelling, "Radioisotope dating of Grand Canyon Rocks" http://www.icr.org.

[144] Example: H. Arp, *Quasars, Redshifts, and Controversies* (Berkeley, CA: Interstellar Media. 1987), and *Seeing Red: Redshifts, Cosmology, and Academic Science* (Montreal: C. Roy Keys, Inc., 2002). E. Lerner, *The Big Bang Never Happened* (New York: Random House, 1991).

nano-seconds of time, then slowing down to our current time, and now seeing the universe, galaxies expanding again some at the speed of light. All this occurs apparently within our existing notions of what constitutes the speed of light.

A similar dilemma exists where scientists consider the same billions of evolutionary years (EY) in areas of meteorite dust accumulation on the planets and moons. Here, estimates include between 1,000 feet to 233,000 feet of cosmic dust on various cosmic bodies. Yet, such cosmic dust remains undetectable in any form anywhere on the Earth, Moon, or any other planets.

Uniformitarian scientists ignore more than a 100 dating methods that suggest drastically more recent time scales. Here we may list: the rates at which the Sun shrinks; Sun's emission of gamma rays; zircon crystal's age which has been determined to be less than 10,000 years. Such crystals contain known lead-leakage rates. What about Earth's slowing rotation; the Earth's diminishing electromagnetic field? The RATE project and many other dating issues raise serious questions about mainstream science's assumptions. Clearly all of these formulas and assumption need to be revisited and placed in perspective within objective and unfettered scientific scope.

Limitations: 4/12 - Proper Tools, Systems, and Procedures

How does a scientist use his scientific tools, systems, and procedures?

When someone describes Noah's flood, one immediately pictures a cartoon image of a miniaturized wooden boat with a house on it, with a couple of giraffes' necks and heads sticking out of the windows. Here we also see Grandpa Noah with his gray hair, who, while checking weather conditions, is about to let a pet dove out for a spin. The Christian Bible, however, depicts a much more dramatic story.

The uniformitarian believer dismisses a global flood scenario. He sees this as a cute little myth that is at best a memory or legend of some local flood. Instead, uniformitarians want the public to believe in yet another story that is portrayed in uniformitarian science. Upon closer examination and scrutiny, the reader will find that such science also qualifies as nothing more than a fable narrated in scientific sounding language.

Uniformitarians consider up to five major ice ages. These five ages lie upon three types of interpretations of evidence. Evidence sourced from: geology (scouring and scratching of rocks, glacial moraines, drumlins, valley cuttings, and the deposition of tillites and glacial erratics)[145]; chemestry (oxygen isotope ratios in sediments, acid concentrations, sedimentary rocks, oceans, and ice sediments)[146]; and paleontology (where and how fossils are distributed away from cold areas). This evidence is used to provide some substance to a long-age period of up to five major ice ages with over thirty[147] intermediate and local ice ages. However, the same evidence substantiates a single recent 500-year ice age that occurred between 2000 BC and 1500 BC - as the recent creation scientists propose.

Table 5. Hypothesized Uniformitarian Ice Ages .

#	Ice Age	Period	Years Ago	Severity
1	Huronian	Early Proterozoic	2.3 billion	
2	Snowball Earth	Cryogenian	1 billion to	Most severe
3	Andean-Saharan	Ordovician & Silurian	460-430 m.	Minor
4	Karoo	Carboniferous/Permian	350-260 m.	Polar ice
5	Glacial, Inter-	Pliocene	2.58 million	North
	Hemisphere			
	Glacial		up to 10K	

Various uniformitarian causes for ice ages have been proposed that are admitted to be controversial by evolution scientists themselves. The quantity of CO^2 in the Earth's atmosphere and volcanic activity seem to play a major role in all uniformitarian ice ages. Other causes for ice ages are attributed to: (a) position and movement of continents which in turn affect ocean currents; (b) changes of the Earth's orbit (Milankovitch cycles[148]; Muller and MacDonald's three-dimensional orbit

---

[145] Doug Macdougall, *Frozen Earth: The Once and Future Story of Ice Ages*, (Berkley: University of California Press, 2004).

[146] "How are past temperatures determined from an ice core?" *Scientific American* (2004), http://www.sciam.com/print_version.cfm?articleID=00001580-C282-1148-828283414B7F012B).

[147] J.P. Kennett, *Marine Geology* (New Jersey: Prentice-Hall, 1982) 747.

[148] M. Milankovitch, "Mathematische klimalehre und astronomische theorie der Klimaschwankungen," in *Handbuch der Klimatologie*, I.W. Koppen and R.

inclinations);[149] and (c) the Sun's energy output.

However, creation scientists identify what few uniformitarian scientists suspect. Evolutionists do not describe, test the causes, nor identify ice ages mechanisms that must account for at least seven key catastrophic requirements. These requirements would also have to leave specific signatures upon geological, chemical, and paleontological evidence that are not addressed by uniformitarian theories. For an ice age to occur there must be:

(1) Massive volcanic and plate tectonic upheavals, which

(2) Leave massive amounts of volcanic aerosol in the atmosphere that contribute to a vast temperature drop by reflecting solar radiation back to space, but continue to

(3) Heat the oceans - thus

(4) Increasing evaporation. A 10 degree C in air-sea temperature difference, with 50% relative humidity, will evaporate seven times more water at a sea-surface temperature of 30 degrees C at 0 degrees C[150].

(5) As volcanic ash covers the Earth, this contributes to the cooling of the atmosphere

(6) These interactions (1 through 5) cause increased precipitation (X50 magnitude of that existing today). These conditions have been simulated on the CRAY computer and,

(7) These conditions must persist for at least two consecutive years.

With these minimal conditions, within 500 years after the worldwide flood, there would be, within a period of two years and thereafter, abundant rains downpours, including black rain falling within the equatorial zones. Snow would start accumulating rapidly at the polar regions and on high mountain tops. In lower valleys, particularly within

---

Geiger, eds., (Berlin: Gerbruder Bontraeger, 1930). A. Berger, S.H. Schneider and J.C. Duplessy, eds., "Oceanic Response to Orbital Forcing in the Later Quaternary: Observational and Experimental Strategies," in *Climate and the Geosciences* (Dordrecht:Kluwer Academic Publishers, 1989). See also, problems with astronomical theory: L. Vardiman, "Ice Cores and the Age of the Earth" (San Diego:Institute for Creation Research, 1993).

[149] "A New Theory of Glacial Cycles" http://muller.lbl.gov/pages/glacialmain.htm.

[150] J.R. Holton, *An Introduction to Dynamic Meteorology* (New York: Academic Press, 1972), 48-51; Michael Oard, "The Ice Age and the Genesis Flood," http://www.icr.org.

the vicinity of the warm and hot oceans, temperature would remain temperate while land would support abundant plant and animal life. This would explain the hundreds of thousands of mammoths frozen in the northern regions of the Earth. No doubt similar conditions existed on the Antarctic continent.

After the 500-year ice age, when the volcanic dust clears out of the Earth's atmosphere, after the Earth cools enough, while the now unclouded atmosphere begins to rise , within 7 – 200 years, the ice age snow packs begin to melt significantly. The total duration of the post-flood ice age would last approximately 700 years with an error margin of 200 years.

Much scientific research has been done in the study of these conditions. Scientists simulated the conditions on the CRAY computer (e.g., Los Alamos laboratories). The software helped them to reconstruct conditions and helped to predict causes and consequences within the context of a single post-global flood ice age on the Earth.[151]

Regarding geological evidence, recent drilling in Greenland and Antarctic ice sheets, revealed ice age durations that measured within thousands of years instead of 100,000s to billions of years.[152]

The above discussion on ice ages provides examples where the proper use of scientific tools, systems, and procedures are key in helping determine accuracy of knowledge. One of the factors that held back science throughout history had been the lack of proper tools, systems, and procedures. Today, these are opening doors. Science policy must not restrict the proper use of tools, systems, and procedures if these help uncover new empirical data. Neither should science policy hide or distort the use and results of tools and data that contributes to accurate knowledge and new discoveries . Today, there's much drilling in the

---

[151] http://www.icr.org, http://www.icr.org , http://www.icr.org , http://www.icr.org , http://www.icr.org , http://www.icr.org , http://www.icr.org , http://www.icr.org.

[152] R.B Alley, "Visual-Stratigraphic Dating of the GISP2 Ice Core: Basis, Reproducibility, and Application," *Journal of Geophysical Research* 102, C12 (1997): 26, 367-26, 381; also, D.A. Meese, A.J. Gow, R.B. Alley., G.A. Zielinski, P.M. Grootes, M. Ram, K.C. Taylor, P.A. Mayewski, J.F. and Bolzan, "The Greenland Ice Sheet Project 2 Depth-Age Scale: Methods and Results," *Journal of Geophysical Research* 102, C12 (1997): 26, 411-26, 423; also, Michael Oard, "Are Polar Ice Sheets Only 4500 Years Old?" http://www.icr.org.

Arctic and Greenland ice and ocean bed floor. Creation scientists have purchased many CRAY computer hours to simulate data and forecasts for the various critical weather conditions.[153]

Limitations: 5/12 - Application of Original Scientific Method

What is scientific? During the past 200 years all kinds of things have been placed within the parameters of what constitutes scientific. We have scientific economics, dialectical materialism (DIAMAT, HISTMAT, FUTURMAT)[154], evolution, laboratory operations and procedures, and classroom exclusive subjects, that are legalized in courts, and appear to have three-to-seven steps that thus describe the scientific method.

At the same time, today evolutionists find it easy to dismiss what they consider to be unscientific or pseudoscience. Here, evolutionists include all the investigative, empirical, laboratory, scientific modeling, and published discoveries done by creation and intelligent design scientists. Some evolutionists give cursory credit to pre-Darwinian works of the ancient Greek philosopher-physicists who sought natural causes and processes, and a few who have contributed to the rationalistic-empiricist cause. Uniformitarian science authority formulate policies which link 'science' with Darwinism in such a way that suggests that science began with Darwin. Uniformitarian policy dismisses creation, intelligent design, and pre-Darwinian scientific contributions on these policy criteria alone.

During the past 200 years uniformitarians have mounted a concerted effort to identify a demarcation line between the sciences and religion.[155]

---

[153] L. Vardiman, "Numerical Simulation of Precipitation induced by Hot Mid-Ocean Ridges," http://www.icr.org ; Larry Vardiman and Karen Bousselot, "Sensitivity Studies on Vapor Canopy Temperature Profiles," http://www.icr.org ; see also, results: K.P. Wise, S.A. Austin, J.R. Baumgardner, D.R. Humphreys, A.A. Snelling and L. Vardiman, "Catastrophic Plate Tectonics: A Global Model of Earth History," *Proceedings of the Third International Conference on Creationism*, R.E. Walsh, ed., (Pittsburgh, PA: Creation Science Fellowship, 1994), 609-622. Also, John R. Braumgardner, "Runaway Subduction as the Driving Mechanism for the Genesis Flood," http://www.icr.org .

[154] George Grebens, *Ivan Efremov's Theory of Science Fiction* (New York: Vantage Press, 1979).

[155] Refer back to Chapter 1 where the works of John William Draper with his book, *History of the Conflict between Religion and Science* (1874), and later Andrew Dickson White with his essay, "A History of the Warfare of Science with

The philosopher of science, Paul Feyerbend, discovered that history shows that there had been more of an eclectic approach to the scientific method. He discovered that scientific research reflected five trends. Scientific research had not been based exclusively upon logical or methodological rules of science that were distinct from sound reasoning. There was no special scientific authority to draw upon - that every scientific procedure had been violated at some time. That science is inseparable from the larger body of human thought and inquiry, and in practice and principle, science had not entirely been empirical. Needless to say, there have been many scientists and historians who questioned Feyerbend's discovery.[156] Upon closer examination, this investigative process becomes clear, when it is placed within the proper DMPS content and environment.

The pursuit of accurate knowledge can be accomplished by a trained and qualified person who uses the 3DMM and DMPS to resolve uncertainty in an effort to achieve conditional certainty. However, the problem rises when this approach is supplemented by, or filtered through, the three-point uniformitarian and reductionist processes.

This method results in having uniformitarian scientists essentially rewrite and reinterpret all history in a hypothesized format that cannot empirically be tested or proved. Inevitably, the hypothesis and process is then perceived as becoming a fact rather than as an alternative (#4) that is yet to be tested. Such is the 'luxury syndrome,' where a desirable alternative is pre-selected before all alternatives have been examined. Such an approach not only eliminates the purpose for the DMPS/scientific method, but also is used to erase the knowledge-base where conditional certainty is managed.

The young earth creation scientists fair much better in the area of the application of the original scientific method. They accept a historical rather than a synthetic view of the 3DMM; recognize a definition of science that includes all stages; and respect the full range of alternatives filtered through executive plans applied during the decision-making and

---

Theology in Christendom" have been brought. The Vienna Circle and Karl Popper and others have been brought.

[156] Alan, B. Spitzer, *Historical Truth and Lies about the Past* (Chapel Hill: University of North Carolina Press, 1996). Keith Jenkins, ed., *The Post-modern History Reader* (London: Routledge, 1997).

problem-solving (DMPS) process.

Dr. Henry M. Morris, the father of the modern young earth creation scientific model, has successfully rescued the original Christian Biblical scientific model by providing it with strategic repositioning within the creation scientific model. This allowed the creation scientists to fight a new battle with the stealthy uniformitarian marketing promoters.

The twentieth century's two World Wars have reshuffled the scientific deck of cards in world politics. Although the West had successfully neutralized most effects of two extreme versions of the application of the Darwinian theory (Marxism and Nazism), the West itself had succumbed to the new atheistic myth, which was bent on destroying the last vestiges of Christendom from which the modern scientific method emerged. It is the uniformitarian theses that are the designing tool that helped achieve these gruesome results. Dressed in scientific garb, the uniformitarian initiative set itself to remove all true science from the civilization's thinking. Where science originally meant pursuit of accurate knowledge, the uniformitarian's science removed all history of reliable 3DMM and designed an artificial history and pre-history by starting with existing conditions, and then extrapolating the physical properties into the past, and then drawing back to the present by adhering to the simple-to-complex, primitive-to-sophisticated process.

The question is how successful have the uniformitarians been in achieving this? By 2000 AD, all mainstream Christian organizations had 'drunk from the glass of uniformitarian wine,' becoming pantheists by converting themselves to theistic evolutionists, progressive creationists, and have become ardent contributing participants in the modernist ecumenical council. With such pantheism, original Christendom, from which originally emerged the quest for true modern scientific method, its quest for accurate knowledge, and contingent certainty, had now converted to becoming 100% proof uniformitarians.

During this migration to uniformitarian realities, the modernist Christian church has forsaken its history, traditions, the qualitative knowledge-base, 3DMM, and the true tools for getting out of uncertainty to certainty. This allows them to play a role in the pluralistic marketing arena. Where originally, Christianity was the only faith that couldn't be made to fit into Caesar's Pantheon of cults, today, with the generous helping of the modernist heresy, it fits into Caesar's Pantheon comfortably.

One would ask, what was the original Christian scientific method designed for?

It has a history that is founded upon geometric natural law, genealogies, executive-based covenants, commandments, statutes, and judgments. This 3DMM knowledge-base contains the formula for establishing the Kingdom of God, and contains the earmarks for identifying the Kingdom of Babylon.

Geometric natural law, when properly understood, contains global engineering management plans; purposes, objectives, strategies, with engineering and infrastructures designs; life-cycles comparisons; rules for husbandry, selective breeding, medicine, property, and economics management, maps, records of kings. It contains, as well, a detailed history of singular events, global cataclysms, world droughts, and documents civilizations populated by giants, and conditions that existed before and after singularities whose effect can be identified in today's geological and paleontological formations. The uniformitarian naïve realism and cynicism may reduce this reality to myths, but, by this very fact, the modernist uniformitarian disqualifies him/herself/itself from discussing issues that pertain to geometric natural law and issues of sub-chromosome information and nano-technology, or issues pertaining to the executive plans and stylistic levels of the 3DMM.

Young earth creation science publications fall within the framework of historical definition of science. They reflect most applications and uses of scientific tools. They successfully, verifiably, and reproducibly move uncertainty towards conditional certainty[157]. When uniformitarian scientists attempt to critique creation-catastrophic interpretations of empirical data, this is done on purely uniformitarian grounds. This is done within a narrowed scope of alternatives, peppered with 'luxury syndrome' logic, and by wearing sun shades that make them overlook much evidence. What uniformitarian critics present are nothing but uniformitarian naïve realism positions. Clearly, it is not based upon justifications that are based upon the original meaning of science. All of this is clearly seen among the more serious high level debates. For example: Mark Isaak's *Problem with a Global Flood*, 2nd ed., (The Talk

---

[157] See the many articles published on www.icr.org., and others, such as: "Journal of Creation," http://creationontheweb.com/content/view/3873/ (previously titled "Creation Ex-Nihilo Technical Journal").

Origins Archive, 1998),http://www.talkorigins.org/faqs/faq-noahs-ark.html ; and the rebuttal by J. Sarfati, 'Problems with a Global Flood?' (1998); http://www. trueorigin.org/arkdefend.asp.

One should take into consideration that over the past 30 years, all debating groups have been repositioning themselves. Their strategies have been adjusted and priorities reset. In order to keep up with the debate, one has to take into consideration the changes that have taken place. This is particularly true with the advent of third players into the debate – the intelligent design group, and more recently the neo-theistic evolution groups: progressive evolution and old earth creationism.

Limitations: 6/1 -. Application of 3DMM (Figure 5)

This sixth interpretative method reflects the best that the 3-D management model details. Certainty in the 3DMM is inversely proportional to the 3DMM's twenty-seven plans and infrastructure's content as it reflects the objective and unfettered scientific method and reflects geometric natural law. A quick review of the first five limitations examined above demonstrates a systematic approach to overcoming scientific gaps. Here, scientists gather, document, and test empirical data, and compare data and information accuracy that they collected globally and now reside in the knowledge-base. Scientist re-examine the knowledge-base to identify gaps, areas of uncertainty, and the potential for establishing DMPS based hypotheses (i.e., alternatives #4). They prioritize and test all alternative's data, information, and knowledge for application and which lead to conditional certainty. In the current sixth stage, scientists test for quality and ascertained/ absolute certainty.

The sixth interpretation of data is set within the plans of the three-dimensional management model (3DMM). This approach views all evidence within a systematic management scope, to ensure that knowledge is accurate and is contingently certain.

As within industrial project management, within this management plan it is then necessary to answer questions of ethics, attitude, and culture that are conducive with scientific research. Under such circumstances it will then be easy to contrast answers that are outside the unfettered scientific system. The unfettered scientific results would, within a 3DMM, allow for easier triangulated answer formulation to key questions that seemed to have been unanswerable until now. Within this 'hypothesis of the hypothesis' approach, the DMPS would lead to issues such as:

- 'What is the origin for this entire marvel or existence?'
- 'How did all this come about and where is it going?'
- 'What is the proper behavior and attitude that should enhance knowledge-base certainty?'
- 'What is a favorable environment that helps ensure long-term accuracy process?'

Such questions would not be limited by such restrictive uniformitarian 'luxury syndromes.' Valid scientific questions continuously emerge when science is properly defined as the 'pursuit of accurate knowledge.' This is why these questions are located within the 3DMM among executive plans on the management design level, and specifically on the management style level. The uniformitarian approach, by definition, eliminates all executive level questions, and specifically the management style issues, as well as, all other stylistic plans. Some of these topics have been discussed above, but discussing these in terms of a 'scientific' context appears unusual today.

The first and second applications of the 'unfettered' scientific method proceeded during the ancient Greek, Christian (East and West), and Moslem times. Though it was true that the context of these world-views had been pantheistic and/or monotheistic, the search for accurate knowledge continued. The momentum continued even with the lack of proper scientific tools, and while fighting uphill battles. Similarly, these civilizations recognized, within their ideological scope, most of the twelve limitations of science, while the uniformitarian method does not. Yet, after this history of successes, the uniformitarian method is oblivious to the twelve limitations of the scientific method (Figure 14).

It was, however, during the sixteenth century in Western Europe that Christendom was challenged in an unsuspecting way[158]. A radically alternate view began to emerge, which questioned the validity of the foundations of all knowledge-base systems and of their contingent certainty. This new emerging approach had:

(a) A truncated knowledge-base system.

---

[158] A similar process emerged at the end of the Moslem Classical period, where Al-Biruni introduced the 'demarcation line' between theology and empirical science (Ahmad Dallal, *Encyclopedia of the Quran*, "Quran & Science"). Similarly, Ibn Tufail's philosophical novel, translated as *Philosphus Autodidactus* (1671), introduced empiricism, tabula rasa, materialism. G.A.Russell, *The "Arabick" Interest of the Natural Philosophers in Seventeenth-Century England* (Brill Publishers, 1994); http://en.wikipedia.org/wiki/Islamic_Golden_Age.

(b) Foundations that were in constant flux exhibited a relative, rather than three categories and process of, conditional certainty. This inevitably established a continuous state of relative uncertainty rather than attempting to achieve conditional certainty.

(c) Actively, not only has this been antagonistic towards, but pursued a strategic replacement policy in all aspects of its rival's approach to its completed 3DMM

(d) Recoined the vocabulary, concepts, standards, and source of authority in the host culture – stressing subjective, substitutional, and diminishing consumerism

(e) Reversed objective and unfettered science by violating the scope of the twelve limitations of science, thus causing an implosion of the 3DMM. Through this it accelerated the dynamics evident in failed civilizations.

Limitations: 7/1 - Four/five mental models, where the 3DMM and the scientific method (DMPS) reflect four to five basic *mental models*

These models help manage the hypothesis, and theory, and have predictive value. For example, the Newtonian and the Cartesian models of thinking reflect mechanical and reductionist forecasting methods. The Bergsonian and Darwinian models reflect an organic model of thinking. Karl Marx's *Das Kapital* reveals the process model. The intelligent design model reflects the information technology and engineering model of thinking.

Mental models can become a hazard with people who misuse facts and evidence. They easily may hamper or arrest scientific development. Scientists achieve this arrest unconsciously or through premeditated policy. A 'fact' without its properly defined framework can lead to absurdity. A few examples:

(a) The concept of a flat Earth is a fact to the naked eye at ground level within the scope of a Mediterranean empire thousands of years ago.

(b) Two parallel lines with a perpendicular line at 90 degree angles run parallel to infinity – this is a fact in plane geometry, but not a fact in Riemannian spherical geometry where the same parallel 90 degree lines cross at both poles of the sphere. Loboshevsky's 'horse saddle' geometry has the same parallel lines in a 90-degree configuration diverge in opposite directions.

Mental models provide a framework of awareness. Mental models describe a reality that helps identify and determine a fact within its scope. At the same time, as long as models reflect algebraic variables, they will remain relative, and appear as points within uncertainty – i.e., they will never lead to conditional certainty.

Limitations: 8/12. Five change levels

Industry recognizes up to five qualitative change levels that describe more than a simple linear change. These change level concepts contain qualitative infrastructures. Sometimes a seemingly simple change process, at a different infrastructural level, can be a qualitatively different change.

The five change levels are: (1) static or copies, (2) change or adaptation, (3) improvement or re-engineering, which also includes supervisory systems, (4) innovation or redesign - purposive executive systems, and (5) invention or third-level change (e.g., hypothesis of the hypothesis).

The uniformitarian / evolutionary concept, for example, in order for it to achieve scientific value and conditional certainty, in areas where allegedly micro- becomes macro-change, the process must describe and test five levels of change. Both evolution and creation may agree on change that occurs at (1), (2) (adaptation), and possibly (3) within an inherited pre-programmed code. However, evolutionists leave the scientific domain when they attempt to explain higher macro-change levels – (3), (4), and (5). Here, evolutionists must address change at several infrastructural and supervisory system levels – an area where statistical and linear methods cause havoc.

Limitation: 9/12. DMPS (Figures 9 thru 13 see related texts).

The comprehensive decision-making and problem-solving process (DMPS) is the foundational tool in the scientific method. This process helps convert uncertainty to conditional certainty. Here also, scientists categorize the hypothesis (alternatives) and theory (quality guarantee) stages. We find that history records various scientific methods. Recently, scientific investigative steps had been procedurized and pre-programmed (e.g., neural systems) that help attain specific solutions and objectives. Others allow wider creative options, exploring quantified alternatives and hypotheses.

Limitations 10/12 - Implementation of ideological assumptions.

Scientists use *assumptions* when they use scientific models, to help interpret data and make predictions. Fair-minded scientists recognize that assumptions are biases - value judgments forced into the scientific investigative process. Scientists and philosophers view this bias as a disguised hypothesis or theory. Assumptions are essentially DMPS procedural filters. In management, such assumptions reflect executive objectives, strategies, and must include purpose. Scientists may begin from any assumption, but should not allow this assumption to violate the original intent of the scientific process, such as to eliminate or distort empirical data by narrowing the scope (see item #12 below)

This is an examination of the situation where the line between ideology and science becomes blurred. This is where ideology may be promoted as science. Science is improperly defined. Its steps are mis-defined, substituted, missing, or overly simplified. Proponents of such a science usually accuse others of not understanding their true science. They continue to modify the process as they go along, all the while explaining the true meaning of this imponderable science. For example, in school a student may ask, 'What is a trilobite?' The packaged answer will include: (a) an oversimplified description – 'a prehistoric sea creature' and this statement will immediately be coupled with (b) the date 'that lived million/billion years ago.'[159] The astronomical date is designed to imply a reality that existed beyond the 6,000 year Biblical creation option. Such answers affect the student's dignity, integrity, and self-determination. This formulation sets up an invisible barrier to any further exploration of alternatives (#4). In other words, such questions and answers remain in a state of uncertainty. Under such conditions students memorize scripted, prescribed, scientific-sounding formulations that must be reproduced in order to pass the science test. So, unless one speaks such uniformitarian magic language and possesses unfathomable thinking, one will demonstrate that: (1) one cannot be scientific or objective; (2) one remains un-programmed, reactive, and

---

[159] On a continuous basis, the media presents the public with paleontological or geological proof that should reinforce the long ages bias. While writing this book the following information was released via Internet: "Japanese and Mongolian scientists have successfully *recovered* the complete skeleton of a seventy-million-year-old young dinosaur, a nature museum announced Thursday," http://news.yahoo.com/s/ap/20080724/ap_on_re_as/japan_dinosaur.

uneducated; or worse, (3) one must harbor some dormant or latent cultist leadings; or (4) one may potentially harbor creationist tendencies.

In uniformitarian states, people with such un-evolutionary views would qualify for immediate intensive psychiatric care. In the United States, scientists who don't adhere to the uniformitarian party line have been legally pronounced as being nothing more than cultist quacks and lost their professional positions and reputations.[160]

Of course, oversimplified religious answers can direct someone off the scientific path too. Such as starting with a conclusion 'evolution scientists are wrong,' 'evolution scientists are all atheists,' 'it's possible to disprove evolutionists' interpretation of evidence in five minutes,' 'if this information is not in the Holy Scriptures, that means that these facts are irrelevant or false.' Countless numbers of people have become confirmed atheists, skeptics, and/or evolutionists because of their exposure to such wrong use of religion. And how many ideologues can't distinguish between a discussion and a dialog? Discussion means that both parties are ready to fight for their position, and let the best man win. In a dialog, both parties recognize that they may have come with half-formed mental models, incomplete knowledge due to limited exposure to issues, or confused about what constitutes the real scientific method (DMPS). So they use the dialog format to examine the 3DMM and listen to and examine all alternatives, the filtering process, and test the applications. In many public debates, it didn't matter what anyone stated, each would simply present one's pre-programmed view. Such misunderstandings appear in areas of the definition, concepts, or scientific method phases. They introduce the 'luxury syndrome' without realizing that the scientific debate turned into an ideological or philosophical soap opera with scientific-sounding commercials.

Here's the typical example where the uniformitarian, atheist, or skeptic simplistically define all theisms and then assume that Christianity fits this simple definition. The atheist's procedure begins with a story such as prior to, and even after, the coming of the uniformitarian and reductionist 'science', people tended to assign metaphysical causalities to all kinds of phenomena that they didn't understand. By extension, this approach was also attributed to Christians. Then atheists would bring even worse

---

[160] *Expelled: No Intelligence Allowed,* starring Ben Stein (2008).

scenarios where Christians were supposed to be guilty of the most depraved human deficiencies, antisocial atrocities, cultist, and antiscientific inclinations. Such perceptions are reflection of uninformed or propagandized individuals. This is a symptom of naïve realist thinking. Such atheists, skeptics, and uniformitarians congregate and associate with each other and re-enforce their convictions that this is almost certainty and actual truth. Such a simplistic view of religion is designed to justify and promote the superiority of the uniformitarian view. This is promoted as an attempt to justify a seeming 'scientific' legitimacy. This is also the single common barrier that must be overcome before any type of science can be discussed. Such a uniformitarian position is axiomatic and an algebraic mode of thinking. Such individuals are most likely not to have ever come across the concept of geometric natural law. Their 'luxury syndrome' is rooted in the rationalistic-empiricist school of thought, and is nested in the supervisory policy (D4) plans within the 3DMM. In this configuration such thinking is designed to bypass the executive level's purpose (D1) with its inherent law, identity, and scope.

The uniformitarian/evolutionary notion of abiogenesis, life emerging from nonlife, has never been proved in the lab, nor does anyone know how such an event can occur. Numerous hypotheses have been proposed and abandoned as soon as counterproposals emerged. There are at least twenty-two such ideas which can be divided into four categories: (1) historical (spontaneous generation, Darwinian proposal of a pre-biotic soup, Haldane and Oparin's - chemical evolution); (2) organic molecules theory – Millers' experiement – the neo-evolutionists' reverse-engineered primordial soup, deep sea vents, Fox's experiment, Eigen-Wachtershouser, homochirality, radioactive beach, self-organization and replication; (3) protocells theory: genes first, metabolism firs, Buggles performance; and (4) other model variations: Clay theory, autocatalysis, deep hot biosphere, primitive extraterrestrial life, lipid world, PAH world, polyphosphates, multiple genesis.[161] All types of science have been devised to prove what turn out to be stories and wishful thinking.

The creation view promotes the centuries' old scientifically proven law of biogenesis which demonstrates that life comes only from life. The

---

[161] See Pier L. Luisi, *Emergence of Life: From Chemical Origins to Synthetic Biology* (Cambridge: Cambridge   University   Press,   2006), http://en.wikipedia.org/wiki/Abiogenesis.

DNA arranges and reproduces all elements of the organism's processes according to pre-programmed 'software.' Life had been created by the supernatural creator in a manner that allows life to exist and adapt within its environment, procreate within the existing physical, environmental, and biological laws. This life is created within the species scope and does not have the internal programming that would to go beyond the scope. Animals pass this genetic code from a living creature to another. There is no spontaneous generation. In most cases adaptation to highly challenging environments leads to the loss of genetic information rather than the formation of new species genetic information.

Intelligent design: Kenyon, the co-writer of *Chemical Predestination*, has identified basic flaws in his book's basic scientific assumptions. He proved that there wasn't a single chance for having biological life to emerge through chemical evolution or chemical predestination. He showed that such notions are founded on the absence of and the function of an information theory. Life is not sustained at the biochemical level only but within greater complexities, including the information technology identified at the sub-chromosomal levels. Here also exists a nano-engineering level, where robotics systems with capabilities to self- copy, replicate, translate, shepherd other components, maintain, manufacture, and self-replicate. None of this could have possibly emerged through statistical–chance occurrences.

This book has shown that the decision-making and problem-solving (DMPS) method is found to be a practical necessity in industry and engineering project management. DMPS is an outgrowth or is interfaced with the three-dimensional management model (3DMM) – knowledge-base (Figure 5) where conditional certainty becomes evident with effective data conversion into information through standards and codes, filtered through quantification and qualification for testing, leading to conditional certainty.

DMPS has been compared and paralleled with the basic scientific method (Figure 11). Both are used to overcome and to convert uncertainty to conditional certainty. (Figure 13). It will also be shown how the DMPS is related to models of thinking (Figure 15), levels of change management (Figure 16), and in the determination of the depth gap (Figure 18).

Limitations: 11/12 - Distinction: DMPS and Uniformitarianism

The *scientific method is not synonymous with uniformitarianism, materialism, naturalism, or reductionism.* These false synonyms are assumptions (# 10). These appear in the role of filters in the DMPS (see Figures 9 thru 13 for detail), yet methodologically, algebraic and axiomatic assumptions control all stages of the DMPS and limit the scope of alternatives. Now, we are daily reminded that the theory of evolution is significantly and legally established as being equal with true science. Other evolution policymakers have pronounced that evolution is so scientific that evolution has achieved the status of almost certainty and definite truth. Yet, upon closer examination, the theory of evolution does not stand on its own merit. Being a theory, it should be located at the quality assessment/guarantee stage of the DMPS (#7). In this condition, theory still resides within the scope of uncertainty. As uncertainty, it requires the DMPS to help it navigate through to three possible types of certainties: (1) complete certainty, (2) conditional certainty, or (3) disproven / falsified conditional certainty.

Dictionaries and encyclopedias provide only an approximate definition of uniformitarianism. Uniformitarianism is usually seen in terms of an assumption, concept, basic principle, generalization, or axiom. Most dictionaries associate the term with geology, while other encyclopedias provide a history of the development of the term. In the late eighteenth century, James Hutton offered the term gradualism to counter the notion of catastrophist causes as an explanation for geologic formations. John Playfair popularized gradualism, while Charles Lyell (1797 – 1875) incorporated gradualism as uniformitarianism in his *Principles of Geology* in 1830. Another concept expressing uniformitarianism is 'actualism' because the term suggests that it is through the current conditions, processes, and rates of change that we can extrapolate any kind of condition that may have occurred in the past – 'the present is the key to the past.' It is this view of geologic deep time that was designed to contrast and replace the notion of recent time . The need to emphasize observation of existing processes influenced Charles Darwin. This gradualism suggested the theory of evolution. The term 'catastrophism' resurged recently as an attempt to explain local or meteoric effects upon a planet. This was prompted by predictions and observations documented by Shoemaker-Levy about the nine comets that plunged into planet Jupiter. It suddenly became apparent that conditions of the surface of the various moons in the solar system, and on many parts of the Earth itself, provide evidence for numerous meteoric catastrophic collisions. However, such momentary catastrophes are not designed to supersede the uniformitarian/ evolutionary process.

The theory of evolution is totally dependent upon the uniformitarian process. The theory of evolution would totally unravel without its uniformitarian foundation. When one meets someone who is totally dedicated to the theory of evolution and would stake his/her reputation and career upon it, it must be recognized that such an individual is foremost a defender of, and believer in, the axiom of uniformitarianism. It is from uniformitarianism that the theory of evolution is conceived as being scientific. Concepts of natural selection, speciation, and macro-evolution, are but extensions, inferences, and window dressings for the uniformitarian axiom. To determine whether uniformitarianism is scientific, it must be compared with the scientific method.

The comparative evidence shows that the uniformitarian axiomatic process violates every step of the original definition of the scientific method (DMPS). Evolution's original conditional certainty is associated with the philosophical position of materialism – an axiomatic position taken from its following step. The uncertainty steps are: (a) materialism, (b) reductionism, and (c) a reactionary view against, and the rejection of, any non-materialistically established knowledge-base (3DMM).

In science, one would think that if mutations occurring within challenging environments would be the single key component that should point to qualitative change from micro- to macro-evolution (i.e., emergence of new genes and new information), the uniformitarian /evolution biologists would jump at the opportunity to use the latest CRAY computers to simulate and produce tests utilizing numerical simulation of mutation and natural selection. If biology evolutionists have already taken advantage of this and actually used CRAY computers to conduct simulations and tested mutation processes, then this information has not trickled out of the laboratories. However, the young earth creation scientists did create such software and did simulate the effects of mutations for this and many of their own population genetics studies. In two articles – Mendel's Accountant: A New Population Genetics Simulation Tool for Studying Mutation and Natural Selection by Dr. Baumgardner and Using Numerical Simulation to Test the Validity of Neo-Darwinian Theory by Dr. John Sanford - both authors study mutations and natural selection in human genetics, plant, and animal breeding and management of endangered species. Both scientists developed this state-of-the-art software jointly with ICR and the 'Feed My Sheep Foundation.' As they describe:

'...a forward-time population genetics model that tracks millions of individual mutations with their unique effects on fitness and unique location within the genome through large numbers of generations....the user chooses values for a large number of parameters such as those specifying the mutation effect distribution, reproduction rate, population size, and variations in environmental conditions.'[162]

Uniformitarian/evolutionary scientists predict that cumulative change proceeds from simple to complex[163], the Mendel's accountant software is used to track such mutations and helps prove that natural selection doesn't detect nor eliminate genetic deterioration due to mutations. Instead these accumulate over multiple generations thus degrading fitness.[164]

Comparative analyses of DMPS application by uniformitarianist, creation, and intelligent design scientists have been made (see Table 6). The results show that the latter two comply with the original scientific method, while uniformitarians violate the process of the original scientific method.

Table 6. **Comparison; DMPS, Uniformitarian, Creation Science Methods.**

DMPS (Fig. 9, 10)	Uniformitarian	Creation
#1 Start with a Knowledge-base (KB) = 3DMM (Figure 5).	3DMM not mentioned. Note: uniformitarian past is 'naïve realism' and an	3DMM legal historical knowledge-base; three singularities occurring during

---

[162] http://www.icr.org. This program is feely available for personal use and can be downloaded from the web at http://mendelsaccount.sourceforge.net. Also, Andres A. Snelling, ed., "Proceedings of The Sixth International Conference on Creationism: Technical Symposium Sessions," (Dallas, TX: Creation Research, 2008).

[163] The reasoning follows that natural selection describes the condition of heritable traits through successful generation of population of reproducing organisms, acts on the phenotype (observable characteristics of an organism), which, with genotypes associated with the favorable phenotypes, increase in frequency and the following generations and adaptations will occur in an ecological niche, thus giving rise to a new species.

[164] http://www.icr.org.

KB + standards = 'contingent certainty.' This includes not only quantitative and qualitative empirical data and information, but also laws, standards, rates, measures, and principles/procedures of economics and mathematics.

extrapolation of current processes, rates (see #3 below). It provides a 'hypothetical' history and 'extrapolated' knowledge-base. Hypothetical is still within the realm of 'uncertainty' and not within 'conditional certainty.' Uniformitarians reject many parts of Christian Catholic knowledge-base (3DMM).

recent historical periods–(a) divine creation of reality, time, geometric natural law, infrastructures, life; (b) drop of energy-density one cycle down the universal cone; (c) initial global hydro-tectonic global catastrophe followed by secondary global geologic, oceanic, climatologically, and other adjustments. Instead of a quantitative progression, there is instead a steady qualitative regression of structures, comparative phenomena.

#2 – Uncertainty – Psychological phase (see Figure 8).

Filtering process (#5) pre-distinguishes and qualifies only the uniformitarian versus the subjective/religious methods. Uniformitarianism seeks a rationalist/empiricist certainty, which is re-enforced by relativism and reductionism.

Preparation for objective and lawful methodology – framed within 3DMM, conditional certainty and resolve uncertainty through DMPS.

#3 – Define – describe gap in terms of desired solution (#6).

Begin with today's (current) condition, processes, and rates. Extrapolate into past, to identify potential cause to current conditions (using simple to complex process, reductionism, relativism). Definition guided by filtration (#5).

Describe gap in terms of desired solution (#6).

#4 – Alternatives (tools, quantitative). Formulate a hypothesis and predictions researching missing yet probable data and quantities. Describe the hypothesis, being within 'uncertainty,' in terms of DMPS phases. Use alternatives to formulate predictions (extrapolations,

Hypothesis formulation to explain phenomenon – make predictions. Hypothesis is usually confused with theory. Under uniformitarian influence, alternatives are reduced through the filtration #5 parameters.

Formulate a hypothesis for missing yet probable data and quantities that is to be researched. The hypothesis, being within 'uncertainty,' must therefore be described in terms of DMPS phases. Alternatives are also used to help formulate predictions (extrapolations, consequences) and interpretations.

consequences) and interpretations.

#5 Filter (priorities, weighing, criteria, consequences, impact). These are derived from the 3DMM's design executive plans (purpose, objectives and strategies).	Filters test for uniformitarian principles or 'naïve realism.' These are objectives and strategies (but exclude purpose) derived from the supervisory level: policies, procedures, rules and regulations. As mentioned above, uniformitarian filters pre-determine the psychology (#2), definition (#3), and alternatives (#4), and applicable tests (#6).	Filter (priorities, weighing, criteria, consequences, impact), these are derived from the 3DMM's management design executive plans (purpose, objectives, strategies).
#6 – Implementation (test, standards, codes) lead to conditional certainty (#7).	Test only for uniformitarian realism (UR) results. Consider other test results as being non-compliant – 'contaminated,' 'inconclusive,' and 'irrelevant.'	Implementation (test, quality, codes) that lead to conditional certainty.
#7 – Quality assessment /guarantee. Verified certainty, may become the foundation of a theory (lawful scopes), or falsifiability.	Theorize but exclude DMPS phases that are used to emerge from uncertainty – thus theory remains at the uncertainty level.	Quality assessment. Guarantee. Verified certainty, or may become the foundation of theory (lawful scopes) or falsifiability.

Historical records of the application of the scientific method do not contradict or interfere with observable, testable, and describable scientific data. The 3DMM is a record of conditional certainty which provides the means for testing both internal and environmental certainty. The DMPS is then used to close uncertainty gaps. Furthermore, the Christian Biblical 3DMM includes those basic law-based qualifies of science that are totally incorrectly defined by, or excluded from, the uniformitarian model.

Limitations: 12/12 - Scientific Lab to Help Reduce Uncertainty

The purpose of scientific laboratories is to provide tools that reduce uncertainty and help promote and ensure conditional certainty.' However, increasingly, scientific lab procedures accomplish the reverse. Here we can commonly find that when predictions are not born out, the lab scientist finds that evidence becomes contaminated, irrelevant, or inconclusive. It is necessary to distinguish between (a) laboratory procedures whose evidence helps reduce uncertainty, and (b) procedures that maintain conditions of uncertainty when predictions are not met due to faulty 'assumptions.' In the latter case, scientists may continue to test not to ensure a more precise certainty but to force the tools and evidence to meet specific predictions. If predictions still do not meet expected objectives, then such scientists will suggest that the results are 'inconclusive' due to 'contamination,' 'anomalies,' and 'insufficient data.'

The scientific lab comes in different shapes, forms, and sizes. The scientific lab is designed to meet different purposes and objectives. Labs may be designed to allow scientists to examine and test phenomena in physics, chemistry, biology, geology, paleontology, and other fields. Here, objects, flows, changes, and samples are measured, made to behave in ways that yields data.

There are other scientific labs that function as scientific models where quantified variables are used to simulate the various processes, reactions, and responses to see if they meet predictions. Some labs/models are used to reverse engineer processes to see if some hypothetical conditions can arise.

Laboratory controlled conditions may be set within territorial parameters, such as one in Tasmania in Australia. It is in this isolated environment that the Tasmanian devil's behavior and changes were studied in isolation. It is here that scientists of the University of Tasmania had been studying since 1996[165] a phenomenon among the Tasmanian devils that had developed a transmittable cancerous facial tumor disease. Because of this disease and early death, the marsupials 'adjusted' their life cycle of five - six-year life span, and the breeding cycle between two and three years to a breeding cycle that began as early as one year to allow the females to take care of their young before an early death (two - three years). However, it was interesting to see how scientists interpreted this phenomenon. University scientists perceived this change as evidence for macro-evolutionary change[166], rather than for micro-evolutionary

---

[165] H. Siddle, 'Transmission of a fatal clonal tumor by biting occurs due to depleted MHC diversity in threatened-carnivorous marsupial,' proceedings of the National Academy of Science, 104(41) (2007):1622-16226.

[166] R. Schmid, 'Cancer forces Tasmanian devils to breed earlier,' Associate Press, July 15, 2008 (web accessed July, 2008); also, M. Jones, 'Life-history change in disease-ravaged Tasmanian devil populations,' proceedings of the National

adaptation.[167] Such a 'scientific' misinterpretation of change by graduates of an accredited university can be understood since the uniformitarian axiom provides for only a linear mechanism for all types of biological change – micro- to macro-evolution. There are no methods for distinguishing between adaptive and processes that are designed to overcome qualitative, infrastructural, re-engineering and redesigning macro-change. To achieve micro-changes there is evident loss and not gain of information at each stage. This is why it is calculated that the affected Tasmanian devils will become extinct within twenty-five years.[168] Whereas, to achieve macro-change, it is necessary to demonstrate new genetic information that would demonstrate required changes in infrastructural, supervisory, as well as provide evidence for re-engineering and redesign into macro-changes.

The dramatic contrasting debates do not occur among the young earth creation and intelligent design scientists. The contrastive and almost irreconcilable debates occur between the young earth creation, intelligent design on one side, and with the evolution, and old earth creation on the other.

The main difference between the two groups is that the latter group of scientists (evolution-uniformitarians) insists on long ages – billions of years progressing through statistical progressive processes. The first group of scientists does not agree with the long ages of statistical progression.

The second group of scientists insists that evolution is equivalent to being science. The first group of scientists shows that uniformitarianism is an ideology and not the scientific method. The first group tries to maintain a close approach to the objective scientific method, and recognize the twelve limitations to the science, although the group may not necessarily be 'unfettered.'

During these debates it became evident that there were two types of scientists who represented the evolution view. The first group had qualified scientists who graduated from accredited universities, loved doing scientific research, and simply went where their research led them. They published in scientific journals and contributed to an accurate

---

Academy of Science, (2008), (ahead of print, accessed July 17, 2008).

[167] Frank Sherwin, "Tasmanian Devils: Extinction not macro-evolution," http://www.icr.org.

[168] Ibid.

scientific knowledge-base. The second group included qualified scientists who also graduated from accredited universities but loved their uniformitarian ideology much more than their scientific research. This second group involved themselves in questionable politics and didn't blink an eye when it came to violating the objective scientific method (DMPS). Their mind was tuned to the luxury syndrome. They recognized the value of uncertainty and hardly ever reached conditional certainty.

The second group of scientists, while debating, exhibit less than scientifically satisfactory lab results. The list below identifies methods that help question the users' scientific method (DMPS) and the users' management style (3DMM):

Incomplete proofs or results (e.g., two of five factors) accounted for during the presentation.

Dissymmetrical comparisons - misinterpretation of data and conditions under which variables function or behave. Here, fraudulent information appears on graphs.

Ascribe motives or methods that are not part of the process. Introduce questionable cause. Data or events appear via unknown means.

Misidentify source of data and processes.

Compare apples with pears. Perform analysis on what is finally interpreted as being 'contaminated' or 'inconclusive.'

Doctor or revise measurements, values, and calibrations.

Mudslinging – nasty pre-/middle conclusions, disrespect, irrelevant information.

Intentional presentation of misinformation, knowing that the audience would not check.

Make emotional mountains out of ant hills.

Present alternatives that have no bearing on the issue. Narrow the scope of alternatives. Change parameters.

Quibble about inconsequential issues.

Allusions to improperly constructed experiments – sources, movement, changes, temperature range behavior.

Misinterpret content and context. Focus on insignificant points in order to obscure a sound structure or body of evidence.

Scientific models established on invalid or limited assumptions For example: focus explanations that are based on conditions that are 'cold' or 'dry' whereas all variable change when temperatures range 400^0F, and the affecting humidity is in the form of melting ice (e.g., conditions on the Moon).

Use of equations with inconsistent dates.

Consider only one cause for real or imaginary fault lines, cracks, uplifts, scratches, demarcation lines, and points.

Application of marketing/sales tactics – 'bait and switch' to attract customers by advertising one desirable product only to sell a product that has lower quality at higher price. [169]

Agree to describe a strategy that excludes the do's and don'ts, but then introduce the do's and don'ts anyway in an attempt to shift the focus off the scope that is to be proved. [170]

Reject the need to read clear proofs and answers in order to submit faulty conclusions. [171]

These eighteen examples are but a few examples of false science that are magnified during many debates. In some quarters, policy-making bodies make such an approach mandatory, including the United States' National Academy of Science.

These examples and high-level policies become the staple sustenance of those who lurk in the dark corners of many websites, where the 'debunking' hopefuls congregate. Similarly, these practices are put to practice in the classroom among the impressionable. One can find articulate motivators in the chat rooms where they can get a crack at exercising their luxury syndrome art. They use syllogistic logic as a preferred tool which allows them to ignore a myriad of pertinent, causal, inferred, or implied context information. Another ploy is to focus and 'debunk' or 'reduce' the meaning of each separate phrase or sentence within a paragraph, thus eliminating contextual or framework meaning

---

[169] A classic example among many: K.R. Henke, "Young earth creationist Helium Diffusion dates" (2005) at http://www.talkorigins.org/faqs/helium/zircons.html; K.R. Henke, "Young earth creationist helium diffusion dates" (2005) at http://www.talkorigins.org/faqs/helium/zirocons.html; and rebuttal by Dr. Russell Humphreys, http://www.talkorigins.org/faqs/helium/original.html; http://www.trueorigin.org/helium01.asp ; and http://www.trueorigin.org/helium02.asp .

[170] Written debate on www.trueorigin.org between Douglas Theobald (evolutionist) who presented his "29 Evidences for Macroevolution," and Ashby Camp (creationist) who responded to fallacies presented in Theobald's work.

[171] Mark Isaak's *Problem with a Global Flood*, and the rebuttal by J. Sarfati, *Problems with a Global Flood?* http://www.trueorigin.org/arkdefend.asp, Ibid.

and value. In such environment, science becomes part of urban legends and soap operas. Contrary to professional logic and examination, winning through intimidation has become a rule (violation of stylistic management – 3DMM).

In such an environment we may meet straight-A science students who may explain the scientific view of the general theory of evolution through well-rehearsed scripts. We may hear or read early microbes began to vary as they adapted to challenging environments. In isolation, genetic variations brought about conditions where the same species were no longer interfertile, and may have become so different from its parent group that the former can no longer be considered to be different of the specie. This process repeats itself until this brings about the emergence of man. During the Q&A session, it becomes evident that the straight-A science student uses syllogisms and provides canned answers for every occasion. However, it is discovered that the student has never been taught to think in terms of alternatives, from a third perspective, nor has he/she been updated by his/her mentors with contingent information. For example, that: (a) this 170-year-old uniformitarian theory had never been designed to attain contingent certainty, or to be used to test or prove anything through empirical scientific lab methods; (b) CRAY computer-based software may have been designed to simulate mutational quantitative processes and generate statistics that would help disprove many uniformitarian assumptions but such information is not available, except through the creationist scientific labs; (c) life forms adapt (micro-change) to challenging environments, but do not re-engineer, redesign, or reinvent themselves (macro-change); (d) genetic change implies loss and not gain of genetic information; (e) the process of natural selection is not designed to detect and eliminate accumulating genetic change debris; and that (f) this genetic debris accumulates and contributes to the steady degradation of the species until its extinction.[172]

Young earth creationist scientists seriously challenge uniformitarians. This is particularly evident in areas of language and concepts where

---

[172] "Mendel's Accountant: A New Population Genetics Simulation Tool for Studying Mutation and Natural Selection" by Dr. Baumgardner; and "Using Numerical Simulation to Test the Validity of Neo-Darwinian Theory" by Dr. John Sanford, http://www.icr.org. This program is feely available for personal use and can be downloaded from the web at http://mendelsaccount.sourceforge.net.

uniformitarians, because of their luxury syndrome, somersault logic and truncated view of the historical knowledge-base (3DMM), have acquired a conceptual language that is punctured with blind spots. The 2,000-year developing Christian scientific culture had helped develop nuances and 3-D legal-based communication. The uniformitarian language, which is similar to Marxist ideological language, has 'speciated' into a separate foreign language, that resembles and reflects a reversed formatted body of values, ethics, attitude, methods, priorities, and culture. The 3-point uniformitarian scientific method has not only significantly narrowed the scope of creative thought, but it perpetually seeks means to polarize and eliminate 3DMM-based users. The very concept and process of the scientific method (DMPS) has been redefined and re-engineered in this uniformitarian environment. One can take as an example – the Marxism-Leninism world-view – whose believers similarly use a dialectical materialist language. It is worth to notice that the uniformitarian democratic notion is not established upon the Christian Ten Commandments or upon geometric natural law but in opposition to these. Notice that the modern uniformitarian practitioner and thinker, like Marxists, use the uniformitarian materialistic view. Uniformitarian principles that are made to work in biological evolution are also made to work in the social arena. When a student graduates from some secular educational institution, he/she must prove and demonstrate a uniformitarian/evolutionist perspective in order to continuously qualify for a job in any science lab and become a catalyst for 'change.' Therefore, such employee and catalyst should never propose an alternate view.

All of this contributes to what one hears at the debates – a reflection on the use of, and what's going on in, the scientific lab. This also clarifies why United States federal courts legally qualify uniformitarians as being 'scientific,' while conversely Christian creation and intelligent design scientists are qualified as being quacks.

RULES AND REGULATIONS – Supervisory level plan (D6).
Business and project management applications

The rules and regulations plan is not defined in terms of suggestions, recommendations, or options. Rules and regulations are short commands that help enforce procedures (D5), and policies (D4). Rules and regulations conform with executive plans (D1 to D3), and are aligned with plans in the column – strategy (D3) and productivity (D9). Vertically, rules and regulations are aligned with implementing (O6) and habit (S6).

Rules can come in the form of: simple one-word commands, phrases, or sentences. Regulations appear in the form of long directives such as those used in customs and ports of entry. Other rules and regulations may be behavior patterns. Rules and regulations can simply be codes that establish borders. Psychologically speaking, this management plan can be seen in terms of where emotions are set and patterned. As with management this plan is used to establish borders. In living beings emotions are where accumulated rules, regulations, and borders reveal patterns of strengths and weaknesses. These can directly and indirectly be linked to other management plans.

Rule and regulations have the least amount of freedom for change. If policies (D4) reflect the widest discretion and procedures (D5) provide examples of best practices, rules and regulations (D6) have room for change. Rules and regulations include checklists, directions, standards, and tests. Cumulatively, rules and regulations are the base for all data, information, instructions, and knowledge that eventually work to define the organization's experience. Inevitably, such data-information reflects a legal character or maintains the organization's safety, security, quality, and legal definition and reputation[173].

The functional management plans (D7 thru D9) are used to track the conversion of inputs into outputs (product – D9), and provide additional measurable feedback information that is used to ensure quality and performance.

Here, within the functional management plans, the research and development (D7) plan is used to monitor quality assurance of input, process, and output as specified within the supervisory management plans (D4, D5, and D6). Data that emerges from quality assessments is reprocessed to adjust performance. It contributes to potential development and change. There may be requirements for internal and external change. Such change appears at potentially five levels of complexity: copies, adaptation, improvement, innovation, and invention.

Economics (D8) is the management accounting, auditing, cost control,

---

[173] For example, the Department of Justice may wish to check all correspondence that went on five years ago to determine whether company management had been aware of the product's safety or health hazard that the company produced.

risk analysis, investment, expenditure, revenues, and profits.

Productivity (D9) is the output, the meeting of objectives, and customer satisfaction. It involves logistics, efficiency, and effectiveness testing, reporting (feedback system), elimination of 'noise' and delays.

Management design (D1 to D9) level is further refined, tested, calibrated, and automated through the columnar screening: directive, process, and infobase functions. For example:

The purpose (D1), policy (D4), and research and development (D7) plans have a directive quality that is designed to provide and set the scope of the marching orders for the following activities in the process plans: objectives (D2), procedures (D5), and economics (D6 and similarly for the infobase column.)

The management design infrastructure (D1 thru D9), when properly automated, is used to facilitate the management of the operational plans (O1 thru O9) and in turn the stylistic plans (S1 thru S9). Similarly, the upper infrastructure's plans help define the plans at the design infrastructure.

RULES AND REGULATIONS – Supervisory level plan (D6). Other applications

Rules and regulations are directly linked with quality control, authorizations, and approvals/rejection. Where executive laws have a permanent character, the supervisory rules and regulations may adjust to the environment, while remaining within the scope of the executive framework. This can be seen in any organization, psychology, and nature of life.

As a knowledge-base (3DMM), the Christian Bible contains sections where rules and regulations are evident. These are ultimately derived from the executive framework. We can see policies, procedures, and rules in areas of economics, engineering, construction, and ethics. Here are rules and procedures on how to become managers worthy of becoming kings and queens. There are supervisory rules on building, maintaining relationships with neighbors, how to manage business, property, agriculture, husbandry, accidents, priesthood functions, health, nutrition, and many others.

Biological life clearly exhibits rules at their genetic code level. Programmed search for specific nutrition includes programs linked to sense interpretation, digestive system, muscular, and wholesale body design to function within the given environment. Many decision-making and strategic functions have also been programmed and coded. Human habits on the stylistic management levels (S6) appear to function like programmed rules and regulations (D6).

Scientific projects and research may consist of many rules and regulations. But national scientific policy may also be expressed and directed through specific rules and regulations. It, therefore, becomes relatively easy to identify the strengths and the weaknesses of a national policy, and inevitably, its scientific executive purpose.

For example, one needs to simply visit websites such as the Science, Evolution and Creationism: National Academy of Sciences by the National Academy of Sciences (NAS).[174] Then follow how NAS rules and regulation for scientific research and interpretation are being implemented by their users - for example the 'true origins' group;[175] and in the many articles that appear in worldwide distribution outlets like Wikipedia.[176] What is being presented in these three sources is duplicated in all of the others. Needless to say, these guidelines and rules are clearly evident during high-level science debates.

The NAS's guidelines also provide a litmus test for two types of scientists. The distinction between the professional scientist who loves his research work and stays away from non-scientific ideological tendencies, and the ideologically polarized scientists who use 'science' to promote uniformitarianism. Where the original scientific method had been a tool that helped identify and objectively convert what has been identified as uncertainty into conditional certainty, the uniformitarian scientists bring up issues about demarcation lines between science and religion – even though there are some true origins website debunkers and atheists, who follow the rules and go out of their way to deceptively claim compatibility between uniformitarian principles and the 'real' Christian tenets.

The NAS provides up to twenty-four rules one is to follow on the path to true science. NAS and kindred national and state organizations function as a veritable scientificist magesterium.

The document entitled, Science, Evolution and Creationism, is one of

---

[174] National Academy of Science, 500 Fifth St., NW, Washington, D.C. http://books.nap.edu/openbook/php?chapselect=yo&page=01&record_id=11876.

[175] http://www.trueorigins.org/arkdefen.asp.

[176] http://www.wikipedia.org.

NAS's foundational documents. A host of participating members from accredited universities, institutes, and colleges endorse this document.

The preface of this document, Science, Evolution and Creationism: A View from the National Academy of Sciences,[177] suggests the following twenty-four rules for gaining the true uniformitarian perception of what distinguishes true science from pseudoscience (specifically, creationism and intelligent design). All evolutionists – science professional, academic administrators, textbook publishers, teachers, government officials, state and federal courts, the media, debaters, most church officials who subscribe to the theistic evolution interpretation, and critics/debunkers use this rules book to express their adherence to NAS's authority and their politically correct position. This NAS document is equivalent to the *Communist Manifesto* and Mao's *Red Book* for the progressive uniformitarians.

The first of NAS's twenty-four rules are grouped into six topics:

Group	Rules	Topic
1	1-7	Strategic and tactical use of terminology, and concepts, providing new definitions for everyday words.
2	8-10	Interpretation of and use of historical data.
3	11-14	Biology and the lab.
4	15-16	Science's framework for progressive religions.
5	17-23	Challenges to creation and intelligent design.
6	24	Summary.

Rule 1: Use syllogisms: (NAS booklet 'preface'- first paragraph):

(a) Suggest a truism – e.g., 'Science and technological advances have had profound effects on human life.'

(b) Provide a negative example: 'In the nineteenth century, most families could expect to lose one or more children to disease.'

(c) Make a deduction: 'Today, in the United States and other developed countries, the death of a child from disease is uncommon.'

(d) Make a lengthy conclusion: every day we rely on technologies made possible through the application of scientific knowledge and processes.

---

[177] http://books.nap.edu/openbook/php?chapselect=yo&page= 01&record_id=11876.

(e) Add four to five additional sentences about the benefits of science: rapid travel, advanced medicines, and higher living standards, orbiting the Earth and trips to the Moon.

Not mentioned here, but developed below, is that science and technological progress is to become synonymous with uniformitarianism. That without the uniformitarian perspective everything will remain at a pre-scientific/technology stage of development and at cultism.

Rule 2: Embed converted terminology and markers that upon the first or second reading would go unnoticed. For example, use terms and concepts like: (1) application of scientific knowledge and processes, which should be interpreted to mean 'uniformitarian materialism and reductionist processes.' The passage (2) 'insights obtained from scientific research' should read 'insights obtained from the simple-to-complex and primitive-to-modern.' Since the 'luxury syndrome' predetermines what is to be considered to be acceptable science, the following sentence (c) '[Science] has given us new ways of thinking about ourselves and the universe' should be read to mean '[Uniformitarianism] has given us new ways of thinking about our primate origins, and the big bang universe.'

If one doubts the 'should read' interpretations, then the next nine paragraphs will remove all doubt about the validity of these should read interpretations. It is here that the hopeful modern scientists receive the truth and revelation of uniformitarian 'science' – its conception and hatching process. NAS's science booklet is endorsed by participating members from accredited universities and institutions. These authorities won't consider anyone or anything to be scientific unless that individual or institution complies with these rules.

Rule 3: Recognize that the cornerstone of modern science is not its 3DMM (knowledge-base, standards) and its DMPS methodology which converts uncertainty to conditional certainty. Instead, NAS focuses our attention on one single branch of science- biology, which is camouflaged in some esoteric terminology – 'evolutionary biology.' Why not simply write uniformitarian approach to the subject of biology?(NAS 'preface' – second paragraph.)

Rule 4: NAS suggests an inductive leap from evolutionary biological approach to ALL sciences. It seems then that all branches of science drive from the evolutionary biological model. Then NAS suggests that evolutionary biology equals all sciences together contribute 'to human well-being,' such as: this combination contributes to prevention and treatment of human disease, development of new agricultural products, creation of industrial innovations, the study of new life forms, the relatedness and diversity of present-day organisms, rapid advances made in life sciences and medicine. NAS does not clarify that the doctrine of 'uniformitarianism' is the foundation to both 'evolutionary biology,' as well as, all of the scientific branches, and must:

(1) Appropriate the works of professional scientists who are not necessarily evolutionists – such as the work of Gregor J. Mendel,[178] that was borrowed as evolutionists went on to construct their 'evolutionary synthesis' (1930s) and 'modern evolutionary synthesis' (1990s). During this, evolutionists leave the impression that Mendel's genetic work on inherited traits, exclusively and uniquely, supports the theory of evolution, and not creation science or intelligent design.

(2) Prematurely give an evolutionary spin on new paleontological, biological, or astronomical discoveries even though soon after, in most cases, evolutionists must retract or remove this evidence when secondary interpretations or new evidence contradict evolutionary predictions.[179]

(3) Ignore evidence that contradicts the uniformitarian mechanical, organic models of thinking. Such evidence may appear in areas of information and nano-robotic technology at sub-chromosomal levels, or as fossils of modern man that are discovered at sedimentary layers below that of the Java Man, or the numerous 'out of place artifacts,' and still as pre-ice age human civilizations, etc..

Rule 5: Place a disclaimer. In its booklet, NAS provides an example

---

[178] Gregor Johann Mendel (1822 – 1884), an Augustinian priest and scientist, is considered to be the father of modern genetics. Genetics is the study and discovery of consistencies, laws of inheritance of traits in peas, and attempted in honeybees. He presented his paper at the Natural History Society of Brunn in Moravia (1985), and published this paper a year later in the proceedings of the Natural History Society of Brunn.

[179] The Associated Press story, on June 26, 2008, reported the finding in Latvia, of a supposedly 365-million-year-old fossilized four-legged water creature – 'ventastega' which is now identified as a 'dead end' because several 'older' tetrapods, with more advanced physical features, have been found earlier. So 'ventastega' could not qualify as a 'missing link;' it was 'out of sequence in timing' (Neil Shubin, professor of biology and anatomy at the University of Chicago). Such discoveries don't match with the uniformitarian geologic column, but do fit perfectly within the creation global catastrophe events.

of such a disclaimer on page XI. Here we find a three-part disclaimer : 'Of course, as with any active area of science, many fascinating questions remain, and this booklet highlights some of the active research that is currently under way that addresses questions about evolution.' This disclaimer focuses on: (1) science doesn't have all the answers; (2) there remain fascinating questions; and 3) active research provides evolutionary answers. Such formulation clearly unveils an ideological (uniformitarian) based faith statement. Here we enter into the realm of hope, faith, and wishful thinking – in an attempt to help fill the 'scientific' gap.

Rule 6: Identify a few inconsequential questions that opponents raise – e.g., 'complexity of life,' proof for 'common descent.' Evolutionists must associate these questions not with scientific but with religious motives and beliefs. Uniformitarians should remind everyone that only scientific issues and explanations must be considered in the school science courses. The uniformitarian scientist should remind everyone that school science should only point to 'scientific'/uniformitarian approaches and explanations – even though the uniformitarian organic thinking model can't account for 'complexity of life' or 'common descent.' NAS recommends that evolution-oriented high-profiled individuals (school board members, science teachers, education leaders, policy makers, and legal scholars) should be involved at the decision-making points and meetings. Such settings should also include: highly-graded school and college students; adults who wish to learn about the evolution 'fact' and 'process' that accounts for the diversity of life on Earth. Such a rule does not mention that:

(1) Such a setting is designed to promote not science but an uniformitarian view (ideology), and may exclude scientific inquiry. The aim is to bend the mind to function along a uniformitarian track.

2) Any opposition to this uniformitarian view is to be interpreted as coming from religious influences (specifically Christian), and that any Christian-based science (e.g., young earth creation or intelligent design) is not science.

This provides evidence for an ideology rather than science.

Furthermore, NAS recommends that 'legal scholars' be included in such quasi-science get-togethers, who will help move the discussion from scientific to legal decisions. The legal tactic is employed as a last ditch skirmish should all other tools fail and evolutionists are clearly unmasked as being ideological uniformitarians.

It should be remembered, in passing, that neither uniformitarians nor many of the United States courts could determine when life begins. Yet based on this lack of knowledge, courts pass decisions in areas of human abortions. These notorious decisions have now led to forty million abortions – an equivalent to genocide.

Uniformitarians have gone to great lengths in their attempt to prove that 'evolution' is 'fact.' Yet, this reasoning works only within the uniformitarian redefined world of mirrors. As mentioned earlier, a fact is contingent on its framework. People have built multi-century world empires on the 'fact' that the Earth is flat. My current book and Table 7 demonstrate that uniformitarians thread the same path as Flat Earth believers.

Uniformitarians are myopic on the issue of how to identify and resolve uncertainty that leads to conditional certainty. They've eliminated the scientific tools that would help them achieve this process. They 'feel' that the hypothesis and theory, if they last long enough, they will become 'fact.' Uniformitarians don't realize that both hypothesis and theory concretely reflect uncertainty and, because of this must, be processed through DMPS in order to attain conditional certainty. Uniformitarians clearly reflect a flat Earth perspective.

Table 7. Similarities: Uniformitarian and Flat Earth Views.

# Uniformitarian	Flat Earth society's
1 Begin with existing conditions, rates, and processes.	Begin with existing conditions, rates and processes.
2 Extrapolate these through uniformitarian materialism and reductionism (mechanical and shape organic mental models) to any starting point (origins) – Big Bang, Steady State.	Extrapolate these through Euclidian mathematics (e.g., parallel lines) to any starting point (border) – whatever the (circular, square, etc.)
3 Draw forward to the present via postulated naturalistic laws using the 'simple-to-complex' doctrine. .math	Draw forward to the current status via natural, observable, measurable, and geographical laws, simple-to-complex
4. Use exclusively a *closed* systems approach. Note: the *open* system	Use exclusively the *Euclidian* systems approach. Note: the *non*-Euclidian system

approach suggests supernatural participatory forces, and users must avoid this approach at all cost.	approach suggests *abstractitis*, and users must avoid this approach at all cost.
5. Evolution is almost certainty truth. and truth.	The flat earth view is almost certainty and truth.
6. Non-evolutionary views are in error, demonstrate latten religious distorted /subjective orientation, and science[180] promote deception.	Non-Flat Earth views are clearly in error demonstrate that science promotes views and is fundamentally pseudo-
7. Evolution is science and religion is illusion or pseudo-science	No position.

Rule 7: A uniformitarian fact becomes fact when:

(1) The fact is accepted by consensus of the scientific community ('scientificist magisterium').

(2) The 'nature of science' (i.e., uniformitarian materialism) is distinguished from religion (subjectivism).

(3) When enough evidence is brought and some religions see the light and conform to the uniformitarian definition of what constitutes to be science (similar to #1 - science by consensus). In other words, when nine/ten of the Christian groups accept the uniformitarian position and one doesn't, then the one becomes heretical and delusionary.

Rule 8: Scientists must emulate NAS's interpretation of history. For example, NAS writes that, The National Academy of Sciences has had a mandate from Congress since 1863 to advise the federal government on issues of science and technology... Note that during the United States Civil War (1863), the United States government did not mandate a uniformitarian interpretation of science. It is necessary to research the history of NAS and identify under what circumstances this un-constitutional uniformitarian ideology was installed into the NAS. This NAS ideology has removed geometric natural law-based constitutional foundations and installed itself as the official state religion/ideology – in

---

[180] http://news.bbc.co.uk/2hi/uk_news/magazine/7540427.stm;
http://ncseweb.org/rncse/21/3-4/flat-earth-society-president-dies;
Flat Earth FAQ, http://theflateearthsociety.org/forum/index.php?topic=69.0

violation of Establishment Clause in the United States Constitution.

Rule 9: Scientists must provide historical re-enforcement whenever they communicate evolutionary topics. This means the scientists must list developments and updates in paleontology. Such updates are to produce 'compelling' evidence about evolutionary history, understanding of molecules, and DNA sequences of human relationships among species. If the fossil record is incomplete (NAS introduces a new field), 'evolutionary developmental biology should show how genetic changes…should fill the gap.'[181]

This general history of uniformitarian developmental 'evidence' for evolution brings about another rule.

Rule 10: Mention historical legal court cases, events, and decisions. When this doesn't quell down issues of 'controversy,' then uniformitarians must simply resort to 'scientific consensuses' - how the 'scientific community' views such 'scientific' issues. Today, such collective bodies' rubber stamps any uniformitarian position. These and other such bodies form what I call the 'scientificist magisterium.'

Rule 11: Chapter 1 in NAS's booklet is entitled, '*Evolution and the Nature of Science,*' and is subtitled, '*The scientific evidence supporting biological evolution continues to grow at a rapid pace.*' This is where the uniformitarians are directed to describe evolutionary mythology. Identify a stratum from which the scientist will bring out an intermediate fossil. Date this fossil form by allocating it several hundreds of millions of years (use the geologic column as reference) – Note: implied here is to never introduce dates that are less than 6,000 years. Then pepper the narrative that describes the form with many 'maybes,' 'probably,' 'it is believed,' etc. Then use the services of a science artist to help create a full-blooded creature that has moved, breathed, and functioned in an unusual and exotic environment. This creature identifies and obtains its nourishment from a setting where there's a zoo of other creatures that coexist with it.

In other words, create a full Hollywood production just as it had been done for the Nebraska man. Here, all you needed is a pig's tooth and an

---

[181] All of these areas have been successfully addressed by the ICR scientists; the reader should be encouraged to visit their website at www.icr.org. It is curious that evolution scientists appear to be ignorant of this vast amount of researched literature that has successfully provided alternate successful and better explanations.

artist. The artist fleshed out a well-rounded reality. The artist will, like any dentist, fill all of the Nebraska man's other missing teeth, identify and describe the man's missing family, will bathe and clothe the family, and provide a comfortable setting for them. All this is achieved through the prophetic predictive features from the evolutionary scientific models.

Rule 12: Chapter 1's subsection is subtitled, 'Biological evolution is the central organizing principle of modern biology.' This gives the scientist another opportunity to drill the evolutionary basics. DNA mutations are triggered by natural selection, as groups of organisms overcome challenging environmental conditions over multiple generations. In this scheme of things, scientists are limited to consider only linear change and cannot speculate on how macro-evolution occurs through re-engineering, redesign, or reinvention. Uniformitarian imagination must be limited to this linear level because all other infrastructural and supervisory systems require non-uniformitarian explanations – e.g., information and nanobot technology and geometric natural law. The luxury syndrome is evident throughout the remaining chapters as NAS's booklet describes this evolutionary mythology.

Rule 13: Scientists, who must fill the uniformitarian bill, are directed by NAS's booklet to draw upon industrial examples. Here principles of natural selection are used to develop new molecules that have specific functions (Page 9 on NAS booklet). In this naturally selected new molecules, nothing had been mentioned about information technology or nano-robotic functions at the sub-chromosomal level as a key requirement for change in the genetic structure.

Rule 14: Another subsection of Chapter 1 is entitled, Scientists seek explanations of natural phenomena based on empirical evidence. This is another opportunity for the evolutionist to make a clear distinction between empirical sciences versus information coming from outside the natural closed system (i.e., religion). This is done without referencing geometric natural law, legal history, 3-D management models, or DMPS. Although NAS talks about testable evidence, reproducible experiments, predictions, and refutability (falsifiability), nothing has addressed the pseudoscientific nature of the uniformitarian process (see the score cards in this book). Furthermore, in this subsection, NAS drills again about the 'fact' of evolution.

Rule 15: The scientist is supposed to show that acceptance of the evidence for evolution can be compatible with religious faith. NAS presents here the various hybrid uniformitarian religious views. With this, NAS booklet contains full page quotations and excerpts of statement by [uniformitarian] scientists. We find full page quotations that include excerpts of statement by [uniformitarian] scientists, who confirm the feasibility of such marriage. Such a marriage of convenience is possible as long as such religions fall within uniformitarian definitions of what constitutes religion (see Rule 22). At the same time, it becomes evident that religions that acquire a uniformitarian realism must, by definition, become pantheistic, whether they had been Christian or of any other variety and conviction.

Rule 16: Most evolutionists claim that the theory of evolution applies strictly to the biological domain. They ridicule their skeptical opponents for not understanding this simple reality. Yet, after having focused our sights on this biological domain, Chapter 2 of NAS's booklet addresses issues of, 'the origin of the universe, our galaxy, and our solar system produced the conditions necessary for the evolution of life on Earth.' Here NAS discusses radiometric dating, living things appearing in the first billion years of Earth's history, how the fossil record helps document the occurrence of evolution, common descent, comparison, and similarities between the chimp and human DNA. NSA consultants go out of the way to talk about fossil footprints in a manner that would help dispel or deflect possible interpretations of dinosaurs and human footprints appearing in the same sedimentary bed (page 33).

What evolutionists fail to note is that when they expand beyond the 'biological' sciences, they still describe reality within evolutionary principles. They are dishonest in this approach since they avoid identifying the foundation of evolutionary concept – the three-point uniformitarian ideology (see Tables 6, 7, and 9). It is within this framework that all non-biological scientific topics are treated.

Rule 17: Chapter 3 in NAS's booklet addresses the creationist and intelligent design perspectives. Under the subtitle, Creationist views reject scientific findings and methods, the rule is to place the creation and intelligent design 'religious' groups into a separate category aside from the hybrid uniformitarians (theistic evolution, progressive evolution, old earth creationists).

Yet it must be remembered NAS believes that 'no scientific evidence supports [hybrid uniformitarian] viewpoints.'[182] This verdict, therefore, in spite of earlier uniformitarian positive pronouncements towards hybrid uniformitarians and other religions, still places the hybrid uniformitarians (listed above) on the eighth or seventh ring of the uniformitarian hell (parallels drawn with Dante's Hell.) Uniformitarians still view hybrid uniformitarians as being cults, just as much as the creation and ID scientists. The difference between the hybrids and creation and ID scientists is that uniformitarians place creation and ID scientists on the lowest, ninth of nine, rings in the uniformitarian hell.

Rule 18: Uniformitarian scientists must be keenly aware that NAS argues that to reject the notions that Earth is about 4.5 billion years old and that the universe is about 14 billion years old, is virtually to reject not just biological evolution but also [the] fundamental discoveries of modern physics, chemistry, astrophysics, and geology.'[183] Evolutionists must therefore reject the worldwide flood, since evolutionists disagree on how sedimentation processes occur and the need for depositing sediments on the top of some of Earth's highest mountains. Rule 18 presents science in terms of axioms that reveal several positions:

(1) That none of the scientific disciplines -- physics, chemistry, astrophysics and geology -- are synonymous with uniformitarian perspectives.

(2) It is the scientific method's role to resolve uncertainty. At the fourth stage of the DMPS process, scientists will describe, quantify, examine, test, apply, and predict the evidence within ALL possible alternatives – from evolutionary to creationist views. Whereas to exclude all or some scientific options is to do so on ideological reasons – e.g., the luxury syndrome – thus rendering the scientific method obsolete (see Figures 10 thru 13).

(3) True science must address the 'twelve limitations of science,' which also includes the 'objective unfettered scientific method' (OUSM). Uniformitarianism violates all of these scientific tools while creationism and intelligent design do not.

(4) Should NAS science consultants have done their homework, they would have realized that creation scientists' positions with regards to sedimentation and the height of mountains had been addressed

---

[182] NAS booklet, Page 38.
[183] Ibid.

scientifically. The mountain ranges that we see today have been uplifted through the various stages of the hydro-tectonic processes during and after the global catastrophic events – third singularity. As described above, these events had successfully been simulated on CRAY computers at the Los Alamos laboratories and provide supporting evidence for the global catastrophic event.

Rule 19: NAS's rules provide a perspective on the fossil record which is rich and extremely detailed record of evolutionary history that paleontologists and other biologists have constructed over the past two centuries and are continuing to construct. Yet, NAS forgets to mention that this view doesn't agree with research results and publications that had been conducted under their own (uniformitarian) auspices.

For example, the fossil record is the single area which disproves evolutions. For example: Goldschmidt proposed to explain vertical macro-change by suggesting an event of instantaneous speciation, saltation, or systemic mutation that produced new groups – now known as the "hopeful monster theory."[184] Niles Eldredge and Stephen Jay Gould,[185] based on Ernst Mayr's[186] theory of geographical speciation, published a work in 1972 where both showed a greater emphasis on the development of a stasis theory – i.e., punctuated equilibrium. This punctuation was to help explain dramatic changes when phenotypic evolution occurs in rarely localized conditions, coupled with rapid events of branching speciation (cladogenesis).

NAS consultants and the founders of the modern evolutionary synthesis axiomatically reject these views and do not falsify them scientifically. What was the reason for discarding such scientific conclusions? The answer is that these views did not match with uniformitarian doctrines and predictions. Yet, the young earth creation scientists have a viable scientific model that helps predict and explain these paleontological gaps. Again, when new techniques, such as computed axial tomography,[187] are used to learn about the internal

---

[184] R. Goldschmidt, *The Material Basis of Evolution,* Ibid ; S.J. Gould, "The Return of Hopeful Monsters," Ibid.

[185] Niles Eldredge and Stephen Jay Gould, *Punctuated equilibria,* Ibid.).

[186] Ernst Mayr, *Speciatonal Evolution,* Ibid.

[187] "A medical imaging technique that generates a three-dimensional view of some object by combining a series of two-dimensioned X-ray image of 'slices' of

structures and composition of delicate bones of fossils, and the Tiktaalik fossil, the uniformitarians – in this case NAS -- substitute science with uniformitarian fiction. By themselves neither the computing axial tomography nor the fossil remains of Tiktaalik fill the fossil gaps. Nor do either of these explain the 'scientific' aspects of evolution theory. If the NAS authorities do not see this distinction, then it is clear that much is to be desired of the accredited education institutions from which the NAS scientists and consultants obtained their diplomas.

Rule 20: NAS wants its proponents to challenge the non-uniformitarians with statements or questions such as: 'Nowhere on Earth are fossils from dinosaurs, which went extinct sixty-five million years ago, found together with fossils from humans, who evolved in just the last few million years.' This statement is variation of the common argument, I dare you to find a human footprint in the Cambrian rock.

The first question that one ought to ask is, If such evidence were to be uncovered , based on uniformitarian past reasoning, methods, NAS's rules, and the scientific manner in which evolutionists handle the 'gaps in the fossil record' (see Rule 18), what would NAS / uniformitarian reaction be if such discoveries were to be made and documented?' What 'scientific' process would the uniformitarian scientists and its magisterium follow to further illuminate this 'out-of-place' scientific evidence and bring it into scientific light? The risks are high that such evidence would never see the light of day.

The second question that one must ask is, "Whether such evidence currently exists?" There is/had been such scientific evidence, before the highly financed and 'accredited' institutions had a chance to lay their authorizing hands on. Such empirical evidence had been documented and did come to light. Such as the clear imprint of a child's moccasin footprint in what is considered to be the Cambrian rock – see Appendix 3 of this book.

Rule 21: NAS writes in its booklet that creationists state that the theory of evolution must remain hypothetical because there aren't any ways to test it scientifically. In reply, NAS restates the direct or empirical scientific process, and then, without realizing, admits that many scientific 'facts' can only be inferred indirectly from existing empirical evidence. For example, evolution on the whole is apparently part of the indirect or

---

that object." (NSA booklet, Ibid.)

inferred body of knowledge/method. NAS suggests scientists use the hypothesis, but forgets to mention that the hypothesis still remains within the realm of 'uncertainty.' This uncertainty in scientific terms must pass through the DMPS/scientific phases, instead of being passed off as being an 'almost certainty, and truth,' through scientific consensus. At the same time, NAS disallows the same hypothesis rights to the creation and intelligent design scientists. In NAS's view, in Creationists' and ID's hands, the hypothesis becomes religion. It is precisely at the hypothesis level that evolutionists are the most vulnerable. It is at this hypothesis level that creation and ID scientists disagree with many of the uniformitarian interpretations, assumptions, and conclusions

NAS's allegation that creation and intelligent design scientists ignore much of the scientific hard 'facts' that evolutionists bring forth, clearly shows that evolutionists are not well read on creation scientific publications. It is the creation and intelligent design scientists who know and follow quite closely all the scientific research that is being done, not only by evolutionists in the United States, but also that conducted around the world.

For example, during the many high-level evolution-creation debates during the late 1970s and early 1980s, the creationist scientist had held a significant advantage over their evolution counterparts because creation debaters, in a major part, quoted the scientific publications that were published by the evolution publishing establishment. Among the evolution scientists, there are hundreds of thousands of honest to goodness scientists who love their investigative scientific work and follow where the evidence leads them. They publish their results that creation scientists study and use in their 'creation scientific models.' Through this, the creation scientists had been able to provide better scientific explanations and prediction than that produced through the evolution scientific model. The 'young earth creation' scientists are very much up-to-date with all published scientific works. They use the same evidence in their creation scientific model, just as evolutionists use in their evolution scientific model. However, the creation scientific model allows for a better interpretation of empirical data, and make better predictions.

On the other hand, in view of what NAS wrote in many parts of its booklet, it has becomes clear that its own scientific experts are not aware of what the 'young earth creation scientists publish.'[188]

Rule 22:   NAS makes questionable allegations of what scientific data creationists accept or reject. Then, based on these questionable evaluations, NAS scientific consultants jump to premature conclusions. For example, NAS writes, 'Creationists reject such scientific facts in part because they do not accept evidence drawn from natural processes that they consider to be at odds with the Bible. But science cannot test supernatural possibilities.' As observed in Rule 21, such a statement clearly shows that NAS's science consultants and authorities have never read or understood the 'creation scientific model.' That is why they misinterpret creation model results and implications.

Let's briefly examine how uniformitarians determine what is supernatural and what is not. Here's the uniformitarian procedure:

(1) Formulate a 'uniformitarian' definition of what is supposed to constitute theism and theistic thinking.[189] The definition provides an open system that allows supernatural participation. The uniformitarian ignores geometric natural law.

(2)   Uniformitarians affirm their closed system view – materialism (closed system) - define uniformitarian science.

(3) Based on (1) and (2), the uniformitarian counteracts to its own view of 'irrational theism.'

4) Contrast 'irrational theism' (1) with uniformitarian science (2). [190]

5) Compare (1) with (4) and conclude that (1) is absurd.

The syllogistic process for this is something like this:

(1) U says that $X = T$

(2) U says that $U = S$

(3) $U = M \neq T$

(4) $X \lesseqgtr M$

(5) $X \lesseqgtr M = U(M)\ [-X\ (T)]$

Being a rationalist/empiricist approach to defining divinity (X), inevitably leads to providing a *pantheistic* definition of divinity. As

---

[188] See research published on www.icr.org.

[189] See Chapter 5 of this book on what constitutes "theism" and religion. Also refer to Table 8.

[190] Figure 11.

described above, within the 3-D management model, this formulation is located at the supervisory policy (D4) row at the management design level and not at the executive purpose (law, identity, scope) row where the original Christian purpose is established. As such, the supervisory policy level can only formulate issues from within time, space, and resource content, and not from the geometric natural law perspective.

Briefly, the rationalist/empiricist approach begins with B (uniformitarianist) defining what X /T are, inevitably perceiving that X is actually T, which is a wrong assumption. This assumption is already pre-filtered for an X perspective (pantheism), i.e., the supervisory (D4). There is no reference to a 3DMM nor DMPS, which define the objective criteria for 'conditional certainty.' In other words, the supervisory approach is a subjective, relative, and algebraic approach - syllogistic argument. There is a missing mechanism for converting 'uncertainty' to 'conditional certainty' (DMPS). Because of the missing DMPS, the pantheist does not refer to the DMPS historical-base, standards, criteria, codes. DMPS requires psychological qualifications, the emphasis on the use of only one alternative (4) (syllogistic, axiomatic, and algebraic) – the pantheist disqualifies him/her/itself on this pre-filtered application. This axiomatic position has no objective (lawful) reference point, just a subjective, ideological one. Such a twisted approach to DMPS and 3DMM enters a high-risk condition. This subjective ideological approach simply reflects 'naïve realism' – pre-determined uniformitarian filtration process (|5| in DMPS). This rejects the executive purpose (D1) and reduces management Style (S1 – S9) to operational management plans. The four-point uniformitarian realism (UR) is naive because, as shown above, the method attempts to short-circuit the DMPS and remains within perpetual uncertainty.

By using the DMPS (see Figure 9) and looking at the given (syllogistic process) we find that:

1.   There is no identifiable knowledge-base (3DMM) which can be used to distinguish certainty from uncertainty. Since the issue is to define theism versus science, the syllogism doesn't contain the starting point – knowledge-base that would help identify and define uncertainty.
2.   Psychological qualifications. The use of the syllogistic process to prove uniformitarian perspectives is already a disqualifier since these identities and qualifiers will not lead from uncertainty to certainty, but

will perpetuate if not multiply uncertainty. The syllogistic statements demonstrate subjective, axiomatic positions that have no objective reference point. This results in the psychological disqualification of B. However, if we let B continue (in spite of his/her disqualification), let's see what will happen on the next DMPS step – definition.

3.　　　Definition: the syllogism reflects the luxury syndrome, i.e., the definition is predefined by the filter (step 5). The filter prescribes or limits the definition's scope. The DMPS process, therefore, ends here. Uncertainty is magnified and enters a high-risk status.

If the process continues, it is possible to see that the filter will also limit alternatives (step 4) to purely reductionist options. The filter will also dictate the scientific-testing process and implementation parameters (step 6). Each of these steps magnifies uncertainty. It escapes conditional certainty the purpose of which is to improve the knowledge-base (3DMM)

This suggests that the uniformitarian approach and view is simply a reflection of 'naïve realism.' This subjective uniformitarian approach ignores a knowledge-base of issues.

The concept of naïve realism is derived from the application of the uniformitarian filters. In the DMPS, filters reflect the executive purpose (D1), objectives (D2), and strategies (D3). However, uniformitarianism reflects a truncated 3DMM, where the executive and stylistic management plans are reduced. The three-point uniformitarian realism (UR) is 'naive' because, as shown above, the method attempts to short-circuit the DMPS.

The uniformitarian realism 'UR' process is best described in the application of the Soviet 'Socialist realist' policy. This filter had affected not only how reality was to be portrayed in the arts (literature, visual, plastic, music), but had also been applied to education, media, history, and daily conversations. The basic Socialist realist directive is to: "Identify in today's world those elements and actions that represent the best examples that will exist in tomorrow's Communist world; and, at the same time, present in degraded forms and content that which will not be seen in the future Communist world.

As mentioned above, during the secular, pagan Roman Empire, Christianity could not be made to fit into the relativistic Pantheon of cults-religions-ideologies because original Christianity had been established upon geometric natural law (see Figures 20 through 26). The same conditions apply in this NAS case (Rule 21). The scope of geometric natural law lies outside the uniformitarian realm since the latter is established upon algebraic rules (see Figures 19 and 23).

Rule 23: NAS portrays intelligent design scientists as being a group that simply represents a variation of the creation model.. Actually, the intelligent design group had emerged from the neo-evolutionary group. These neo-evolution scientists became dissatisfied with the nineteenth century pseudoscientific baggage that the evolutionary theory carried – specifically – uniformitarianism. Intelligent design scientists, with the help of their super-high-tech laboratory equipment, were able to penetrate into scientific depths and 'data,' 'information' that has never been suspected or even dreamed of. The intelligent design group in search of a scientific model went beyond the mechanistic, organic, and process mental models. They explored the 'information mental model.' It is within this context that they began to speak a new scientific language whose existence had not been suspected prior to the 1980s. These neo-evolutionists discovered an unimaginable world at the nano-level. This level within the organic model boggles the human mind. Here we have nothing that resembles advanced engineering so complex, refined, and precise with unimaginable management and engineering codes and standards. One begins to see clearly that the organic and process models that are at the foundation of the uniformitarian model are totally out of league in areas of explaining information-based technology and nano-robotics. The honest scientist can only use superlatives and conceive an intelligent designer concept – a teleological[191] view of this scientific realm.

At the same time, evolutionists continue to attempt to explain this information-based model with their mechanistic, biological, and process models. By analogy, it is like attempting to repair a computer chip with a magnetized Philips screwdriver. So the best outlet that uniformitarians can

---

[191] The concept of teleology precedes Darwinian evolution. 'Telos' (Greek) for 'end, purpose' implies that everything has a design and that this design reflects a purpose – a bird as an aircraft is designed to fly through the air – the design implies the purpose. In other words, there's an inherent final cause (purpose) – 'telos' in every design. Where Plato and Aristotle identified a final cause, Lucretius (Democritus) conceived of metaphysical naturalism (materialism) or accidentalism – precursor of uniformitarianism. In the modern world, teleology can be seen as thermodynamics in physics, fitness of elements within a complexity framework in chemistry, vital force in biology, and process-driven systems (teleonomy) in communication and control.

have is to simply close the door on this research and accuse the ID scientists of becoming religious freaks.

Rule 24: NAS concludes by ruling that scientists bring back, once more, issues of: (a) the curriculum ruled for the public school; (b) remind the public of specific court decisions that ruled in favor of evolution versus religion; (c) emphasize the separation of church and state; d) re-iterate the propaganda that evolution is science while religion is pseudoscience. NAS writes, Learning about evolution is an excellent way to help students understand the nature, processes, and limits of science in addition to concepts about this fundamentally important contribution to scientific knowledge. This sentence concludes by emphasizing that only the uniformitarian materialist ideology is the acceptable and authorized world-view. Yet, this ideology is an algebraic, rule-based approach that reflects a truncated 3-D management model, excludes executive plans, and reinterprets all management style plans that affect ethics, attitude, and culture. This process and its filters are used to continuously brainwash individuals, groups, and societies into a reductionist condition. Every issue the users address, they must reduce it to a purely local and subjective hands-on application. Predictably users will react to anything that does not enforce or support this subjectivism.

The courts issue has been addressed in Rule 6; it is worth noting that the true United States constitutional law is based upon geometric natural law. Yet, it is purposefully ignored and bypassed through various intermediary precedents. Evolutionists glorify themselves on such court-based decisions, but fail to notify the public of its dangerous direction. Such uniformitarian-based directions have been seen in the twentieth century when other uniformitarian secular, 'scientific,' and court systems had been established in Communist and Nazi countries. And here too, the uniformitarian-based court decisions justified genocides, concentration camps, relativist morality, secular state education, and, above all, initiatives to eliminate Christendom.

These are at least twenty-four rules that the NAS has established for authorized uniformitarian scientific work and a world-view. Each scientist, publisher, teacher, administrator, court judge, educational institution, curriculum designer, university professor, and deans must conform to these rules in order to remain in good standing. This uniformitarianism also lies at the foundation of the accreditation process for educational institutions. Deviators from these rules are automatically considered to be pseudoscientists, religious fanatics, and heretics, who will never have access to inner research material, publish in scientific journals, teach, or research in accredited institutions.

It is now easy to understand where debunkers get their confidence and inspiration when they tackle creation and intelligent design scientific works and beliefs. These critics now don't even have to research creation or intelligent design scientific works. Or if they have done some research, they no doubt interpret it through their uniformitarian filters.[192] By wearing uniformitarian glasses, they will almost find it impossible to find their way to the objective and unfettered scientific method. One needs to read the difficulty that the ID scientists had experienced before they set themselves to discover the objective, unfettered scientific method.

Where the NAS may be right in one respect is when it identifies contemporary non-uniformitarian scientists being affiliated mainly with the Protestant fundamental denominations. But NAS uniformitarians miss the point that these fundamentalist scientists represent the views of what Christendom had recognized for two millennia. This includes a distinction between Christian versus pagan world-views, recent creation with three historical singularities, discoverable physical natural laws that are set within Creation and which function as the fabric of all of Creation: that man was made in the image of the eternal Lord God and not in the image of a primate. Man daily qualifies for the Kingdom of God, and can also create, by discovering natural laws and standards, a better civilization — a Kingdom of God on Earth rather than to qualify for and participate in the construction of the Kingdom of Babylon.

If most of Christendom has drunk of from Babylon's wine, it does not mean that truth resides in that wine for everyone. Christendom had created a civilization where there was an opportunity to pursue accuracy of knowledge. Manage the tools that helps convert uncertainty into

---

[192] A good student of this school, who follows the rules to a 't,' can be identified most anywhere — as mentioned above. However, a classic case of this approach has appeared on http://en.wikipedia.org/wiki/Objections_to_evolution. The author of this article has put his heart and mind to follow the rules, and, for this alone, he/she should receive an award for this effort. However, the deficiencies of the uniformitarian / evolutionary rules are also evident in every sentence and paragraph, and for this the author has my sincere sympathy.

conditional certainty instead of leaving it all in uncertainty, and then claim that this uncertainty is reaching to or is 'almost certainty, and is truth.'

What are the original Christian creation management rules as they pertain to science, and which are in-part represented today by the young earth creation scientists? These rules are evident in:

Table 6	Comparison: DMPS, Uniformitarian, Creation Scientific Method
Table 8	Religion and Ideology: Similarities
Figure 14	The Twelve Limitations of Science a Scored Comparison
Figure 22	Qualitative Infrastructure and Energy Densities
Figure 24	A Comparison of Geometric Law – Derived or Revealed
Figure 25	Comparison of Filters – Evolution and Creation Science
Figure 26	Genesis Creation: Seven-Day Infrastructural GNL Interpretation

4.5 Change, Models, Alignment – Productivity: Functional Plans

FUNCTIONAL PLANS [R&D (D7), Economics (D8), and Productivity (D9)].
Business and Other Applications.

Functional plans are used to track how inputs are converted into products (D9), and provide additional measurable information that is used to ensure quality and performance. All of 3DMM is designed and focused upon quality controlled productivity for which the purpose had been designed. All steps from purpose (D1) on the design management level, and all that come through from ethics (S1) on the style level, is tested in the productivity plan. At the same time, sensors, gauges, and feedback from productivity (D9) lead to strategy for conformance measurement.

It is now easier to recognize the full value, for example, of these management methods when these are recognized as having been founded on the functional design management level (R&D, economics, and production). Similarly, the management plans have provided definitional value to these function design plans. The three columnar functions: directive, process, and infobase respectively, make it clear that any type of information flow reflects direct or indirect relationships among the plans on the three infrastructural levels. Just as in an engineering project, it is necessary to establish R&D-optimization-quality/linear links, economics-finance-dignity, integrity and self-determination link, and productivity-QC-dependence/growth link. These functional levels are used to convert raw material to useful products.

Research And Development – Functional Plans Level
Business Management and other Applications.

Research and Development (D7) is a general term for monitoring quality of input, process, and output within specified processes (D5) and rules (D6). Data that emerges (history) from quality assessment is used to adjust performance, and contribute to possible development and change.

Christendom prioritized requirements for R&D that helped yield feedback on performance quality assurance and quality control. A coordinated effort was established to not succumb to secular mercantile-marketing-consumer distractions that led to much of social degradation, disease, or invasion. When the pagan/secular empire converted to Christianity, it was necessary to run against the tide in establishing quality institutions that would reflect higher management style performance. Conversion of the pagan tribes and their assimilation into a Christian network of commerce and civilization were centered on the church and monasteries. These were instrumental in significantly reducing destructive conflicts, forming a barrier against invasion by pagan invaders, maintaining a stability that contributed to the growth of knowledge accuracy, and means of reducing uncertainty.

About 1,000 years after the Roman Empire had been Christianized, there began to emerge counter R&D values and standards. The new trend was designed to reintroduce and reinstall the commercial centered pagan/secular system. This began to gain momentum with a new approach to banking, commerce coupled with the rationalist/empiricist trend of thought. This management orientation focused on the supervisory and functional rather than stylistic management levels. Economic materialism replaced the value of man as a unique resource whose purpose was to produce perfection through R&D in every area of civilization. Economic materialism marginalized social values and reduced creative thought to utilitarian non-ending reductionism. Economic materialism immediately set out to reduce human populations, R&D initiatives, and qualitative scientific and technological growth. Factually, the new trend reduced human value by reinterpreting existing social achievements in terms of servitude, relativized rights, and targeting Christianity, that brought these renaissance values to the human awareness and implementation, for extinction.

Within the living creatures, R&D is a key component that is used to enhance survival. Genetic programming, management infrastructures, and plans are set for continuous response to environmental and internal change and balance. Various default values have been built into the biological, DNA, and operations programming to emerge as an adaptive measure within the limits of the system's scope. The key component is not the gene alone but a network that contains coordinated programmed scopes and limitations.

Four of the Five Mental Models

Mental models[193] are presented here to expand the DMPS process and compare how people tend to interpret a similar event. Mental models form patterns, values, and competencies for processing data, information, and knowledge into behavior and conclusions. There are companies, organizations, and individuals that excel in some areas of performance through the use of advanced mental models. However, mental models become an issue when they are misapplied to the applications – e.g., biological mental models applied to interpret information-base processes that contain sophisticated networks of supervisory, self-re-engineering, self-design, and other features.

There are many ways to categorize the manner in which the human brain arranges its knowledge-base, conducts decisions, and solves problems. As an example, we can think of Jungian archetypes and Meyer/ Briggs personality types.[194] [195]. However, if philosophies reflect how the

---

[193] The fifth model of thinking will be presented in greater detail – see related text accompanying Figures 22 and 23.

[194] David West Keirsey, *Please Understand Me II* (1998).

[195] Theorists and "cognition" scientists have provided different approaches to mental models when the term first appeared in K.J.W. Craik, *The Nature of Explanation* (Cambridge: Cambridge University Press, 1943). In 1983 two books appeared by the same name, *Mental Models*. Johnson-Laird described the process by which humans solve problems by various combinations of premises and possible conclusions. P.N. Johnson-Laird, *Mental Models - Towards a Cognitive Science of Language, Inference and Consciousness* (Cambridge MA: Harvard University Press,

human minds work, perceive, analyze, and organize ideas, then it is easy to recognize the repetition of consistent mental models.

The mechanistic mind, for example, views reality in terms of machine functions. Here we have concepts such as parts, components, assemblies, units, systems, efficiency, productivity, inventory, power, gears, preventive maintenance, procedures, and operating manuals. Rene Descartes and Newton's works are good examples of this kind of the mechanical mental model.

The organic model, such as that used by Bergson, Darwin, Hegelians, and Teilard de Chardin, visualizes the world in terms of organic growth, development, life cycles, evolution, environmental and genetic concepts, élan vitale, and dynamic movement into the future from the simple to the complex.

The process model presents a systemic approach, such as that offered by the modern industrialists. They may not necessarily know where the process begins. They focus only on what is logistically necessary as inputs to be processed into necessary target outputs[196]. The system has quality assurance controls and feedback mechanisms that allow for self-adjustments. They measure this process. They seek to improve and may re-engineer this process for better performance.

The fourth group is the information processing-based mental model. The scientist or information-robotics engineer recognizes a reality that is intricately filled with networks, software, feedback systems, controls, a knowledge-base, and learning system. These scientists and engineers recognize supervisory systems, robotics, and goal-seeking systems. They seek to refine the operations of consciousness that function within a fixed or changing environment.

1983).. On the other hand Gentner and Stevens described how mental models provide man with information on how physical systems work by generalizing a number of situations and behaviors that man encounters in a working environments. Dedre Gentner and Albert L. Stevens, eds., *Mental Models* (Hillsdale NJ: Lawrence Erlbaum Associates, 1983). Today, such mental models are scale models of the external world, a knowledge-base or perceptions, problem-solving strategies, are able to "learn" (change and adapt), and provide feedback. This leads to simulations with neural and artificial intelligence. Arthur B. Markham, *Knowledge Representation* Mahwah NJ: Lawrence Erlbaum Associates, 1999).

[196] See Figure 18 for an illustration of a typical process model.

Figure 15. Models of Thinking (Mental Models).

MECHANICAL	ORGANIC	PROCESS	INFORMATION
Sum of parts	Interrelatedness	Systemic flow	Communication
Maintenance	Nurturing	Management	Re-engineering
Quantitative	Qualitative	Statistical Assurance	Cycles, goal seeking
Manufactures	Organic birth	In-/output, process	Sensory input feedb.
Wear and tear	Life cycles	Preventive maint.	Supervisory systems
Rational	Evolutionary	Project plan	Neural, knowledge
Matter and energy	Biochemistry	Resource, time, money	Dignity
Balance	Stability	Optimum perform.	Integrity
Algebraic	Relative	Economic	Geometric

It's easy to recognize these mental models in every walk of life, including literature, management styles, philosophy, and ideology, or religion. It is also curious to recognize these mental models during contract negotiations, business round table discussions, and debates. Once a mental model is chosen, its logic and the manner by which conclusions are reached become almost predetermined. Gaps in communication may emerge solely on the basis of mental model differences. For example, how would each proponent of the different mental models view an organization?

Mechanical:

An organization is an integral structure of operational and maintainable units, components, assemblies, and systems. These elements function efficiently and effectively to generate work and products, and function within physico-chemical laws.

Organic:

An organization is an organism that reflects functional patterns so that it would meet environmental and internal challenges. The organism may undergoes life-cycle adaptations and changes while performing specific function(s) in a competitive environment, while functioning with bio-ecological laws.

Process:

An organization is a systemic process with five fundamental functions that convert inputs into qualitative outputs, ensuring standards, controlled feedback, while attempting to limit delays, noise, and waste (entropy), while functioning within customer economic laws.

Infobase:

An organization reflects timed communication, controls, and goal-seeking systems. It implies capabilities for learning, decision-making and problem-solving, recognition, and anticipation. It includes three feedback levels: at the functional (integrating), supervisory (network automating), and executive (functioning within neural networks and servo-stylistic laws) levels that allow optimized behavior within an environment

With these views, it is easy to see why some scientific data, information, framework, and facts would fit differently. Using one mental model instead of another brings different results. For example:

An inordinate number of 'unexplained' anomalies.

Uncovered 'out-of-place' artifacts or fossils.

Prematurely force the lab technician to ignore or shelve what may be interpreted as being contaminated samples. Warehouses of such contaminated or inconclusive samples exist.

Discover and interpret certain fossils in some questionable positions, locations, and orientations simply because geologists and archeologists were authorized to find and discover them.

Identify widely divergent or even contradictory results on dating. When different dating methods are applied on the same samples from the same locations, dramatic difference emerged.

These examples emerge when it is clear that the wrong mental model and consequent procedures and predetermined conclusions are made.

Needless to say gaps appear and it is necessary to determine the nature of the gaps. On the surface a situation may be steady, but the knowledge-base or standards may point to potential or actual gaps in the system. One method of identifying the gap may be the use of the gap-depth determination (see Figure 18).

Five Levels / Qualities of Change

All phenomena or information is made to fit into some framework. Infrastructures separate each qualitative level (copy, adaptation, re-engineering, redesign, invention). Operations at each level have their own unique specificity - standards, codes, software, etc. If so programmed, each phenomena or the framework itself may be made to function as a catalyst for change within or between infrastructures.

Figure 16 is used to help identify at least five qualitative infrastructures. When it comes to change within these parameters, any infrastructural change will be unique to that infrastructure. A seeming simple change within each of the infrastructures will have different causalities, links, processes, standards, and codes within their respective infrastructures.

Infrastructural differences exist within industrial projects. The nature of change at each of the five levels is unique. Totally different engineering processes, codes, and costs are evident when one copies, adapts, re-engineers, redesigns, and invents. Implementation of qualitative change reflects differences among the twenty-seven plans in the 3DMM.

The genetic code exhibits four layers where change occurs. Change in the code is not linear but clearly reflects multiple-layered codes system. In order to meet requirements at these various infrastructures, DNA contains information storage with data compression. The first level RNA reads series of four instruction letters (C, G, T, and A). Second level information has multiple instruction pieces from different points on different genes. Third level information is 3-D formatted information reading structure (poly-constrained information). Supervisory genes exist at multiple levels. Kimura's 'no selection zone' with 'selection noise' guarantees that almost all deleterious and essentially all positive mutations will never be selected by natural selection. The significantly higher mutation rate than has been expected guarantees a decline of all terrestrial organisms' fitness. This trend, which creates a limit of about 300 generations, cannot be reversed.[197]

Proponents of the theory of evolution prioritize a relativistic management of statistical progressive movement across several infrastructural levels. This is an 'a-priori' condition.

One feature about evolution scientists is that after 100 years of theorizing and experimentation, they have never really addressed issues that should be addressed as a normal course of action. For example, there's a library on the evolution's statistical progression (random, mutational micro- to macro-change). But should anyone mention that change can be multidirectional, and can have things devolving downward, an evolutionist will emerge and, in an accusatory tone, demonstrate that such observers don't understand evolutionary science. Then they explain devolution, and underline the linear evolutionary view. To checkmate any misunderstanding, why wouldn't evolutionists explain, test, and make scientific prediction for all types of change? Why not address the twenty-

---

[197] J.C. Sanford, *Genetic Entropy & the Mystery of the Genome* (Ivan Press, 2005).

three other English synonyms for change?[198] And why not contrast these within the parameter of eighteen antonyms of change?[199] Clearly, change does not occur in a vacuum. So, why not account for at least fifty change conditions and drivers?[200] These synonyms, antonyms, and conditions may be listed with a tongue in cheek, but this is exactly the extremes to which evolution writers have gone to somehow prove the 'almost certainty' of their scientific theory. Yet, Figure 16 shows the basic requirements that evolution scientists must address and demonstrate to prove their theory to be truth.

Figure 16 summarizes key requirements for change at five infrastructural levels[201]. The figure provides the basic components that allow us to understand, recognize, design, gauge, measure, and implement change at five qualitative levels of complexity. Proponents of evolutionary biology, while describing micro- to macro- change, are obligated to account for such change. Linear simple mutations are totally inadequate as scientific proof for changes at five qualitative levels. Linear 'explanations' promote uncertainty rather than proven certainty.

Many scientists can describe nature's life cycles and complex ecological interrelationships. Nature provides examples of programmed finished goods. It's easy to recognize plant and animal life's infrastructural levels, design engineering that allows flight, navigation, decision-making, communication, information programming, and nanobots self-replication.

Here, we are also amazed with the sophisticated data conversion

---

[198] For example: alternation, modification, variation movement, transformation, turn, transition, exchange, barter, variety, innovation, difference, novelty, variance, diversity, shifting, turnaround, substitution, conversion, permutation, trade, switch, interchange, resolution.

[199] For example: constancy, stability, immutability, firmness, tenacity, persistence, steadfastness, determination, resolution, faithfulness, devolution, loyalty, allegiance, obstinacy, fortitude, immutability, perseverance, firmness.

[200] For example: barriers, culture, creation, competencies, corporate, drag, improvement, objectives, purpose, practical, rules, system, redesign, breakpoints, quality, continuous, complexity, competition, diagnosis, un-/learning, natural, policies, process, success, structure, breakthrough, conversion courage, diversity, intervention, leadership, paradigm, procedures, proactive, strategy, customer, re-engineer, reinvent, reawaken, traps, transition, remap, recast, resistance, triggers, value, reshaped, transition, turbulence, vision.

[201] Figures 22 and 23 complement Figure 17.

systems, photosynthesis, and finished goods (e.g., nests, birth, digestive systems, among others). What about the revolutionary yet programmed physiological and psychological transformations accomplished by the caterpillar to butterfly process? Or where land spiders create submarine oxygen diving bells to dwell in?

Similarly, many systems and processes can be inferred and identified through the fossil record: Tyrannosaurus Rex's lung capacity that requires double our current air pressure for this animal to breathe and live. All these provide evidence for not only one linear, but up to five levels of qualitative information change processes. The creation scientific model includes and predicts devolution for originally higher physical and organic designs, higher air pressure, electromagnetic fields surrounding the Earth, features of gigantism among all living creatures, longer life spans, and features that block solar radiation on pre-flood Earth. The evolution scientific model and scientific literature doesn't describe any of the Creation predictions, nor is it able to predict statistical progressive processes beyond the linear approach to the scientific qualitative re-engineering, redesigning, and reinventing processes at the different infrastructural levels.

Investigators who use Figure 16 will find that the evolution model, which restricts itself to reductionist linear change only – i.e., mutation plus families of species plus challenging and isolating environment – will never be able to account for the billions of challenging and isolating environments on Earth. These environments must be restricted to occur over billions of years. These environments must exist to account for the billions of families of species that exist today. Such a condition requires the activity of zillions of coordinated mutations at four qualitative change levels. If all this should occur, as the evolution model suggests, it would require that today, investigators would find a significantly less stable cellular and much more fluid physiological structures to accommodate such qualitative change rates. If such qualitative change rates should occur, they would cause havoc at the sub-chromosomal information and nano-robotic levels, since such mutations and qualitative changes would have to occur at speeds faster than that of light. The evolution model has set itself a task that borders on alchemy.

Figure 16 summarizes prerequisites for the five qualitative change levels. A scientific approach must provide proof for each change. Uniformitarian scientists have opened themselves up for the most difficult scientific task. Unnecessarily, they have positioned themselves with the necessity to demonstrate quantifiable, reproducible, and predictable processes that must be proved, tested, and reproduced for progress from the copy through all of the five change levels. They now must go beyond the economics of statistical probability or possibility. They must go beyond simply referring to hypotheses and theories without applying DMPS phases to these areas of uncertainty. They must go beyond what now appears to be nothing but simple secular leaps of faith. They must devise tools to predict specific information and super high-tech engineering processes. Similarly, in order to be scientific, they must go beyond the artistic level and identify which environmental conditions, information programming laws exist that will drive specific speciation changes. Hypothetical formulations that never move beyond the descriptive level do not and are not synonymous with scientific solutions that help resolve uncertainty. Reductionism is not a refined enough tool to address information software at sub-chromosome levels. One can forgive an eighteenth century scientist who used mechanical, organic, and philosophical process models to help generalize and attempt to explain some sub-microscopic processes. There's no excuse for offering 100-year old philosophical generalizations that are decked with scientific terminology today. Evolutionists can't even provide reverse-engineered models to help demonstrate and explain the super complexities that they suggest evolved.

Figures 17 'Production Process' and 18 'Gap Depth Analysis' (see explanation below) help us understand a little better the conversion process. Such a process leads from one qualitative level to another (Figure 16). Supervisory and executive infrastructures are inevitable barriers. To overcome them, engineering design specifications and information programs are necessary. Specific programmed conversion processes allow movement from one management level to the next. Within 3DMM, such precise movement contributes to conditional certainty. Here the process maintains, updates, standardizes, and conditions.

Figure 16. Study of Qualitative Change Types.

#	Change Type	FLOWCHART	OBSERVATION
1	NO CHANGE Copy	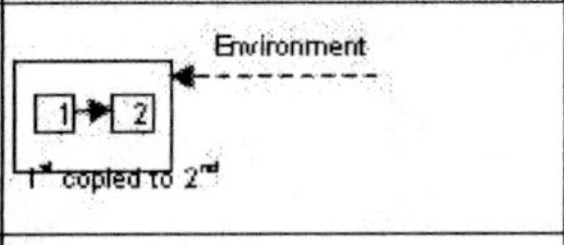 Environment 1 → 2 1st copied to 2nd	The duplicate is identical to the original's design, content, processes, and information. Duplicates function similarly in the environments.
2	CHANGE Adaptation Re-alignment Micro-change	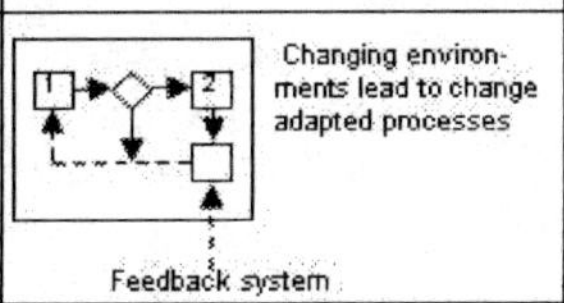 Changing environments lead to change adapted processes Feedback system	Entity changes within its 'programmed' scope Adjusts in response to feedback (internal, external). New patterns identified to either reflect programmed cycled changes, or permanent change
3	IMPROVEMENT Re-engineering Macro-change	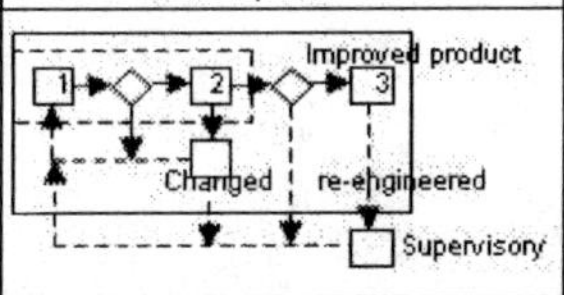 Improved product Changed re-engineered Supervisory	Supervisory function is the 2nd level feedback process that crosses an infrastructure. It not only deals with original and copies (2) but also re-engineers new standards, resources for improvements.
4	INNOCATION Re-design Mega-change	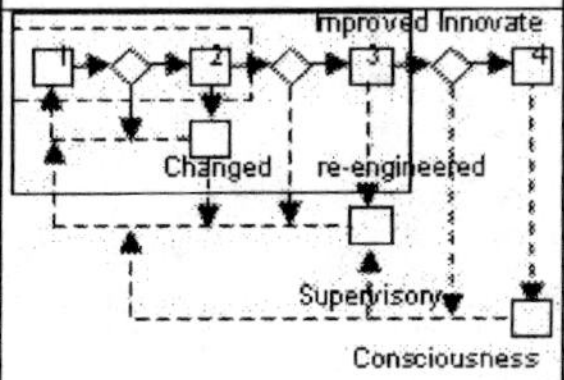 Improved Innovate Changed re-engineered Supervisory Consciousness	3D Management self-awareness (consciousness) – modifies re-designs supervisory functions to overcome real and potential internal/ external challenges. This includes, re-mapping, several re-engineering and self-redesign changes within a cultural setting. Codes, standards, s/w, power/energy densities
5	INVENTION Breakthrough Conscious self-change	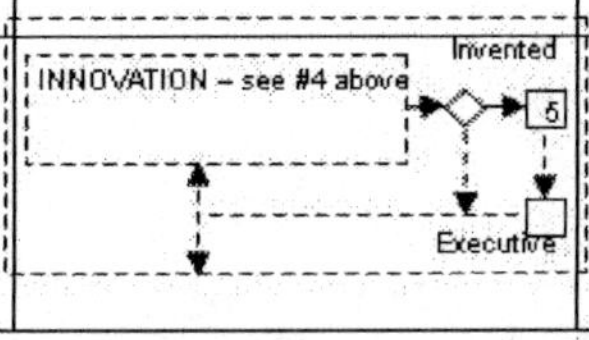 Invented INNOVATION – see #4 above 5 Executive	Theoretical re-examination of laws, conscious (design) concepts. Executive faculties: purpose, objectives & strategies. See qualitative cone's energy/density levels – see Figure 22.

ECONOMICS. Functional plans level.

Business and project management applications and other applications.

This subject has been briefly addressed in Figure 4 and helps explain the scope of how economics, law, and mathematics are used. This subject will perhaps be addressed in greater detail in the next book.

PRODUCTIVITY. Functional plans level.
  Business, project management and other applications
Productivity (D9) is the meeting of objectives and customer satisfaction. It is also a test for efficiency and effectiveness. Productivity is the end product of what has been conceived at the purpose (D1) level. All the intermediate plans between purpose (D1) and productivity (D9) are the conversion mechanisms.

Productivity is, at least, a four-stage process that must work perfectly together under a supervisory system with proper feedbacks (#4) to ensure the desired output (#3). This process begins with the proper selection of inputs (#1). Quality assurance parameters, which lead from product sourcing (#1) through processing (#2) to output (#3), are established at this point. The raw resources (#1) are processed (#2) into the final product (#3) to meet the specific product objectives - quality assurance (#1), control (#4), and customer satisfaction (#4).

The productivity process (#2) includes specific procedures, processes, flowcharted steps, checklists, mechanization, automation, robotization, and artificial intelligence. All of which can be automated. This is evident in many plants and in living creatures.

The productivity process, which is presented here, is but a generalized schematic of what occurs at the information and nano-robotic engineering sub-chromosomal level. All scientists must address these issues, and particularly the evolution scientists who have theoretically built in a mechanism of mutation and natural selection as the tools of choice to account for the changes that occur at not only one level, but also to all qualitative levels as described in Figure 16. Both the creation and intelligent design scientists don't have to tackle this statistical progressive concept, since it is not an adequate scientific concept to address all levels of change. Some validity can be ascribed to copies, adaptive and properly defined improvement levels. Here a distinction must be made between purely statistical and pre-programmed (genetic) change.

Figure 17. Production Process.

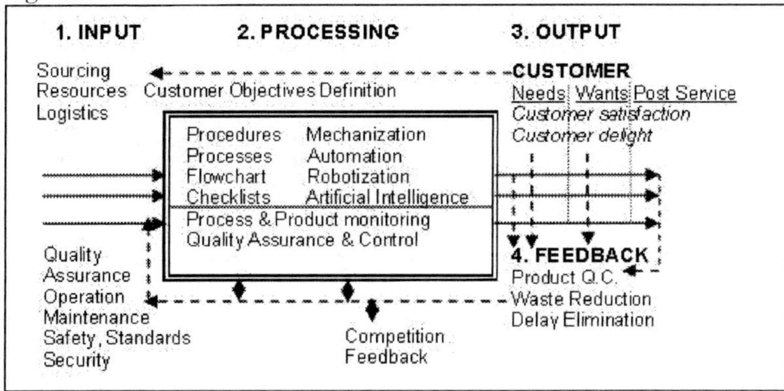

As mentioned earlier with regards to Figure 16, Figures 17 and 18 become useful in helping us understand the conversion process from one qualitative level to another. Located at the infrastructural barriers where qualitative work must be performed, where supervisory and the executive infrastructural changes are considered, these involve conversion processes. These interplay within the knowledge-base – the 3DMM – where conditional certainty is established, maintained, updated, standardized, and conditioned.

Figure 18. Gap Depth Determination

Gap = 'Is' (minus) 'Should Be' (G=I-S)

DEPTH 1 (cause):

(a) Performance: Minimum performance standards met? Before and while doing.

(a) Scientific Process: Data collection. Standards met.

DEPTH 2 (cause):

(b) Performance: Work expectations met? While and after doing.

(b)Scientific Process: Quality and documentation.

DEPTH 3 (cause):

(c) Performance: Methods appropriate? Why / what is actually being done?

(c) Scientific Process: Comparative ▪ Global ▪ Id gaps ▪ Hypothesis.

DEPTH 4 (cause):

(d) Performance: Conducive environment ▪ Research ▪ DMPS ▪ Objective.
(d) Scientific Process: **Causal alternatives:** ▪ Strategy ▪ Culture ▪ Implementation
▪ Test   ▪ Theory.

DEPTH 5 (cause):

(e) Performance: Organization's purpose, operation, and style.
(e) Scientific Process: 3DMM; ▪ Origins   ▪ How.

The gap depth determination is used to help identify where performance gaps emerge. By identifying a gap between what IS and what SHOULD BE, one can go through several levels of causes for the gap to find solutions. In other words, we have a process that has been designed to work within precise specifications. Inevitably, quality and performance gaps emerge in a changing environment. Scientists and engineers can predict most of these gaps and can easily compensate through various contingent plans.

This minimal gap is identified as #1 in Figure 18. It is considered to either meet or not meet minimum standards. In the scientific realm (see right column on Figure 18), this first level is used to establish and ensure that empirical data collection complies with standardization and documentation of empirical data.

If the minimum standards are met (#1), then the gap may be identified at the second level (#2). The second level gap relates to work expectations – the manner or means of doing the work may cause unnecessary delay or expense. In the 'scientific' column, #2 is the comparative approach to multifaceted quality of data/information/knowledge documentation. Such comparative analysis can identify information, procedural, prediction gaps. Procedural and predictive gaps may involve introducing premature ideological filters. An example of this can be seen where uniformitarian filters pre-evaluate and prevent scientific discoveries from being properly compared. Such is the case where, in Mongolia, scientists excavated a mother dinosaur fossil that was brooding upon twenty-two eggs. These eggs still contained the presence of protein – a surprising condition considering the chemical instability of proteins.[202] Such a discovery is 'surprising' only because the uniformitarian filter prematurely 'forces'

---

[202] Ariel A. Roth, *Origins* (Hagerstown, MD: Review and Herald Publishing Association, 1998), 242-243.

millions of years upon such fossils. At this stage in the 'gap depth determination' (Figure 18), this questionable time scale violates #1 and #2 on the twelve limitations of science (Figure 14).

If the first and second gaps are found not to be the issue, then the third-level gap may be the cause. In management the third-level gap relates to methodology – why and what is actually being done? The answer may be found in improving the process and product.

In the scientific column, the third-level gap focuses on the investigator's duty to select causal alternatives, which include strategic and cultural (management) approaches. This should provide the means for proper testing, implementation so as to ensure conditional certainty.

The fourth gap relates to whether the environment is conducive to scientific research – attainment of conditional certainty. Related to the 3DMM, the environment should allow for proper research processes, implementation of productive policies, and exercise of DMPS and the guarantee of achievable objectives. Under these proper circumstances, the fourth-level gap disappears. The issue of origins and the reconstruction of pre-/historical events can substantially be re-enforced not only with the products of first, second, and third knowledge, but also with the 3DMM twenty-seven management plans, infrastructures, and other inherent features of the 3DMM features and environment.

5. Religion Everywhere

For thirty-five years, hundreds of evolution, young earth creation, intelligent design, and hybrid uniformitarian books, videos, textbooks, and other media have been produced to justify, confirm, and critique the various approaches to science. Much can be stated on what has been under- or overstated, sidetracked, incorrectly defined, missed, or overlooked by the groups. The outcomes of court decisions[203], however, clearly indicate that the definitions of what constitutes science and religion are based on definitions that are promoted by the materialists, naturalists, or secularists, and not upon the original United States Constitution that had been established upon geometric natural law.

Perhaps three representative journalistic questions may help shed some light on this issue.

(1) Do you think that teaching evolution goes against religious beliefs?

(2) State and federal courts ruled in favor of evolution's approach to science rather than that of intelligent design, creation, or hybrid uniformitarians. How do you interpret this ruling?'

---

[203] Supreme Court rule in *Epperson v. Arkansas,* 393 U.S. 97 (1968), invalidating laws that prohibited the teaching of evolution in the classroom – issue of Establishment Clause; *Edwards v. Aguillard,* 482 U.S. 578 (1987), ruling that invalidated laws that required equal time for teaching creationism and evolution; *McLean v. Arkansas Board of Education,* 529 F. Supp. 1255 (1982) – Establishment Clause; *Kitzmiller v. Dover Area School District* – federal court ruled that intelligent design is not appropriate for inclusion in science classrooms and is essentially religious in nature; *Selman v. Cobb Country School District* (2005) – disclaimer stickers to be placed into biology books that stated that evolution was only a theory and not a fact, was ruled by Federal District Judge Clarence Cooper to be unconstitutional and in violation of the Establishment Clause of the United States Constitution.

(3) Any other related issues?

Upon closer examination, the editor's first question contains at least twenty-one assumptions, inferences, and interpretations – see details in Appendix 3 of this book. These assumptions, inferences, and interpretations are also evident in the court decisions.

To examine these questions, it is necessary to define the basic terms and concepts. Among these are:

(A) Ideology's similarities with religion.

(B) Evolution-creation and intelligent design compliance with objective and 'unfettered' scientific method.

(C) Awareness of the economic-mythological vehicle within society.

(D) Man's_brain's prioritizing capacity.

(E) Algebraic versus geometric approach to constructing reality.

Ideology's Similarities with Religion

The twenty-one editorial/court assumptions, inferences, and pre-built conclusions clearly reflect an ideological view rather than a scientific one. This is particularly true since these twenty-one-based pre-built conclusions reflect the uniformitarian axiomatic structure.[204] Here uniformitarianism: (a) arbitrarily rejects or negates several 3DMM management plans, infrastructure thus introducing reductionism and relativism; (b) preempts the alternative process (#4) by its filtering values (#5) – thus introducing the luxury syndrome; (c) by narrowing the alternatives options it creates 'naïve realism;' (d) pre-determines the 'validity' of results, thus maintains 'uncertainty' instead of allowing the process to reach conditional certainty; (e) does not pass the hypothesis and theory's 'uncertainty' through the DMPS stages. With this in place, uniformitarians ascribe an almost certainty to hypothetical and theoretical 'uncertainty' factors.

These deficient factors, which violate scientific method procedures, clearly remove uniformitarianism from the scientific realm into the ideological realm. The differences between ideology and religion are very narrow. Table 8 'Religion and Ideology: Similarities' clearly demonstrates the similarities between religion and ideology.

---

[204] See also, Table 6.

Table 8. Religion and Ideology: Similarities.[205]

RELIGION	IDEOLOGY
Body of beliefs, doctrines	
A set of beliefs concerning the cause, nature, and purpose of the universe, esp. when considered as the creature of a superhuman agency or agencies, usually involving devotional and ritual observances, and often containing a moral code government the conduct of human affairs.	The body of doctrine, myth, belief, etc, that guides an individual, social movement, institution, class or large group. In the philosophical area: it is the study of the nature and origin of ideas. Exercise of theorizing of a visionary or impractical nature.
Social contribution and Adherence	
A specific fundamental set of beliefs and practices generally agree upon by a number of persons or sects. A defined body of persons that adhere to a particular set of beliefs and practices, e.g., World Council of Religions.	This is a body of doctrine, myth, etc., with reference to some political and social plan, as that of Fascism or Communism. Included are the devices for putting it into operation.

In either case, it is beliefs, doctrines, and policy that move societies and individuals. If religions identify a supernatural component, we can also find the supernatural's equivalent in ideology – i.e., philosophy, which helps outline ideas, causalities, and purposes. In both cases, it is where vision and the 'impractical' can be accepted.

However, both religion and ideology are a necessary cohesive component that establishes an 'economic-mythological' vehicle that helps carry society through the challenges of uncertainty (for more detail, see

---

[205] www.dictionary.com is used here for the following reasons. This web-based dictionary: (1) doesn't vary from the lexical and source standards identified in other authoritative dictionaries, encyclopedias, and thesaurus; (2) provides a fresh approach to definitions; (3) terms are contextualized in a comparative framework; for example, religion is not primarily established upon a belief in a supernatural entity, since religions can also be "atheistic" – for example, the Buddhist focus on behavioral ethics and rule-based structures. Comparisons can be made within synonymic derivations – e.g., religion and ideology.

Section 5.3 below). Uniformitarianism doesn't identify this relationship.

Awareness – Economic-Mythological Vehicles

The human mind seeks to confirm its self-awareness within its environment. The human mind affirms its environmental awareness through various tools. These tools must function effectively, efficiently, and competitively. From the limits of what animals can achieve, mankind expands its awareness to multiple areas that improve survival. With the use of tools, identified landmarks, documented history of stellar observations, and creation of navigational charts that help measure distances and identify universal, stellar, lunar, and local time, mankind continuously refines a knowledge-base. Mankind develops scientific instruments that help confirm, interpret, and predict locations, processes, causes, and outcomes.

Mankind is awed by the universe's structure, its mathematicability, and what it has to offer. Mankind uses this structure to set schedules for seasonal and agricultural cycles. With it mankind makes improvements in order to achieve higher productivity, precise navigation into unknown and changing environments. Also, it designs precise calendars that allow for the forecasting of realities through which it must be prepared to pass.

Today, we may be better equipped to observe stellar, galactic, multiple and mega-clusters of galactic phenomena, but we are simply continuing the long tradition that had started at the dawn of time.

This synchronized awareness of the celestial, temporal, and economic phenomena has been refined, coordinated, and incorporated into practice by, what can tentatively be called, the mythological event. These are procedures at various operational levels. The combination of the mythology-economics infrastructures become the vehicle that its passengers use to travel on a quality assured course.

This vehicle reflects a hierarchy of values that everyone recognizes as 'reality.' Reality allows mankind to identify and manage borders, prevent accidents, and to prosper. Production, distribution, construction, and discovery sustained existence. This has occurred everywhere civilizations emerged.

By tracking the road to the roots of civilizations, we begin to see how the management of mythology has helped coordinate or not coordinate reality. Through a number of means, citizens of any of these civilizations were able to adjust, subdue, force, direct, organize, and motivate individuals, groups, social classes, or management on any given economic infrastructure. Mythologies, infrastructures, and economics helped manage and introduce different levels of outcomes. Such outcomes remained stable, static, or dynamic platforms of civilization. Or these outcomes may have served to integrate, galvanize, or deteriorate societies. Some have been used to establish benevolent or exploitative conditions. These civilizations presented a universe in terms of rational, organizational, and eternally discoverable contents or in terms of accidents.

History has helped identify five social structures that have helped coordinate management, economy, labor, and their corresponding myths:

The **first** – Master-slave model identifies a privileged master class ruling over unprivileged masses of labor, slaves, and the vanquished. The slaves' nose-close-to-the-ground myth includes state-devised myths that reflect polytheistic realms. This realm contrasts divine gods and the masses' awe of the seemingly visible interplay between the divine and human. Such interplay evokes and overreaches all aspects of life from conception to the grave, and provides a purpose for existence. This is expressed in forms of materialistic or mystical polytheism.

Second - the warlord maintains a centralized, imposing, yet relative and capricious power. This affects all classes: merchants, trades persons, owners, and serfs/slaves. These conform, reflect, and entertain adaptive and interpretive behavioral patterns. These do not wish to appear to fall outside the task of fulfilling the ruler's will. Myths stress material opportunism and polytheism, coupled with mediating mystical powers.

Third - coalitions of city-states with or without a single ruler. It is supported by a visible presence of merchant families and trades persons. The prevailing polytheistic myth attempts to experiment with a theism that includes rules of conduct, some underlying principles of economics, social contract, and etiquette of convenience.

Fourth – Expansion of rules, procedures, and policy-based associations helped expand the economy. A mercantile-banking system and think tanks had perhaps expanded to an imperial scope. Citizens, merchants, and consumers conceive some pluralistic myths that include atheism, polytheism, and various mono-theisms. These myths function in, and help promote, a temporary intermediate democratic filtering system. Eventually, overburdened by the wishes of the people, the now culturally debased and bankrupt civilization settles for an emerging dictatorship. This new rule promotes just-cause solutions that eventually function on a lower infrastructural level, such as those described above. Ever newer common denominators become new democratic standards.

Fifth – this is the original definition of the republic that is founded upon the universal and objective principles of geometric natural law. With its program of continuous improvement and search for breakthrough science and technology, it increases an accurate knowledge base that ensures that the population and representative government function within the ever discoverable geometric laws. This is an initiative towards self-improvement. Natural laws are either discovered or revealed through special creation, incorporated with natural law, covenant law contractual precedents.

These economic-mythological vehicles establish and contain four continuous conditions that mankind has adapted for its own awareness:

(1).Matter (cosmos, economics, tool, management, and resources).

(2).Interpretation (decision-making and problem-solving, cause, trends, quality, systems, priorities, and value).

(3).Degree and nature of change (static, life cycles, time, measurements, five qualitative levels, improvement, and prediction).

(4).Supernatural (objective versus subjective, affirmation versus negation, lawful versus relative, invented versus revealed, and various hybrid positions).

These four help identify two foundational (1 and 4) and two intellectual factors (2 and 3). Among the foundational, matter (1) reflects the relative, changing, measurable, and temporally-based 'is.' The non-mythological (4) – i.e., the supernatural, reflects geometric natural law, the objective, and reflects the personal-based 'I am' with its temporal, changeable, and discoverable creation. Both of these foundational factors are recognized by their existence 'is' and 'I am.'

The two intellectually perceived conditions (2 and 3) come to bridge the unbridgeable 'is' and 'I am' to the 'ought to be.' Both the 'is' and the 'I am' reflect management systems that reflect certainty. The two intellectually perceived conditions, interpretation (2) and change (3), include operations and tools that move us from 'uncertainty' to 'conditional certainty.' The operations and tools are management, decision-making, and problem-solving. More specifically, these are knowledge-based scientific models, and the uncertainty resolution tools -

DMPS. These are tools and the human mind's quest to identify what 'ought to.'

The same operations of interpretation (2) and change (3) are evident in the formulation of the myth. Myth is an interpretation (2) with its own hierarchy of priorities and values, that are filtered through 'is' and 'I am' as it attempts to meet specific 'ought to be' requirements. Based on matter (1) it reflects matter's attributes. At the same time, myth is not based on geometric natural law. Myths may, therefore, appear to be pantheistic or polytheistic and express mysticism, new age, and a wide assortment of monotheisms. This is why the Roman Pantheon was so accommodating to these religions or cults.

If myth is identical with matter's attributes, then what is the nature of matter? (1) The pre-Socratic philosopher, Empedocles (490-430 BC), suggested that matter is made up of four elements: water, earth, air, and fire. These 'elements' can easily be viewed as 'states' of matter. Modern features of matter are described in terms of something that:

(a) Has weight and takes up space,

(b) Has mass, energy, and particles,

(c) Is constituted of elementary fermions with electrons, protons, and neutrons that make up most of matter; matter contains baryons and mesons, and

(d) Has a physicist speculate about anti-matter and dark matter

Within this context, matter is considered to be a 'solid,' yet upon further microscopic analysis, matter eventually begins to appear as 'nothing' at its core.

Matter's origins can be interpreted from existing evidence. Some thinkers propose that matter can also move from simple-to-complex or in any direction due to challenging environments. These changes are attributed to various causes, including originating from single to multiple or eternal (steady state) conditions, parallel and hybrid conditions, or created out of nothing. For example, those who propose the big bang simply offer a rework of the algebraic, Aristotelian model (see Figure 23). This philosophical and algebraic, rather than scientific, model was devised during the fourth century BC and as early as 2000 BC. The big bang theorists[206] begin from 'nothing (ness).' Then they redefine nothingness

---

[206] Originated by George Lemaitre (1927) and expanded by George Gamow, R.A. Alpher, and R. Herman.

into 'somethingness' by attributing nothingness with physical features. The original definition of the term 'nothingness' is 'the state of being nothing' (see this and other definitions at www.dictionary.com), yet the uniformitarian's big bang's nothingness suddenly acquires, as if by magic, physical properties such as the ability to: (a) 'condense' due to (b) 'gravity' into a (c) single minuscule 'dot.' Where did nothingness acquire these physical features? Certainly nothingness does not include   dimension, quantity, extension (space), or time, which these big bang physical features imply. The reader is supposed to open his/her mind to over sixty additional definitional absurdities that fail scientific, theoretical, and experimental prerequisites[207]. The imaginative, speculative, and synthetic big bang theory, however, passes tests in fiction, imaginary tales, leaps of faith, and myth. Like the banking system that creates money out of thin air and charges usury, here uniformitarian scientists create physical reality out of nothingness and use courts to enforce this 'almost certainty and as truth.' Although various evolutionists will argue that evolution is multidirectional, the main thrust of the theory is statistical progression (simple-to-complex), since this must lead to conditions, processes, and rates that exist today. This is an uphill struggle that, due to the inherent uniformitarian need for reductionism, must be accomplished linearly through statistical means. This 'means' is devoid of any qualitative change mechanisms that help overcome qualitative infrastructural changes. In other words, evolution must climb up but does not recognize any ladders to get there, except hopes to rise by piling linear debris.

In contrast to the uniformitarian view of origins, interpreters propose a geometric natural law-based origin. Constructed within this geometric

---

[207] In addition to those examples presented earlier, and contrasted to the geometric natural law (see Figure 24), there are vacuum versus density; ignition mechanism (which implies external processes) that nothingness and vacuum does not have; expansion assumes linear expansion that diverge through space rather than merge (note Euclidian parallel lines, and flat Earth inclination); where does heat appear where there are no standards for extremes. This expansion leads not to continuous existence but leads to extinction since the original source no longer exists to generate continuous "explosion" source life. For whatever particles, energy, gravity should continue to expand, the existence of anti-matter would neutralize any type of positive matter/reality that may exist. If reality should continue to expand linearly, it would not combine into atomic structures but continue increased rarification, etc.

'canvas,' it implies infrastructures within geometric solids (see Figure 26) and suggests that complexity is established during the course of the first singularity. This includes the creation of time, space, 'firmness,' gravity, movement all the way to diverse syngameonic life and all of its 3-D management systems, infrastructures, and plans (see Figures 20, 21, 22 and 26). This perfection includes infrastructural default conditions for lower level operations that were initiated while adapting to conditions initiated during the second singularity (energy-cycle drops) and third singularity (primary hydro-tectonic world events and secondary mega adjustments). It is here that we can anticipate a rapid 'programmed' adaptation to rapidly deteriorating environmental conditions that occurred during the second and third singularities. An example of inherent adaptive defaults is a bird's straight beak that upon x-ray examination also revealed an inherent 'teeth'-like beak within the straight beak. Depending to what environment the original syngameonic life has to adapt, it would bring about corresponding adaptive default features. In the beginning, there may be greater diverse opportunities for adaptive change. Yet these options become limited the further down the adaptive stair the life forms must adapt to. This is the top-down adaptation in contrast to the evolutionary multidimensional, yet specifically the upward direction (simple-to-complex).[208].

Both matter interpreters apply different decision-making filters to suggest their conclusions.

The hybrid uniformitarian version attempts to present a uniformitarian and three-singularity, though algebraic approach. Those who propose a hybrid interpretation may redefine some terms and concepts in order that they may suggest more limited pantheistic versions of: material dynamism or of spiritual materialism. Here we see mixed attributes of matter and of mythological forces and, thus, inevitably provide a pantheistic and algebraic-based view.

Today, matter is expressed in mythological terms. We hear terms like 'evolution proves, wants, rises, improves,' and mythology expressed in materialistic terms (divine participation facilitates simple-to-complex diversification of speciation). We have situations that, not scientific proof,

---

[208] Singularity — event, condition, or state of having to happen once - unique, uncommon, unusual, distinct, and nonrepeatable.

but group consensus may authorize that certain uncertainty should become certainty or near-truth. Then, third parties use this new 'certainty' to erect second and third level 'scientific' evidence for additional 'certainties.' Such construction may be seen as being 'scientific,' but, without a third objective view, such multiple constructions can be nothing more than simple science fiction or myth. Without objective standards and building codes, it will be difficult, if not impossible, to verify or validate any of these 'certainties.'

Conditions during the twentieth and twenty-first centuries have shifted the meaning of the terms 'science,' 'knowledge,' and 'reality.' In our information-saturated society, we can easily find ourselves in a 'virtual' reality. Effective marketing strategies and legally enforced taboos have helped rewrite history. Millennia of historical qualitative values that had propelled our civilization to great heights are being challenged. Questionable subjective standards that throughout history had been at the root of failed civilizations are today being legislated as relativist social concern and truth that is derived from the democratic reality. All this is done in the name of 'science' and 'democracy.' This democracy has become the bedrock for bringing about principles of failed civilizations.

These developments touch upon the underlying nature and principles of what constitutes the 'scientific method.' Imperceptible redefinitions introduced through 'reductionism,' and through the loosening of historic anchors, have given way to six areas that need to be re-examined:

(1) Knowledge-base and standards management that reflect 'certainty,'

(2) Decision-making and problem-solving tools for managing 'uncertainty' until it can return to conditional certainty (1),

(3) Five levels of qualitative infrastructural change.

(4) Mental models – mechanical, organic, processive, information tech,

(5) Eight-point dynamic decision-making and problem-solving steps,

(6) Qualitative and geometric tools.

5.1 Man's Brain's Prioritizing Capacity

Myth is a manageable resource. As such, one can conceive of an intellectual think tank where all myths are created, ritualized, documented, and marketed. Then have various groups of consultants, social activists, and true believers put these into practice and monitored for quality performance. Then, after comparing the results with objectives, these would be improved or discarded – as any other manufacturing process or product. After all, in a social and business management environment, such considerations as visions, myth, religion, and ideology are equally manageable resources that function together with economics, products, human resources, technology, demographics, and politics.

The human brain is the media where myth is managed. The human brain is a management and decision-making tool that daily seeks certainty in an environment of uncertainty. Once a level of certainty is attained, there emerges a sense of comfort, stability, satisfaction, and even happiness. In a condition of uncertainty the human brain uses the decision-making and problem-solving process and other tools to help resolve paradoxes and implement solutions.

The brain must eventually prioritize information and possible alternatives. The brain will filter these into a hierarchy of priorities. Inevitably, having identified the highest priority, the mind will de-priorities all other priorities and values. This process shows that the mind manages all of this. The exercise of forming hierarchies of priorities and the identification of the highest priority has a byproduct: management. Inevitably, the mind recognizes the dynamics of the 3-D management model. Much of the content, priorities, and management methods are simply accepted, researched, optimized, or reduced. However, the highest value remains as the guiding light that will be defended with our lives.

The highest priority is derived from experience and values derived from the environment. In this decision-making process, it is inevitable that the highest priority leads towards establishing an executive purpose (D1)[209], objectives (D2), and strategies (D3) that motivate the person, society, and culture to dedicate or to sacrifice its very life for this highest value.

As an information management tool, the brain automatically converts this highest priority into levels of action:

(1) The executive level (which helps formulate the purpose, objectives, and strategies),

(2) The supervisory level establishing: (a) policy – functions of the intellect/reason; (b) procedures – functions of the will; and the (c)

---

[209] See Figure 5 and Table 3.

data/information base, i.e., rules and regulations – functions of the emotions),

(3) The functional level (where it can be used to perform research and development; economics; and deliver productivity).

With these three management levels and twenty-seven plans, it is now easier to understand the content of the terms:

(1) Religion, ideology, and faith (S1 to S9) (highest priority – purpose, objectives, and strategies),

(2) Ritual and practices (O1 to O9) operations management, policies, procedures, and rules

(3) Ethics (S1) management style, practices - management functions (D1 to D9), research and development, economics, and productivity.

We should give credit to the ancients, whom we have underestimated in their ability to identify the highest priority and who metaphorically have identified this highest priority to be a god with its derived management levels of subpriorities. The ancients have recognized a pluralistic and relative meaning of the highest priority/values – gods. Their gallery of the highest executive priorities represents total management systems. For example, we have the epicureans or stoics with their respective highest priorities (gods) and a philosophical/management system that sustain their highest priority, and from which they acquire a hierarchy of values and decision-making and problem-solving means for interpreting and solving challenges.

Even the theory of evolution reflects five gods (highest values): Dionysus (chaos) + Fortuna (chance) + Chronos (time) + Nike (victory – survival of the fittest) and these four gods compete with Apollo (form and art – creative features). Evolutionists defend their faith or attack their perceived enemy – Creationists -- just as any theist does. Evolutionists have developed apologetics and exhibit symptoms of apoplexy when discussing seemingly scientific topics.

Historically, the ancients had recognized that collectively, these gods reflect their corresponding management plans and levels. Once we recognize our highest value (god), our 3DMM gets into gear to accommodate us to our environment. The Russian culture, for example, has accumulated centuries of high-quality literature written by geniuses of the arts. When you meet a Russian who has absorbed this culture, it takes the Russian less than five minutes to figure you out better than your mother ever has. How does this cultured Russian do it? He/she knows what to look for in an individual. They're able to spot the highest value (the 'god' you worship) and the corresponding management behavioral patterns. Since this god has already been profiled in one or two of the Russian novels - manner of thought, deed, interaction -- it is then very easy to predict behavior. I met people who described how they felt 'naked' before a Russian after having said only a few sentences. The Russian seemed to have worked through their minds, because the Russian was answering questions before the questions were asked.

In spite of the spin that the media, academia, and social science offers about the 'scientific' certainty, the uniformitarian simple-to-complex evolution offers, in the past the same evolutionary views were evident among early Greeks. Such evolutionary views were pure mythology. Greek philosophers[210] - specifically Aristotle --as well as today's pantheistic religious world-views[211] have not changed. We see this in such expressions such as, evolution 'plans,' 'changes,' and 'decides.' This may, of course, be a simple metaphorical expression, but we also find that at the United Nations, there are plans to ensure that all people would '*believe in evolution*'[212](my emphasis) This conviction that evolution 'lives' is found through consensus among most modern scientists. This belief has come to influence even mainstream Christian churches and denominations. The mighty Roman Catholic Church and many Christian

---

[210] The term 'evolution' has not been used but the processes have been described: Thales suggests that all things originated from water; Anaximenes refers to the thickening and thinning of the air principle; Anaximander focuses on the concept of development from moisture under the influence of warmth, suggests long periods or change between animal to man. Empedocles, Epicarus, and Lucretius build on this and suggest a type of natural selection. Heraclitus conceives a teleological rational development involving air to water and to Earth with the involvement of the Logos who refines the process. See also, http://www.iep.utm.edu./e/evolutio.htm.

[211] Ernest L. Abel, *Ancient Views on the Origin of Life* (NJ: Fairleigh Dickinson University Press, 1973); also, Stanley L. Jaki, "Science: Western or What?" *Intercollegiate Review* 26, (1990); also, James Lovelock, *The Ages of Gaia* (New York: W.W. Norton, 1988); also, Wolfgang Smith, *Teilhardism and the New Religion* (Rockford, Illinois: Tan Books and Publishers, 1988).

[212] Robert Muller, as cited in "United Nations' Robert Muller – a Vision of Global Spirituality," by Kristin Murphy, *The Movement Newspaper*, (1983): 10.

Orthodox churches have succumbed. Pius XII (*Humani Generis*, 1950) has reflected that a speciation occurred within the Roman Catholic Church. This is evident in Pope John Paul II, who was influenced by and immersed in the writings of the modernists, and has succumbed to the evolutionary, or more specifically, theistic evolutionary theories (i.e., hybrid uniformitarianism.).

How did the modernist uniformitarian view originate and progress to its fruition in the modern world? There are historical events, church authority practices, demographic changes that have brought about influences. These posed challenges that were 'solved' in the fourteenth – sixteenth centuries in West Europe within a context of a hidden agenda. It is a 'hidden agenda' because, if, for example, some quasi-protestants didn't like papal administration why didn't they become Orthodox Christians – a religion that earlier existed among the Celts?[213] This may be a separate question, but it is generic to the 'hidden agenda' of the times.

Briefly, the Christian understanding of apostolic succession, which is modeled on the system that existed under the Old Testament – the marriage covenant that was maintained through patriarchs, kings, and prophets who were the Israel tribes[214] Many can imitate some aspects of Israelite covenant[215] but such imitations would not be covered under the divine covenant with Abraham, Isaac, and Jacob.

Constantine the Great, upon Christianizing the pagan Roman Empire, initiates original ecumenical councils to help resolve issues that increasingly splintered the Christians. Many Christians had most of the New Testament books, but many didn't because there were no guidelines as to what constituted the complete authorized scriptures. Constantine convened Christian bishops and presbyters (priests) to pray, function under apostolic authority, and resolve these scriptural and other issues

---

[213] http://www.canto.ru/calendar/index_en.php is a calendar that contains the history and names of saints throughout Christian orthodoxy including the Celtic world. This is one of the most complete and comprehensive records among many others.

[214] These Israelites are not to be confused with those of the contemporary State of Israel.

[215] For example, as those non-Israelites that occupied the Israelite territories after the Israelites had been taken into captivity and then returned seventy years later under Ezra, Nehemiah, to find non-Israelites practiced Israelite beliefs and practices.

once and for all. Eventually, the canonical scriptures were identified and the format of Christian doctrines and functions were established.

A thousand years later Protestants questioned the three key Christian foundations: holy/sacred apostolic traditions, Church authority, and the canonicity of the Holy Scriptures. Luther's hidden agenda provided the formula to reprioritize, i.e., dismantle the Christian knowledge-base - the source of accurate knowledge and conditional certainty.

Within a century, sixteenth century rationalism and empiricism took a philosophical route to identify certainty. This trend led to the establishment of uniformitarianism, reductionism, and modernism.[216] This momentum eventually included social revolutions, world wars that had removed all Christian authority from the face of Europe and America.

It is also worth noting similarities in cult-building methods used by Luther, the rationalists, empiricists, reductionists, and modernists, free-/masonry and Talmudism. They all sing from the same music sheet. The process becomes clear when the 3DMM is used as a standard. This cult building process needs to: (1) remove geometric natural law and replace it with algebraic rules and axioms; (2) change existing purposes, laws, objectives, strategies, history (executive); (3) replace all authority, priorities, standards (objectives); (4) structure all beliefs and social norms on economic, narrower scopes of naïve realism (e.g., relativistic interpretation, sensory-based reason and accommodating social conveniences, relativistic, materialistic policies, procedures and rules/regulations and traditions; mystery and secrecy); (5) establish arbitrary standards for determining self-development, improvement, and self-perfection; (6) establish ambiguous notions of long-term economics; and (7) unstable criteria and use of output.[217]

Martin Luther's subjectivism led to Kant's idealism - pure reason (see 'Romanticism exalting the cult of the self and raising sentiment over reason'), and then more specifically to works and philosophies of: Ferdinand Christian Bauer (1792-1860), David Friedrich Strauss (1808-74), Renan 1823-1892) with their view on the 'mythical view of Christ' (a

---

[216] Abbe Dominique Bournaud, "Cent ans de modernisme" Genealogies du concile Vatican II.

[217] Check these with management design plans, as well as with 3DMM and DMPS.

Gnostic tradition),[218] Friedrich Ernst Daniel Schleiermacher (1768-1834) (revelation is a subjective fruit), Ritschel (1822-89), Henry Bergson's (1859-1941) evolutionary philosophy – reality is not the stable being which we know with our minds but a pure becoming to which intuition is our only guide[219]. Maurice Blondel – who in *Action* (1893) developed the principle of intellectual autonomy according to which man cannot be subjected to an outside truth. Fr. Alfred Loisy (1857-1940) depicted an opposition between the Christ of history and the Christ of faith. George Tyrrell (1861-1909) – personal mysticism with a theology of intuition over intelligence – revelation belongs to the category of impression and not expression. Teilhard de Chardin heralded the coming of a new Messiah – super-humanity destined to rule in place of Jesus Christ, reaching the final omega point (qualities of God himself). Two existentialists: Kierkegaard, Husserl and Martin Heidegger (1889-1976) (phenomenology – facts of consciousness) and also moralists: Father Wojtyla (future John Paul II), Max Scheler, and personalists: Maritain, Mounier and later: Camus, Simone de Beauvoir, and Sartre. Among the neo-modernists three are: Ricaeur, Rahner, and Father Henri de Lubac (1892-1991) continued on the foundations laid by Teilhard de Chardin, and reaches out to the whole world – other religions who may have some truth – a pioneer of Vatican II. Both Ratzinger and John Paul II had been De Lubac's intellectual heirs. Rudolf Bultman (1884-1976) investigated historical formation of the Gospel by applying a scalpel to cut the Gospels into a thousand pieces. Karl Rahner establishes a new theology - pure existentialism. anthropological inversion – Joseph Ratzinger's future professor, who promoted the subjectivist view in opposition to Church authority and traditions. It should be noted that Vatican II was forced into session by the modernists who dominated it and set its agenda, creating the most unusually Catholic council in the history of the Roman Catholic Church. This same trend is becoming visible via the modernist ecumenical councils and the World Council of Churches among many the Christian Orthodox Church and Protestant denominations – specifically among those who promote the mid- and full-liberal trend.

---

[218] St Irenaeus, "Conte les Heresise" in M-C. Ceruti-Cenrier, *Les Evangiles Sont des Reportages* (Paris: Tequi, 1997) 324-25.

[219] Henri Bergson, *Creative Evolution'*, translated by Arthur Mitchell (New York: The Modern Library, 1944).

This may explain one side of why modern Christendom opted for theistic evolution. The other is that modern Christendom is involved in the 'modernist' ecumenical council (MEC) initiatives.

There's a significant difference between the original Christian ecumenical councils (e.g., held between the fourth and the seventh centuries AD) and today's modernist ecumenical councils (MEC). One single difference is that now the dialog is not so much among Christian churches and denominations as it includes non-Christian religions and cults. Within this context, Christians (not only Roman Catholics) should ask themselves at least eight questions:

(1) Are all members of MEC working towards Christian Orthodox truth? Is this the core of this new agenda?

(2) Are Christians not Christian enough and therefore need to improve their Christianity and/or Orthodoxy by participating in the MEC? Is this a therapeutic exercise!

(3) Who are those who oppose or support the MEC? What is the illusive middle ground that would lead to a union and resolve divisions?

(4) Who has set the MEC's standards and agenda during the past multiple decades? What are the standards and long-term agenda?

(5) What is the ultimate purpose of the MEC? It was easy to determine the purpose and agenda in the early years of the original Christian ecumenical councils: (a) identify the true apostolic faith in view of the many opposing views that began to emerge; and (b) establish the canons, dogmas (universal divine laws), purpose, objectives, and strategy. Certainly these are not the points that are being addressed at the MEC.

(6) From the time that the MEC emerged, why have the participating 'Christian' groups multiplied a thousand fold – from 1,000 to 44,000+ denominations today? Why have familiar faces at some earlier councils moved to represent other denominations?

(7) Even if one were to demonstrate the true Christian path, how would this position be presented? What other barriers prevent others from subscribing to the new formula?

(8) In an ever increasingly secularized world, wouldn't it be nice to have all Christians unite under a common initiative and effectively set the world right? Do any of the MEC members have the formula for accomplishing this? Or is there some underlying agenda that runs counter to all that Christianity has ever offered? How about the emergence of a Roman modernist church?

The mind is temporal and thus can only generate temporal and pseudo-infinite scopes. Furthermore, temporal worldview is conditioned by the dynamics that are three times removed (singularities) from a perfect creation. When communicating about the highest values and priorities, the mind tends to use superlatives, anthropomorphic projections, and emotional, economic, and esthetically mystical descriptions to depict the highest values. If a constructive dialog should continue, the debaters will eventually realize the limitations of their linguistic scope. They will then explore and find that there are two basic mathematical models that can be used: algebraic and/or geometric. These may provide starting points in their quest to find reality.

5.2 Algebraic vs. Geometric Approaches to Constructing Reality

How can words, sentences, or concepts be made firm and concrete? How can these reflect a reality that serves as a platform or foundation upon which additional words, sentences, or concepts can be built upon? If words, sentences, and concepts can be backed by laws, that would solve the problem. If logic can be geometrically fibered to reflect verifiable laws, then language will become useful. Such an approach will help provide workable, refined, and measurable definitions that could be used scientifically. If such laws were not to exist, then laws become relative rules, and language becomes a subjective expression.

There are two competing and contrasting world-views that are established upon two separate mathematical constructs. There are two mathematical constructs that underlie and reflect separate philosophies, ideologies, religions, and beliefs. There are the algebraic and the geometric fundamentals that underlie all that is expressed in words, grammar, syntax, stylistics, metaphors, symbols, concepts, etc.[220]

The algebraic world[221] begins with a 'point' from which the mind constructs all rational possibilities. These can be expressed as symbolic extensions – $a^2 * b^2 = c^2$. The algebraist's mind fills 'points' through the required extensions to formulate what become subjective and relative

---

[220] During the European classical period, these have been recognized to be the foundational tools of Aristotle (algebraic) and Plato (geometric).

[221] NOTE: The mathematical discipline of algebra should not be confused with the ideological implications that are being ascribed to algebra.

reality, which are unbound, and reflect 'rules.' The algebraist's world is then either dominated by a single totalitarian view of algebraic reality, or the pluralistic, democratic, or collectivist view. These variables may express theistic or non-theistic realities. Pantheistic and atheistic world-views, for example, emerge from the algebraic approach.

Figure 19. Algebraic Reality.

---

(1) –   '•'   The 'point' is where reality begins.

(2) – '• • • • • • • • •' 'Points' extended to form an abstract 'line' or other subjective forms: e.g., triangles, circles, etc. – axiomatic statements.

(3) – $a^2 \times b^2 = c^2$ – algebraic representation is used for deductive, axiomatic, and postulate thinking. Each of the variables can be used to 'prove' materialistic or theological issues – this is how relative such an approach is.

In contrast to the algebraic world-view, an earlier method had existed known as the geometric approach (Figure 20 below). The geometric view begins not with a 'point' but with 'infinity' - geometrically represented as a 'circle' where there is no beginning, end, numbers, nor extension. It is when the circle is folded that the circle forms a diagonal AB. AB is a sub-eternity, i.e., it is the creation of time, space on either side of the diagonal, and quantity, two areas on either side of diagonal AB (time). Fold the circle perpendicularly to line AB, a second diagonal CD. Where two diagonals (AB and CD) cross, we have 'point' E.[222] From this, creating a triangle is easy – fold by bringing side B to the point E forming lines FG. From F and from G, make two separate folds aligned with A, thus forming the equilateral triangle AFG.

---

[222] NOTE: In other words, the true position of the algebraic "point" is really contingent on at least five geometric conditions within the infinite circle: (1) time (diagonal AB); 2) extension (space) on either side of the temporal diagonal AB; (3) numerics; (4) a second "fold" creating diagonal CD; and (5) at the crossroads of AB and CD there is the "point" E.

Figure 20. Geometric Reality.

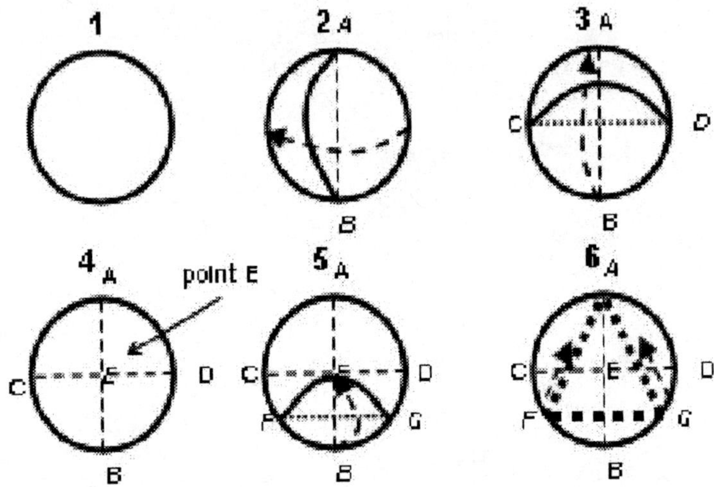

This brief constructing exercise shows that the geometric eternal circle is the foundation for defining reality. The history of everything that unfolds follows the 'inheritance principle.' In other words, each geometric configuration within the circle is a base for constructing the next. So you can trace one geometric structure through a series of earlier formed foundational structures - triangles, pentagons, octagons, the golden mean (see Figure 21), as well as, the three-dimensional cone (see Figure 22) with its qualitative infrastructures, which evidence higher energy-densities[223].

This is a lawful geometric system that is reflected consistently in the Christian Bible (details in Figures 24 and 25).

---

[223] This also points to the prerequisite infrastructures of energy densities that must be identified within nature and within the organisms that would allow for qualitative jumps up the energy density infrastructures to meet "evolutionary" criteria; and this includes changes in the dynamics of the geometric solids that are relevant to structures (see Figure 23).

Figure 21. Geometric Solids.

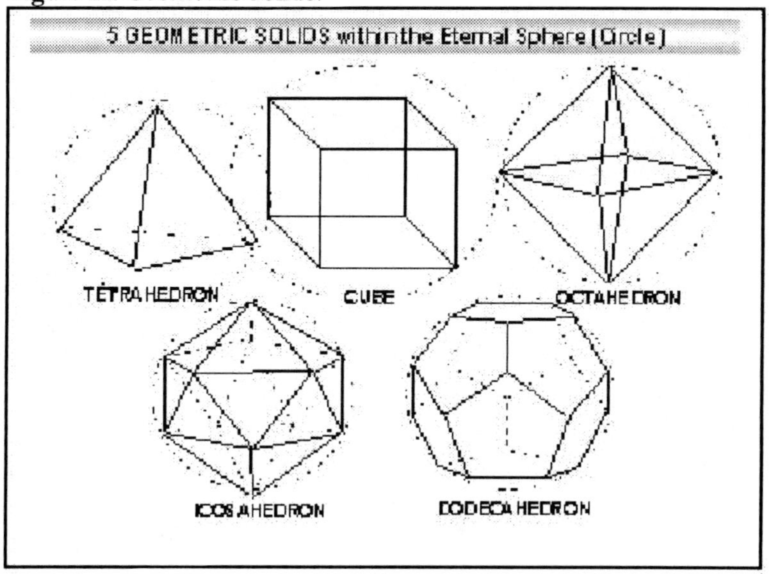

Figure 22. Qualitative Infrastructures & Energy Densities.

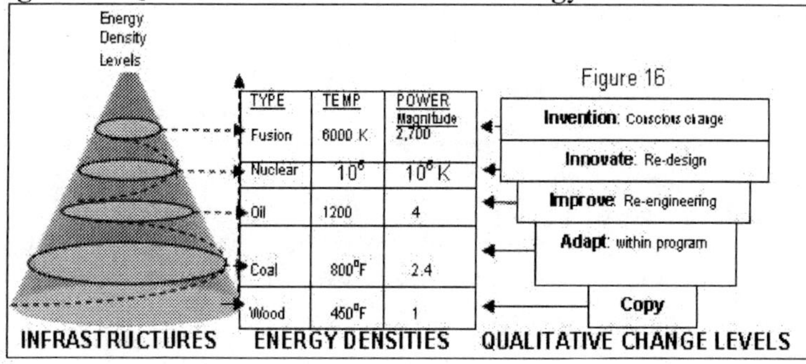

One of the reasons why original Christianity could not have been made to fit into the 'pagan Roman Pantheon of cults,' is because Christianity's geometric natural law identifies the infinity of the true supra-god that supersedes all other temporal algebraically derived pantheistic gods. In other words, materialism, atheism, and agnosticism are nothing but reflections of algebraic highest priorities – derived by the temporal mind of man – from which we derive the original pantheism.

The algebraic 'point' (Figure 19) is not really independent from the infinite circle (see Figure 20, #4 'point' 'E'). This algebraic 'point' is really contingent on five conditions within the geometric circle. It becomes clear that any human algebraic constructs that deny the existence of these five preconditions automatically become subjective and relative constructs. Any decision-making 'highest priority' that is conceived by a human temporal mind, while excluding the circle's preconditions, automatically establishes algebraic sub-infinite temporal conditions. Thus, priorities derived from this algebraic and temporal condition are at best pantheistic. Pantheism is the deification of temporal existence - nature.

As it has been demonstrated, as the human mind identifies the highest priority, this highest priority acquires deified qualities. This occurs because this highest priority derives executive management purposes and legal functions. Whether the highest priority is theistic, polytheistic, animalistic, ideological, or materialist, all of these algebraic relativist views reflect essentially the worship of a sub-infinite – i.e., a temporal (Figure 20.2) priority rather than infinite priority (Figure 20.1). Thus, all temporal highest priorities are essentially pantheistic. This also means that all other algebraic pluralistic and relative highest priorities – whether they are theistic, polytheistic, non-theistic, animistic, philosophical, or mystical world-views -- are essentially derived from the pantheistic world-view. This even places many of the denominational and non-denominational Christianities into this Pantheon of pluralistic cults, because these Christianities adhere to the algebraic rather than the geometric foundations. Similarly, there are those who claim that they recognize the existence of infinity, but then begin, to provide an algebraic definition. Certainly, it's possible to talk about general infinity and use Euclidian methods to talk about parallel likes extending into infinity. This in reality simply becomes an abstraction, a creative leap of the mind or faith. The real geometric infinity must be described with the recognition of the inheritance principle, and with the proper positioning of the self and one's environment.

It becomes necessary, therefore, to determine the character and framework of the algebraic and geometric priorities. Which one of these mathematical methods -- algebraic or geometric --really helps us define the scientific method? What are the prerequisites, facts, and evidence presented by these mathematical models? How does man's decision-making and problem-solving mind interpret reality that these mathematical models suggest?

Algebraic or Geometric Scientific Method

Perhaps the best way to compare the algebraic and geometric approach to the scientific method is by examining two basic figures (16 and 22) and their explanations that are at the heart of the scientific method definition.

Figures 16, 20, and 22 have been used to describe requirements for establishing or identifying qualitative change. These have also been used to provide an example of infrastructural scientific and technical requirements involving qualitative change. Here we can visualize events and processes at various infrastructural levels of energy-density, temperature, and power-magnitude levels – in areas of energy production and control. These same figures can be used in multiple ways and uses. For example, identify weather patterns on Earth, planets, and stars; new structural development under high level of rotary velocities; software programming involving robotics. Inevitably this will include workings of executive faculties, not only quantitative but also qualitative economics, and as it will be shown below - qualitative development of scientific knowledge and research.

These five energy-density levels can reflect realities in many fields.

The first energy-density level is copy. Students, scientists, and leaders simply duplicate what they have learned. The aim is to maintain and apply existing knowledge, standards, and thinking. Students learn, are tested, and demonstrate that they can 'copy.' Scientists follow procedures and leaders maintain a steady course.

The second energy-density level identifies gaps – the difference between 'what is' and 'what ought to be.' Such comparatives search for adaptations and realignments. Students are taught, scientists improvise, and leaders refine processes in using existing resources to help overcome anomalies that appear in existing systems. They seek to meet new quality, performance, and productivity benchmarks. Students, scientists, and leaders re-examine the knowledge-base for opportunities.

The third energy-density level is improving or re-engineering. While performing second-level adaptations and re-alignments, some areas of education, scientific policy, and leadership initiatives have set up the groundwork for improving or re-engineering resources, systems, and strategies. Proactive students, scientists, and leaders anticipate new novel measureable qualitative approaches.

The fourth energy-density level is innovating and redesigning. In a fast paced environment where re-engineering is a standard, the student, scientist, and leader soon realize that re-engineering is but a sub-component of redesign. Multiple trends reveal new patterns of packaging flows, information technology. Subatomic components, flight, and submarine navigation have similar and unique process and infrastructural features. New engine, information, and automation designs help achieve significant variations on economy of scale – more bang per buck.

The fifth energy-density level is invention or consciousness. In this context redesign is a sub-component of invention. This is where all aspects of the knowledge-base, all geometric natural laws, are re-examined for executive level refinement. Students, scientists, and leaders decipher the refinements of geometric natural law.

There are counterfeit conditions for each of these levels. An improver may consider him/her/itself to be an innovator rather an improver, and may cause havoc by targeting the knowledge-base, the DMPS, and the legitimacy of an authority. While using 'improvement' terminology, the improver may wonder why no one understands his claimed innovative concepts.

Although such conditions can be found throughout history around the world, one must be careful with the sources and authorities that interpret these events. For example, the Protestant Reformation, Freemasonic, and Talmudic sources have frequently targeted the Roman Catholic Church's (RCC) conduct and strayed far in their interpretation of historical and knowledge-base accuracy. Casting the RCC in an arch enemy role, the three justified their right for introducing 'adaptations,' 'realignment,' 'improvements,' and 'innovations' apart of the existing historical knowledge-base. Until that time, this knowledge-base represented conditional certainty. Besides the perception of flaws in the theological position, there was a recurrent theme of perceptions of historical events.

In the Galileo versus Vatican case (in the sixteenth century, Italy), we have the prolific writer, Arthur Koestler, who among many other writers on the subject, brought in his *The Sleepwalker* (Arkana, 1989), a totally different view of this case. The Copernican heliocentric view was not a new idea to anyone during Galileo's time. The problem with the theory was that no one had been able to successfully reconcile this logical theory with the known stellar movements, that were so well covered by other views. Hundreds of year of experience, observation, predictions, and navigational applications had been verified many times over, even though the theories had not been validated. Galileo, with his questionable record for accuracy, presented the heliocentric theory as certainty without providing the conversion calculations from existing theories. In spite of the many cardinals and the new pope's favorable predisposition to Galileo's ideas, Galileo went out of his way to: (a) ridicule the pope; (b) did not provide the necessary conversion calculations, verification, or methods for validation; and (c) insisted that his heliocentric view was close to certainty and is truth." Galileo's approach was definitely not scientific, and in fact was pseudoscientific. During this process, Galileo totally ignored Tycho de Brahe, who had brought in some significant and proven innovation that could have supported the heliocentric view. Examining Figure 13, we see that, methodologically, Galileo started with one option (C), ignored standards (E), and insisted, that based on this flimsy record, 'his' theory was to be placed for implementation (F), and automatically should get the stamp of approval for passing quality assessment (G). It is worth noting similarities between the demands made by Galileo and those presented by the multiple top-evolution authorities who claim and insist on viewing the theory of evolution as 'fact[224] The heliocentric view was eventually reconciled and adjusted scientifically by others. Whereas the theory of evolution, for over 100 years, has not been reconciled with scientific evidence, but is moving further away from ever being reconciled scientifically.

Rewriting history for the Crusades' objectives and events is a common topic. One simply needs to present an analogy. Imagine that an invading force has occupied the eastern third of the United States. This invading force converted the population by the sword, and proclaimed its intention

---

[224] A classical representation of this type of argument can be found in http://en.wikipedia.org/wiki/Evolution, and also at the National Academy of Sciences (NAS), whose "scientists treat the occurrence of evolution as one of the most securely established of scientific facts" - see introduction, page 1: http://books.nap.edu/openbook.php?chapselect=yo&page=o1&record_id=1187 6.

that within the next decade(s) intends to do the same to the rest of the United States. What would the United States population do? If the United States took arms and attempted to either stop this invasion or push back the invaders, the critics would see this as a crusade that had bloody, genocidal, and exhibiting dire purposes.

Yet, the 'innovators' have rewritten history and cast the Roman and Byzantine Christian powers as the villains in this conflict.

In the case of the Spanish Inquisition with its alleged millions of victims, we find a similar case of rewritten history. During the 1980s - 1990s the Vatican's archives were examined by a cross section of secular and religious scholars. Having examined up to 10,000 well dated and certified documents, it was discovered that the inquisitions were simple inquiries or investigations of data, information, behavior, and events. It was discovered that in Western Europe these inquisitorial courts were the most humane and just that existed during this period of European history. Furthermore, in unrelated cases, most law violators demanded to be prosecuted under these courts of inquiry (inquisition) rather than under any other courts that existed at that time.

This is an example of 'medieval' legal practices and actions that have been misinterpreted for the past 500 years. Such misinterpretation of historical events is not an isolated case. It is the rule! Such modern misinterpretations and rewriting of history happen repeatedly in every area – depiction of questionable management (rulership) and culture in European courts, their apparent misbehavior, and the low morals in monasteries, churches, and general community life. In these examples, a few indiscrete incidents were portrayed as being the norm.

These distortions are also evident in modern America, where the pseudo-scientific Kinsey Report left a profound negative effect on the view of American morals. These details were discussed in college classes. Based on this prime source, secondary works were established to further distort American culture and propose legislation in all areas.

This approach to the last 500-year rewritten history and strategy to disqualify the knowledge-base had been a staple source of information for decision-making in Soviet Russia. Here we have identical preconceived uniformitarian notions of primitive versus modern knowledge. Here, just as in the United States and Europe, if someone questions the modern uniformitarian establishment, it can only be due to your wish to promote the primitive, pseudoscientific world.

We are permeated with 'uniformitarian' interpretations of history, morals, and psychology. Notions of 'primitive illiterate-to-modern man' help socially re-engineer the democratic masses. Through subtlety, this approach embeds the compulsion to comply with uniformitarian standards and scripts. As described in Chapter 2.1, the set pattern of 'evolutionary / uniformitarian realism,' is drilled into people 24/7. This is seen in children's shows, K-12, and college education, the media works together to adjust our thinking. The modern and tolerant 'good' and 'free' is contrasted to the primitive racist past. We now think in UR/ER terms.

These examples have shown how and to what extent the five change levels, the qualitative 3DMM infrastructures, and gap depth determinations can be arrested, reversed, and made nonexistent.

By presenting these figures, tables, and options, it will be possible to determine the distinction between what constitutes science and ideology, identify incremental increase of an accurate knowledge-base, and how to identify uncertainty and lead it through DMPS and 3DMM to conditional certainty.

Algebraic Subjective Realities

Figure 23 provides the pattern for paradox. The algebraic mathematical method cannot logically account for at least twenty-four conditions that must be linked through lawful relationships. It can, however, provide a structurally fragmented, subjectively 'assumed,' relationship.

Figure 23 - Algebraic Subjective Realities

Existence of an abstract **'point'** but not recognize subjective assumptions for the existence of :	Extend the 'point' producing lines, triangles, circles subjectively to fit a desired shape, while assuming the existence for:	Algebra deals with symbols, variables, values that can be substituted for any type concepts or values:
Time	**Direction**	**Materialistic**
Space	**Infinity**	**Relational**
Dimension	**Force**	**Mental**
Quantity (math)	**Gravity**	**Reduction**
Extension	**Pressure**	**Leaps of Faith**
Comparison	**Motion**	**Theological**
Reflection	Among others	**Divine**
Tension		**Mystical**
Relation		Among others
Logic		
Among others		

Algebraic variables may be used to represent materialist as well a mystical concepts. These and every condition in between represent subjective and relative conditions. They are subjective because there aren't any objective foundation or reference points to anchor upon. Variables a^2, b^2 and c^2 can represent anything that the conceiver wishes the variables to mean. If the conceiver musters enough authoritarian power, then the conceiver becomes an objective enforcer, until he/she/it is replaced by another relative enforcer with subjectively derived definitions and variables. These variables are not anchored on objective, lawful, verifiable, testable system. A conceiver may state that variables represent materialistic variables that can be described, measured, tabulated, and quantified, and become 'facts.' But these 'facts' reflect a framework that will be subjective and tentative, and thus a realm of 'uncertainty.'

This represents a fragmented approach, moving with the waves and whims of authority. Truth will vary with authority's whims. Today something is true, but tomorrow you better adjust yourself to reject it as error because authority has now established a new truth. An algebraic approach reductionist seeks to provide mechanistic explanations for complexity, and is fragmenting because any mechanical explanation should do. The algebraic method is used to reduce and fragment reality. The reductionists and users will have to exhibit symptoms of amnesia and perpetually live in a world of relativity and uncertainty.

The algebraic approach limits the content of the 3DMM by functioning from the supervisory level. It also eliminates the stylistic infrastructure and its management plans. Evolutionist's history is viewed from the four-point uniformitarian notions. The knowledge-base will therefore be filtered for and is designed to reflect criteria or doctrine of 'evolutionist realism.' It was, therefore, easy for the Marxists in the Union of Soviet Socialist Republics to develop their doctrine of 'Socialist realism' because the uniformitarian and reductionist materialism were pre-established. The doctrine or policy of Socialist realism affected not only how reality was to be portrayed in the arts but also in all of education, media, and daily conversations. A Socialist realist must identify in today's world those elements and actions that represent the best examples of what will exist in tomorrow's Communist world. Also, degrade all that will not be in the future. Similarly, this rule is valid in comparing the primitive elements of the past with the advanced elements in the present.[225]

Since algebraists are relativists, subjectivists, and do not recognize universal and geometric natural laws, but only 'authorized' rules and policy, then the scientific method and DMPS will be subject to the same reductionist applications. For example the eight-point DMPS / scientific method will be filtered through the same 'evolutionist realism' criteria. Such an approach leads to a ten-point formula for failed civilizations.

Table 9. Formula for Failed and Successful Civilizations.

Reference: Figures 11, 13; Tables 4, 6, 7, 8 and others (see below)

SUCCESSFUL CIVILIZATION	FAILED CIVILIZATION
1. User/civilization refines all aspects of DMPS. Recognizes the '12 limitations of Science;' no limitations to alternatives and processes the hypothesis and theory through DMPS phases. A Successful Civilization recognizes all aspects of the 3DMM – 27 plans, 3 x 3 rows – executive, supervisory, functional, at the three infrastructural levels (design, operations and style). This includes the directive, processive & info-base columns.	1. Guided by the 'Luxury Syndrome'-filter pre-determines DMPS process – psychology, definitions, alternatives; from the filtering phase. Excludes 3DMM's historical value; reduces the 3DMM's executive plans and Stylistic level plans - infrastructure. Pre-determines theory and hypothesis and maximizes the scope of 'uncertainty' within DMPS. Reference: Tables 6 and 7; Figures 9, 10, 12, 13
2. For example, the Creation Scientific Model accounts for multiple alternatives. This also includes legal historical documented evidence that includes interpretations and predictions within the scope of a recent history, and up to 3 singularities	2. For example, the Uniformitarian Scientific Model arbitrarily filters reality and history through concepts that the present is key to interpreting conditions, processes, and rates that existed in the past; statistical progression - simple-to-complex and closed systems. Reference: Table 4

---

[225] Quickly reference Chapter 2 of this book where the dynamics of Socialist realism are compared with evolutionist realisms, orchestrated by journalist, Henry Louis Mencken, and the American Civil Liberties Union in 1925 during the "Scopes Trials."

3. Maintains an Open System derived from Geometric Natural Law; also in compliance with OUSM.	**3.** Maintains a Materialistic closed system. Excludes OUSM and promotes UR, ER, and SR - naïve realism. Reference: Figures 19, 23
4. Maintains Geometric natural law; inheritance law. Authority derived from these that provide support to ensure that uncertainty converted to conditional certainty.	4. Maintains an Algebraic reality. Axioms theorems, a-priori; Authority based upon these rules – e.g., NAS in areas of sciences, and a-/Gnosticism in philosophical issues. Reference: Figures: 16, 20, 21, 22, 23, 24, 26
5. Enhances search and provision of means for infrastructural conversion methods	**5.** Will be unable to identify or distinguish between linear and qualitative change methods at five qualitative levels of change. Reference: Table 3
6. Seeks to identify, design, maintenance, calibration and management of all 3DMM processes	**6.** Will maintain a reduced or truncated view of management plans, rows, infrastructures and columnar directive function. It will also truncate human mind modeling; remove executive plans and stylistic infrastructure from the 3DMM. Prioritize supervisory functions (e.g., behaviorism). Reference: Figures 19, 23
7. Will use processes and gap depth determinations as tools to help convert uncertainty to conditional certainty.	**7.** Will oversimplify the 'input-processing-output-feedback' system, and limitation of the Gap Depth Determination, 18

Instead of adhering to 'engineering' laws that pursue knowledge by resolving uncertainty through DMPS tools, the above ten points extend and guarantee the perpetuation of 'uncertainty.'

The following can be derived and inferred from the above ten points. If people conform to the United States Constitution and do not conform to the uniformitarian world-view, then judges, politicians, educators, and corporate executives will see such constitutionalists as rebels, cultists, and racist supremacists because they believe that they are 'created by God.' Human beings having evolved from primates, according to the uniformitarian doctrine, have no executive management infrastructure (see 3DMM[226]) for establishing the purpose (law, identity, scope) (D1), objectives (D2), strategies (D3) or most of the management stylistic plans. In other words, there is always a contrast between human beings who recognize that they are: (a) nothing but beasts of burden versus those who are racist supremacists (uniformitarians); (b) proletariat versus bourgeoisie/capitalists (Marxism); (c) inferior versus superior races (Nazism). This is why the uniformitarian high priests wage an unceasing war against the original definition of Christianity and the United States Constitution. Both suggest that man is endowed with inalienable rights given by God. What does this new uniformitarian priesthood and its subordinates wish to achieve through their occult science? The Christian Bible specifies that there are two kingdoms – one can be a citizen in the Kingdom of God or the Kingdom of Babylon. The first offers presents, self-perfection, and change to spiritual beings, while the second offers a reductionist economic system staffed with cultist priesthood, phallic worshiping temples, physical and mental slavery, and eternal uncertainty.

Where, on the one hand, the Christian world for 2,000 years has been emerging and reconstructing a geometrically-based natural law based civilization, 'evolutionist realism' is designed to return this Christian culture back to the original pantheistic culture. The multi-trillion dollar de-civilizing project penetrates all spheres of leadership around the world. This de-civilizing force that establishes a materialist economic base has identified its methodology through a world depopulation scheme and an anti-Christian worldwide authority. A reality has descended upon the world that establishes a world dictatorship of the final Dark Age. It is a Dark Age that will be worse than that which descended upon Western Europe after the fall of the Roman Empire and that which existed during the Black Plague in the fourteenth century. In both cases, we see that it is Christianity that brought the Western world back to the light of the Renaissance. It is not surprising why today it is Christianity that is increasingly being criminalized in the courts. The Ten Commandments are outlawed, while church and state secular interpretations lead to unrealistic views. In secular schools, the mention of the word *god* is automatically reported to the commissariat for corrective action. Such a distorted world redefines marriage, rewrites United States history, attacks religious rights, and silences the church. On the other hand, policies

---

[226] See Figure 5 and Table 3.

enforced through court action prove that secularism is nothing more than a phallic worshiping religion. Here we find that, by gagging the overwhelming majority of the population under various 'hate crime' legislation is allowed to pass alternate sex-management? Is this the picture of the democracy that the United States is exporting to the world?

In contrast to the limited, subjective, and relative algebraic pantheist's approach to the scientific method, the geometric supra-monotheistic method accounts for and accepts all of the 3DMM and DMPS phases and infrastructures. Early America understood the qualitative and quantitative values of the three 'I's: improvement, innovation, and invention.

Geometric Objective Lawfulness

In contrast to the algebraic pantheistic relativist method, the geometric method suggests not only the true foundations for the scientific method through all of its DMPS, 3DMM and other methods, but also expands the realm of inquiry based on lawful principles.

One can conceive that there may be two approaches to the geometric natural law ways of defining the scientific method: (1) the derived supra-monotheism from the geometric approach[227]; and/or (2) the revealed supra-monotheism as uniquely depicted in the original Christian Bible. The original Christian Bible is the only historical document that describes the geometric natural law-based supra-monotheism. Other theisms and atheisms reflect algebraic and supervisory causalities.

The derived and revealed geometric views are compared below. Both demonstrate the inherent scientific approach and method. The Christian Bible stands in significant contrast to all other literatures and records such as the Babylonian Talmud, Greek philosophies, Sanskrit, and other world literatures. The Christian Bible contains unique features: it is

A legal document with an Old and New Testament that require a testator and inheritor.

Two legal covenants of marriage between the prime legal party (the eternal Lord God/Jesus Christ) and the second legal party - genealogically tracked through the parties - the righteous, who adhere to the covenant terms, conditions, and prophecies.

The prime party makes additional covenants and/or agreements with:

---

[227] As mentioned earlier, the works of Plato have described this non-Biblical approach to geometric natural law.

(1) prime individuals and families that lead to the marriage covenant of the genealogical line [(see (a)]; and (2) with some who are in proximity and are not of the prime genealogical line (e.g., Esau/Edom, Ishmael, Nineveh, the King of Babylon, etc.)

This documented knowledge-base (D) identifies a 3DMM design management structure. From this one can derive the operational and stylistic management plans, links, and infrastructures. This 3DMM represents a typology from which other realities can be constructed: psychology, national identities, the identity and mission of the Messiah, history, and others – see 'Tabernacle in the Wilderness'[228] and partially in the 'Temple of Solomon.'[229]

These are designed to help the righteous to: (1) manage the Kingdom of God, which provides a net contrast to that of the Kingdom of Babylon contract; (2) determine psychology, executive functions – spirit, supervisory functions - psyche (soul), and functional (physical); (3) identify the responsibilities, functions of executives, priests, and authorities.

Provide a document that records a 4,000 to 6,000-year history, precedents, case histories, civilizations, forecasts, applications based on geometric natural law (e.g., Decalogue),[230] identification of the righteous personalities and multitudes of people who carry the original Kingdom covenant and Christian message to the end of time[231]. The Christian

---

[228] See Exod. 25:8 ff, where there is a description of the Tabernacle's layout and features. The 3MM can be derived from this layout and objects, where all of these correspond to the management design of the 3DMM (see Figure 1). The operational and stylistic management levels are derived through the corresponding activities, performance, judgments, attitudes, outcomes, and others that follow.

[229] See the Tabernacle built by Solomon (1 Kings 8:4 and following). This Temple contained the Ark of the Covenant but the ark itself only contained the Ten Commandments provided by Moses, and neither the rod of Aaron nor the dish of manna

[230] Briefly, these are summarized in Deut. 26-28 – contains a listing of the blessings and curses for following or not following the Decalogue, among others.

[231] Note that Jesus Christ commissioned his apostles and disciples to go to the 'lost sheep of Israel' (Matt. 10:5-6). He recognized that he has been sent to the same 'lost sheep of the house of Israel' (Matt. 15:24). Curiously, we can find that it is most of the European nations that have converted to Christianity and proclaimed Jesus Christ and His Kingdom mission to the world for 2,000 years.

Bible's stylistic uniqueness and originality has not been duplicated or surpassed in any world philosophy or literatures. This includes a combined narrative style, poetry, total musicality from Genesis to Revelation, and mathematical stylistic patterns.

The first chapter of the Christian Bible reveals a legal text. Beginning from the first verse and continuing until Chapter 2:3 reflect geometric natural law as the self-identified Creator creates a canvas with underlying fibers. The Creator creates His highest creature - made in His image.[232] This image is the executive functions and creative capabilities. Man identifies the Creator (prime party to the covenant) as the 'Eternal Lord God' in Genesis 2:4, identifying Him by his eternal nature, His supreme governing responsibility, and His nature, divinity, God.

The original letter-number value provides an additional layer of communication, music, relationships, and identification of individual's positive or negative character prototypes that are evident in other participating characters.

All this and more highlights the revealed portion in the Christian Bible, which may further show the relationship on how: (1) the first six geometric process figures match lawfully with (2) the corresponding first three verses in Genesis. This suggests the lawful elements in the scientific method and scientific evidence.

5.3. Comparison of Geometric Law - Derived and Revealed

NOTE 1: Geometry is a mathematical branch, whose term is derived from the Greek concept of 'land measuring.' It also extends to encompass all lawful referential relationships. In contrast to Euclidean/ Aristotelian geometry, which is established upon axioms and postulates that are derived through deductive methods of reasons, the Greek Platonic geometry relies on proof acquired through rigorous methods of construction. These are derived from the eternal circle and through the inheritance principle.

NOTE 2: While reading Figure 24, follow along on Figure 20. Figure 26 parallels the beginning (Figure 24) and continues with an analysis of the remaining six days, including the use of geometric solids (Figure 21). These solids provide the foundation of the infrastructural devices between the creations in each day.

---

[232] Gen. 2:7

Figure 24. Comparison: Geometric Natural Law: Derived and Revealed.

#	GEOMETRIC NATURAL LAW	CHRISTIAN BIBLICAL GEOMETRIC NATURAL LAW
1	The infinite dynamic circle, which has no beginning nor end, numbers nor space, is the best rational construction that the temporal human mind can understand about infinity and from which time (a subsystem of eternity) is structurally initiated as a base for all other structures within eternity.	Two translation versions for Genesis 1:1, follow also Figure 20, #1 and #2: a) '*In the beginning* [time] *God* [infinite circle - without beginning or end] *created...;*' or b) '*God* [infinite circle - #1], *in the beginning* (time (sub-infinity) - #2] *created..*'. From other Biblical passages, we find that together with *sub-infinity* (time) within *infinity* (God), God also created the '*corner-stone*' (Job 38:6-8) (i.e., geometric natural law) and identifies Himself - 'God', 'Creator'. 'Time' starts the clock ticking (schedules) for events: creation of '*heaven*' or its dual version '*heavens*' with its two components: 1) heavenly realm of angels − (Job 38:6-8 − 'cornerstone' and '*angels of God shout for joy*'; and b) the heaven of empty space − 'canvas' for the forthcoming universe. Biblical God provides His own name − 'God', the 'Creator'. No man observed this creation except God. In Gen 2 Adam sees God as the '*Eternal Lord God*'. Later, John (1:1) identifies another aspect of the Creator's name - the '*Word*' − the formulator, a management and organizing function. Later Adam 'names' Eden's animals. When speaking with Moses, God identifies Himself as the '*I Am*' (eternity) − the condition of permanently being.
2	Law is viewed as infinite geometric constructs - the infinite circle or sphere. Time emerges when the circle is 'folded,' with two areas formed by the temporal	Law is viewed in terms of geometric constructs - In addition to: a) ticking and scheduling/project planning **time**, b) geometric natural law, c) heavens (angelic and dimensional), now God creates '...earth...' (Gen. 2). Since planet Earth cannot exist without electromagnetic fields

diagonal. From the managerial point (3DMM) of view, the executive plan reflects the purpose (D1) composed of Law, Identity and scope. Note: distinction must be made between Executive 'Law' (D1) and Supervisory 'rules' (D6). Specifically, rules pertain to the database of information, while laws to the executive fabric of Creation. Since algebraists do not begin with the infinite circle, they commonly misapply the term 'rules' as 'law' - Figure 5.

and gravity initiated by the Holy Spirit's 'movement' 'hovering' of the face of the 'waters' (atomic elements) (Gen. 1:3); the 'earth' (Gen. 2) must refer to geometric 'firmness.' Figure 20, #4, form the 'point' E (earth/firmness) at the crossing of diagonals AB (time, quantity) and CD (dimensions, space, and quality).These created features – form the very fabric of all of Creation – God, the Word, infinite circle 'geometry', time, space, quantity - fibered within geometric natural law. Management kicks in as soon as there is more than 1 (3DMM). At the Executive level, (D1 thru D3) Law is an integral part of Purpose (D1). Here, within Purpose, Law couples with Identity and Scope. It is important to distinguish Executive purposive Law (D1) from Supervisory rules (D6) which miss-defined as 'laws.'

3 Divine Law can be understood by constructing, theorizing and hypothesizing, and by reflecting upon Geometric Natural Law (see below). Reflecting and extending the attributes of natural law can help approximate divine law. For example, the nature of infinity (without beginning or end) must represent an eternal presence – i.e., the act of being, total perfection, wisdom, and knowledge since all is created and originates from, and no other source other than infinity. There is nothing in time that is un-knowable within infinity, because

Divine Law – is <u>revealed</u> to man through the intermediary of geometric natural law and covenant law (Holy/ Sacred Scriptures & Traditions). Mankind, having been made is subject to geometric natural law, understands communication that complies with the Divine and natural laws. Man, with his temporal faculties cannot recognize the nature of infinity and total Divine Law. Similarly, the features of divinely revealed law, His perfect creation and communication, are evident from Genesis 1:1 through Revelation 22. In fact, the content of Genesis' first chapter is written from the Creator's point of view since man had not been there from the 'beginning' (creation of time). Evidence of the 10 Commandments is clearly laid out from the first three chapters of the book of Genesis and concurred by evidence in other Biblical books. Note: there are algebraists who play with geometric circles, but the

time is a sub-set of infinity.

axiomatic algebraic circle is not set within an inheritance structure.

4 Natural Law – derived geometric law constructs become evident in, and become the very fabric in all of creation and the structure of and definition of reality and sanity. These are discoverable laws and are at the foundations of all mathematics, science, technology, engineering, government, society, history, psychology, communication and development (Kepler)

Natural Law (law of nature) derives from geometric law constructs. The law of nature becomes evident in, and becomes the very fabric in all of creation and the structure of and definition of reality. These are discoverable laws and are at the foundation of all mathematics, science, technology, engineering, government, society, history, psychology, communication and development.

5 Natural Law – Language, communication, and mathematics are languages with their own: Words (data, information, concepts, and definitions); sentence (formulas); grammar (rules); syntax (specific formula constructs – sentences and rules: simple, complex, subordinates, compound, integral, etc.);

Stylistics: strategic arrangement to ensure clarity, accuracy and purpose of message).

Geometric natural law – reflects not only documented but also ascertained tradition. Some tradition is documented in terms of the original Christian Bible (scriptures). Documented transmission of Divine communication with man is evident from the earliest patriarchs down to Christ's apostles; through Covenants, agreements, testaments, history, management plans, genealogies, missions and forecasts. The Christian Bible tracks covenants and precedents, by writers in the genealogies of the righteous and historical events. As a legal document - it contains a starting point – the signing of the covenant by legal parties, case studies, judgments, statutes, history, strategies, policies, practices, rules, development, research, economics, productivity, quality standards, defense, science, engineering, sociology, psychology.

6 Geometric natural law and law of nature – the creation of time (diagonal AB - see #2 in Figure 20 – Geometric Reality) creates conditions of: 'Counting,' numerics, mathematics. Two areas of space on either side of the temporal fold diagonal (AB); extension; direction

7 Geometric natural law – By folding the circle a second time to form a second diagonal CD (see #3, Figure 20), that is placed perpendicularly to the first diagonal AB. The geometric field lines allow for the creation of: comparison, reflection, texture, relations, logic

8	Natural Law – Identify Point 'E'. Where the two diagonals cross (AB; CD), we have 'point' E (see #4 in Figure 20 – Geometric Reality). This is a geometric force field focus within dimensional or spherical space.	Geometric natural law and law of nature – '...and the earth. [Gen 1: verse 2], now the earth was formless and empty, darkness was over the face of the deep...' (Gen 1:1-2).: Didn't have any shape (form) since it was a condition of two field foci. Was 'empty' ('firmness with no content of itself). Occupied a place in space 'where darkness was over the face of the deep/abyss (space)'. At this stage, this 'field/fold' didn't affect space with any type of energy – (see verse 3 for this energy).
9	Equilateral Triangle – Figure 20 - # 5 & # 6. Create an equilateral triangle, by folding and bringing side B to the point E thus forming line F and G (5). From F and from G lead two lines to A, thus forming the equilateral triangle AFG (#6); this suggests interplay of the existing geometric lines, to create a geometric 'force-field', that form bounded gravitational forces and preconditions for the electromagnetic spectrum.	Equilateral Triangle – Figure 20 # 5 & # 6. In Genesis 1:2 – '...and the Spirit of God (mighty wind) was hovering (moved) over the (the face of the) waters.' This is where the third person of the Trinity is introduced – the 'Spirit of God/the mighty wind). This Spirit introduces: a) movement – to move what was a static condition until now; b) to introduce change; c) among the multitudes (waters) of 'points' – 'firmnesses' (earth) in the vast expanses of dark space. We see: d) gravitational forces forming among the 'waters' (numberless 'firmnesses') coming together within the geometric lines and gravitational or field forces (geometric triangles) to create solids and bodies. It is with the formation of the geometric diagonals and specifically equilateral triangle (gravity and force fields) that the necessary pre-conditions appear for the creation of; e) Electromagnetism, sub-atomic, atomic and molecular hard bodies in space in Genesis 1:3 - the appearance of light.'

This brief analysis of the first three Biblical verses, describes the beginning of geometric natural law. Geometric natural law continues into chapter 2. Both the 'derived' and 'revealed' explanations demonstrate the interweaving of geometric reality with its incremental development within geometric solids (Figures 21 and 26), and qualitative infrastructural and energy density (Figure 22). Geometric #1 through #9 (Figure 20 to 22) suggest at least 70 additional constructional derivatives:

10   Motivation and intent – wish to communicate and to listen
11   Duration – continuous time (in the past, present and future)
12   Tenses and aspects – simple 'exist' (-ed; will) includes the beginning and end of the activity – whether present, past, future); continuous' existing' (action continues as long as it is/was/will be done); perfect (have/had/will have existed' (indefinite continuing action towards completion), and other tenses.

13	Beginning (start)	14	Process
15	End – (completion)	16	Quantity – numerical, relational, formula
17	Quality – infrastructural. & graded (Fig. 22)	18	Measurability – reference to standards
19	Dimension – size, volume, proportions	20	Comparativeness – now with n or x
21	Division – at least 2 areas on either side of line AB	22	Historical – past quantities and conditions – in inheritance principle

23   Forecasting – potential, future quantities and conditions
24-   Project management executrices: plan, schedule, contract, law, timelines, functions,
40   activities, resources, controls, mechanisms, logistics, resource utilization, objectives, goals, policies, procedures, rules, development, economics, productivity, etc.

41	Dimensions – at three +	42	Sub-and atomic matter
43	Molecular	44	Velocity speed – time, distance, rate
45	Pressure	46	Temperature
47	Forum-Structure-Design	48	Frequency
49	Calculus	50	Electromagnetics

#51 - 70) +. In a separate study, the 7 days of Creation of the first week correspond to the entire set of Geometric Solids' (see Figure 26). For example plant life reflects the structure and dynamics of the pentagon-based icosahedrons, while man and woman (6th day), the seventh day of rest; Adam (eighth day of the second week) correspond to the highest life-based system reflecting a dodecahedron creation design. See: geometric solids (Figure 21) and the qualitative infrastructures of energy densities (Figure 22).

Geometric fields and solids (Figure 20) suggest that all reality is installed or composed of lawful geometric fields and infrastructural energy densities. They are built into reality's structures - 'fabric,' or 'canvas'. These geometric fields, solids and energy densities are evident not only at the sub-atomic, molecular, natural and animal life, but also within human life. Scientists are deciphering similar results in the solar system (see the works of J. Kepler), intergalactic, galactic clusters, supra-clusters, network of supra-clusters, new structure appearing within the high-speed rotary systems and at information processes and at the chromosome levels.

Clearly, the definition of the scientific method acquires substance in the integral geometric law of creation. It is not evident in the narrow subjective, algebraic and materialistic economy that cannot ascend above the empirical and a two-dimensional theoretical level, based on supervisory rules - uniformitarianism.

Returning to the journalist/editor/court's 1st question 'Do you think that teaching evolution goes against religious beliefs?' This one sided and ideological view is not a scientific question. First, one must address the implied 22 ideological inferences (see Appendix 1) before formulating a properly scientific question. Having addressed these many issues, one can properly formulate a more realistic question - 'Do you think that teaching pantheism goes against the original geometric law-based definition of the scientific method, and against supra-monotheism?' The answer is clearly in the affirmative.

6. Score Cards, Filters and Solutions

The second question[233] that a newspaper editor may ask a writer who wishes to write an article on the 'evolution, creation, and intelligent design': *"State and federal courts ruled in favor of evolution's approach to science rather than that of intelligent design, creation, or hybrid uniformitarians. How do you interpret this ruling?"*

6.1 UNIFORMITARIAN COURTS

Courts interpret that the theory of evolution is a 'religion-free' approach to 'science'. On the surface, this appears to be a safe position in view of the alternative – a religion-tainted science. Even though the decision seems to have addressed 'science versus religion'[234] and 'church and state'[235] issues, the decision did not address the 'science-ideology' relationship[236]. Similarly, court stated reasons for their decisions are devoid of an investigation into the nature and scope of an 'objective and unfettered science and scientific method.' Due to this, courts default and subscribe to the notions that evolution-is-science and creation and intelligent design are religions.

By posturing on this surface platform, courts fail a **second** time, by not looking at what lurks beneath the evolutionary-science platform. Identify the infrastructure upon which the theory of evolution is erected? Yet for over 200 years, it has been clear that Evolution's infrastructure is its three-point uniformitarian *ideology*. And that this infrastructure is supported by the five-century-old pillars of rationalism, empiricism,

---

[233] Chapter 5 of this book addresses the editor's first question.

[234] Demarcation problem (see Chapter 1 of this book, Page 21)

[235] Establishment Clause, which refers to the first of several statements in the First Amendment to the United States Constitution.

[236] See Table 8.

materialism, reductionism, and modernism. These five philosophies stand in opposition to the principles and interpretation of the United States Constitution, which reflects geometric natural law.

Third flaw lies in that if these judges wish to promote uniformitarianism, then they overlook the opportunity provided by the best used uniformitarian model - Marxism. Methodologically, the Marxist uniformitarian approach is significantly more systematic than the secular American one. Marxist uniformitarianism is totally atheistic, anti-religious, materialistic, reductionist, is economics-based and provides a forecast based on its uniformitarian/economics foundation. It is just as 'scientific' as that promoted by uniformitarians in the United States. Similarly, this uniformitarian Marxist science is guaranteed to be viewed to be a superior science than that offered by creation and intelligent design scientists, who graduated from top United States accredited institutions of higher learning. Classical Darwinism was used to justify social-Darwinist social programs such as those offered by the Marxism, Fascism, socialism, secularism and democracy groups. Clearly, there's a link between neo-Darwinism, socialism/democracy - materialist uniformitarian three-points. Judges seem to be ignorant of this pseudo-scientific connection.

It is evident that none of these uniformitarian groups have ever used, but reject the objective and unfettered science and scientific method, the 3DMM and DMPS. Instead, we see a perverted and truncated scientific method compromised by UR, ER, SR and more specifically the 'luxury syndrome' – i.e., mind control. Where the true objective of the scientific method is to convert uncertainty into conditional certainty, the uniformitarian approach ensures that all science remains at various phases of uncertainty.

Fourth flaw - based on the above three deficiencies, the United States courts pass decisions upon something judges can't define: (a) what constitutes the original meaning of true science and the scientific method; (b) what are the similarities and differences among the operational definitions of: ideology, philosophy and religion. This deficiency is evident because these judges have shelved USA constitutional law, which is derived from geometric natural law. This is a common trend among all the 'activist' judges in every other field.

Fifth flaw - due to the above four constraints, judges do not help resolve, through their decisions, the lingering questions whose mission this book addresses:

a) Had the original scientific method been improperly defined?

b) Had the method or the nature of science changed with time?

c) Wasn't the scientific method supposed to provide a constant – an authoritative anchor?

d) Has science and the scientific method been misapplied by some or all scientists?

e) Has science's content been misunderstood, blended, or mutated into economics, philosophy, or ideology?

f) Perhaps science and the scientific method had not been designed to fulfill a role that most thought it should fulfill?

g) Has the scientific method expanded beyond its procedural scope?

h) Does science now provide evidence for scientific misconduct or intellectual dishonesty?

i) Have influential forces hijacked science and lead it to fulfill other purposes?

The answer to each question is in the affirmative and judges, inevitably, decide that Uncertainty must reign supreme. Most areas of the United States judicial system have bought into this filtering process.

Today, we find historic perspective has been relativized; this is why USA Constitutional Law has illegally been neutralized. All standards have been reset to reflect 'naïve realism.'[237] It had become evident, early in the last century that this new application of 'realism' in the United States social and natural sciences was to ensure that 'uncertainty' reigned supreme. Certainty has been renamed to be nothing more than an extended undeterminable flow of uncertainty – see 'evolution is almost certain, and is truth.' This is an Orwellian redefinition of terms. These may be understandable within a socialist and relativistic environment, but not within a culture that had devised accurate knowledge base (science, conditional certainty) and DMPS tools to resolve uncertainty. Such a

---

[237] 'Naïve realism' is derived from the application of the uniformitarian filters (UR, ER, and/or SR). These emerged in the U.S. during the "Scopes Trials" in 1925, applied by the journalist, Henry Luis Mencken. See Chapter 2 of this book for details.

culture would immediately recognize such an Orwellian approach as a reflection of insanity.

Two groups of scientists – the 'young earth creationists' and the 'intelligent design' - saw the handwriting on the wall. These scientists attempt to maintain the original historical scientific filters. They update their scientific models and perused the effort to maintain the original science and the scientific method. They distinguish between uniformitarian and the objective-unfettered scientific methods and results.

Uniformitarians claim that non-evolutionists find it difficult or too complicated to understand their 'evolutionist realism' (ER). But, clearly, non-evolutionists understand the uniformitarian stance perfectly. They recognize the uniformitarian 'naïve realism' axioms, theorems and postulates that reflect mechanical, organic and process mental models only. An uniformitarian foundation is secular thinking. We can see evolution, uniformitarianism, secularism in the concepts of class struggle (Marxism), race (Nazism), gender, generations, gender and modernism (Americanism). Court decisions based upon such uniformitarian foundations have until recent history legitimized concentration camps and genocidal programs on a massive scale. We can point to the proactive policies signed at the Club of Rome (1975) for the next 50 years. Upon its implementation we will see the following results: a) centralization of the world banking system; b) de-industrialization of world; c) world depopulation to $1/6^{th}$ or today's population. It becomes evident that uniformitarian objectives are to convert the masses into controllable, de-educated 'producers' (labor) and an economically manageable resource.

6th Flaw - this disproportional battle that evolutionists wage is not so much to promote 'science' and the 'scientific method.' Instead, these 'naïve realists' target: a) Christian knowledge base; b) successful application of science, scientific method; and c) the 3DMM; d) target and wish to truncate the 3DMMs executive and style infrastructures.

The Christian 2,000-year-old creationist model has provided a practical legal and historical foundation that led to measureable solutions. It is Christendom that allowed civilizations to revive and survive after sever challenges. Christendom established a workable knowledge base, standards, and several management systems to overcome irrationalism, reductionism, subjectivism and barbarism. It resolved these through such activities as those of Augustinian concepts of the 'City of God,' (fifth century AD), the Byzantine Empire, Christian Celtic networks, the re-introduction of the Renaissance (fifteenth century) qualitative methods and recognition of man's design in the 'image of God.' This opened the way to the development of engineering, sciences, technology, arts and letters, exploration, and discovery. Here, the need to perfect man, society, and civilization in the image of God's standards led to the rediscovery of geometric natural laws and the scientific method. It is this that has motivated the battle against the pagan theories and their program to reintroduce elements of failed civilizations and the dark ages.

Figure 25. Comparison: Filters – Evolution and Creation Science.

UNIFORMITARIAN EVOLUTIONARY	CREATION SCIENCE
Gradual development within statistical progressive rules that exist today. Extrapolate existing physical rules and tolerances (e.g., speed of light) to an original explosive beginning (Big Bang) or a Steady State, and apply rules of simple-to-complex; primitive-modern. This provides a synthetic pre-/history to explain contemporary conditions	Conditional certainty recorded as a knowledge base, which is legally documented as history (scriptures) – identifies geometric natural law, universal physical infrastructure, three singularities – first provides an 'open system' allowing for extra-materialistic participation or influence. Second singularity is a universal drop on an energy-density cone. Third singularity - an initial global hydro-tectonic catastrophe of short duration (12 months) and sequence self-adjusting global mega-changes over thousands of years leading to our current conditions, which are subject for empirical analysis, modeling and predictions
Materialism – economics-based reality	Geometric natural law – objective with inheritance tracking.
Reductionism – reduce all processes to mechanical, organic and processive levels	Qualitative energy-density infrastructures, re-engineering, re-design.
Survival of the fittest	Self-perfection through man's executive faculties and geometric natural law.

| Genocide of any variety: classes (Marxism), race (Nazism), age, gender, ideology, abortion (Secularism) | Multiplication of population supported by applied qualitative technological invention and 'manufacturers' (Alexander Hamilton) |

The intelligent design group as it emerged from the neo-Darwinian group it found a scientific position through the teleological approach. With the assistance of high-tech research, ID scientists discovered anomalies in the theory of evolution's ability to predict and explain complexities at the DNA/RNA and cosmological level. Without entering into the theological issues, the ID group provided a scientific hypothesis of an intelligent designer that helped explain the new info-based complexities.[238] This allowed the ID scientists to continue with their scientific research without being stalled by artificial uniformitarian realist (UR) filters and limited mental models.

6.2 Report Cards

When evolutionists pontificate on what constitutes 'science vs. cultism', or 'scientific method vs. reality', such an approach divides scientists into several camps. There are the 'evolutionist realist true believers,' such as Richard Dawkins, who professes a 'methodological materialism.' Stephen Jay Gould remained neutral from extreme materialism and theism. There are those who pursue 'hybrid' positions; and subsets of 'theistic' or teleological positions (I.D). Other scientists play a progressive role by balancing long-ages with 'creative reasons' or progressive evolutionism. There are others, who allow billions of years of pre-/history and consider evidence for universal fine tuning and physical constants of nature (Denton). And among these, they may also embrace

---

[238] It is ludicrous to see how uniformitarians address the complexity of information and nano-robotic engineering at sub-chromosome levels. Most still argue from the organic model, talking about gene duplication, mutations, nylon-eating bacteria (I. Baldwin Musgrave, 'Information Theory and Creationism,' (http://www.talkorigins.org/faqs/information/infotheory.html) (Retrieved 2008-03-24). Or simply continue to present the trial-and-error, statistical progressive argument for information since this is a "part the genome functioning within an environment, describing about the proportions of neutral, beneficial and harmful mutations," (Bergstrom and Lachmann, "The fitness value of information," (2006) (http://arxiv.org/pdf/q-bio.PE/0510007).

universal common descent.

There are also the 'Young Earth Creationists' (YEC), who in this environment of re-scientification[239] appear like an odd group that sits on the fringes. Yet they are the ones whose scientific model balances scientific evidence, taking into consideration legal historical documentation and successfully predict from their creation scientific model.

The atheistic and hybrid uniformitarians see the Christian Bible through uniformitarian eyeglasses. They see the Bible as any other world literature. Such literature may have anthropological and ethnological value but has little to do with 'science.' Such literature is strictly artistic, subjective and provides a mythological view of the reality. Such literature is valid only if it can be made to support the uniformitarian time scales and events.

Uniformitarian 'science' fails on the 'scientific report card'[240] because such science fails to meet OUSM, DMPS criteria, and have no valid approach to or truncate the 3DMM. At best, uniformitarians simply provide an uniformitarian interpretation of all reality.

Such is the situation in the case of Christian Biblical analysis. In uniformitarian (modernist) hands the Bible had not escaped the reductionists' critique and scrutiny. For over 200 years, proponents of proto- and current 'Evolutionary Realism' (ER) used 'primitive-to-complex' concept and other uniformitarian modernist views to chip at Christendom's 3DMM historical database. Despite this cynical chiseling in areas of linguistics, archeology, geology, dating methods, and anthropology, these and other circumstances provided 'last minute' discoveries and evidence that confirmed the Bible's described evidence and the erroneous assumptions and alleged evidence offered by the modernist.

For example, some ER scholars suggested that there had been three sources of the book of Genesis. Yet, due to the legal, Covenantal and

---

[239] This term is used to bring out the fact that the true scientific method has been replaced by a pseudo-scientific ideological one. See the function of the 'filter' in DMPS.

[240] Report card topics, items, and issues for measurement are summarized in figure and table formats in this book. These include: the OUSM (objective unfettered scientific method); the 'twelve limitations of science' (Figure 14); DMPS (Figure 13); 3DMM (Figure 5); (Figures 15 and 16) 'scientific models of thinking' (Figure 17) 'study of change types;' Figures 20-25, 26 and others.

testament style of the book of Genesis, we find that there are up to ten pre-flood and fourteen post-flood writers, patriarchs who left written records. Such authors have been documented: Adam, Seth (Genesis 5:1 to 5:7), Enosh (Genesis 5:8 to 5:10), Canain (Genesis 5:11 to 5:13), Mahaleel (Genesis 5:14 to 5:16). The list of authors continues. Their writings were finally summarized by the prince of Egypt - Moses. Being of Levitical background he smmarizing the voluminous documentation that had been carried around by the patriarchs from before the flood, through a voyage on the Ark, and continued after the Flood until the time of Joseph - the Israelite ruler in Egypt. This became the book of Genesis, written in Egyptian script. These writings reflected the covenant requirements – genealogies, laws, statutes, commandments, judgments. This included precedents and key quantitative descriptions of three singularities that existed pre-during and post-conditions.

The first chapter of Genesis is clearly a text that reflects a structure that was based on geometric natural law (Figure 24), included resourced infrastructures and geometric solids (Figures 24 & 26). Within this first chapter we find a 'GANTT chart' of scheduled ('evening' and 'morning') functions, activities, tasks, resource loading, quality control, functions, activities, dependencies, contingencies, establishment of supervisory systems – e.g., sixth day man. The writings of the second party to the covenant (Genesis 2:4 thru 4:26) – i.e., Adam identifies: the names of the Covenant participants; terms and conditions; executive choice (free will), that reflect issues of the resurrection form death (causes of the second singularity) and many other issues discussed above. This clearly goes beyond the scope of what cults, religions, philosophies and ideologies reflect.

It is not surprising that for over 200 years the uniformitarian realist (UR, ER) scholars, who promoted themselves as being 'higher criticism,' 'modernists,' have, as the wizards of Babylon, become blind to all of these Christian 3DMM foundations and formal facts. Their reductionist method could not identify the prime contractor, the existence of a covenant, the divine and human abilities to write, record, decide, and interpret issues that affected the condition of all of creation, the true descent of man - made in the image of the eternal Lord God.

Instead, these modernists theorize that modern man is made in the image of primates, through chance and through the struggle for existence life emerged and developed adapting to environmental challenges. These neo-interpreters prefer to promote myths that are derived from the three-point uniformitarian model. This totally disqualifies them from interpreting the Christian Bible. At best, their views can only be seen as interpretations derived from the three-point uniformitarian perspective and not from scientific evidence.

If the Christian Bible were to be examined within the OUSM, DMPS, and 3DMM parameters, then it's easy to identify geometric natural law-based scientific foundations. Today, 'Young Earth Creationists' [241](YEC) have the modern 'creation science model' that helps them process, interpret and predict all empirical data. The YEC's scientific model is set within parameters of recent historical events, as it has also been recognized by the early church fathers and two millennial Christendom. This includes the legal historical documentation of three recent singularities. They used the original understanding of science and have been refining the decision-making and problem-solving method (DMPS). With this, the Young Earth Creationists and their creation scientific model succeeds on multiple 'Scientific Report Card.' The YEC does not distort the fundamental framework of objective or 'unfettered' scientific method (OUSM). In its longer scope – historical two millennial Christendom has included – geometric natural law, as well as, the holy/sacred traditions and authority. So we can see the Genesis creation with its geometric law/solids application from Genesis 1:1 (see Figure 26)

Figure 26. Genesis' Creation Seven-day's Infrastructures: Geometric Natural Law Interpretation. Infrastructures, resources and networked systems.

Day 1: **Tetrahedron – i.e., three triangles (**Refer to Figure 21 – Geometric Solids).

---

[241] The original creation scientists renamed themselves as 'Young Earth Creationists' (YEC) in the late 1980s to distinguish themselves from then emerging new hybrid uniformitarian groups: the progressive creation or old-age creationism.

(a) *God creates time* - Within infinity God creates sub-infinity, i.e., time + geometric natural law – simultaneous.

(b) *Heavens* (dual) – quantification and extension – 3-D (see 'deep' below next column) - The dual form of the term heavens suggests: Creation of numeric concepts, two extensions: physical space - two areas and the heavenly abode (angels – see Job 38:7).

(c) *Firmness* - 'earth' - Crossing of geometric fields – without form (waste), empty (no substance), waters (numerous quantities randomness); darkness; deep (3-D) – spherical.

(d) *Spirit of God* hovered over 'waters' introducing movement. Light (energized) darkness (structured emptiness) - designates day and night. Movement introduced in the randomness (waters) gravitational attraction (geometric – triangle): energized = light; division or distinction between empty space (darkness) and energized gravitated and moving fields.

Day 2: **Cube,** i.e., **four sides; one top and one bottom squares.**

Genesis description: Expanse in the midst of two areas of waters – above the expanse 'heaven' and that below the expanse: (*Geometric interpretation*) waters being the myriads of crossing geometric fields are separated into two 'waters' – (geometric crossing fields – 'firmness') one above the expanse – called 'heaven,' and the other 'waters' below the expanse.

Day 3: **Octahedron,** i.e., **four top and four bottom triangles connected by a square. Part 1 of 2** - *Genesis description:* waters under heaven to be collected in one place (dry land): Earth and collection of waters: seas; Earth is to yield tender grass, herb sowing seed, fruit trees – after its kind. *Geometric interpretation*: in the crisscross of energized fields (pre-atomic) - now within geometric natural law (gravity) forms atomically organized matter forms, soil, dry land and seas. This energized land now has structure, elements to produce distinctive species (kinds) of plan life, herbs with its seeds, and fruit trees. Here, life has its own genetic code, information system, nano-robotic engineering, conversion, and reproductive systems.

Day 4: **Octahedron: i.e., four top and four bottom triangles connected by a square. Part 2/2** *Genesis description*: Luminaries in the heavens as a calendar for days, seasons, and years. The great (Sun) light and the small (Moon) light to illuminate the Earth. Geometric interpretation: Levels luminaries purposes: distinguish between day/night, seasons (quarterly measure of Earth's orbit around the Sun), and year (God's calendar was focused on a solar year); no calendar measurement for the Moon. However, the Moon is used as a night luminary along with the stars, while the Sun for daytime. These luminaries rule (manage by laws) in the sky.

Day 5: **Icosahedron: i.e., twenty triangles and two pentagons arranged in: five lower triangles connected via a common pentagon to ten middle triangles, which are in turn are connected via common second pentagon to**

five upper triangles. *Genesis description*: Waters to teem with living creatures, the Earth's heaven with flying creatures. Also, includes 'monsters and creeping living creatures'. All are to multiply and fill oceans and the Earth's heavens. *Geometric interpretation*: The waters are filled with living creatures, great monsters and things that creep, while the air is filled with flying 'fowl' creatures. All are to multiply and fill the seas and the air. There is a distinction between the Day 5 (sea and air creatures) and Day 6 land creatures.

Day 6: **Dodecahedron: (Pentagons: one bottom, five middle bottom, five middle top and one top = twelve). Part 1 of 2** *Genesis description*: The Earth brings forth living creatures, each according to its species, cattle, creeping things, and beast of the earth – all within their species. The 6th day man - made in God's image - to rule over the creatures in the sea, air, earth (day 5 and 6 creatures). *Geometric interpretation*: These are 'living creatures' as distinct from the material creations (waters, earth, sea, air, etc). The hierarchy of living creatures has awareness, volition, emotions – they have the capacity to react as well as to various degrees, make 'decisions' among choices/options. Each creature is made according to its genetic code, species for specific purposes within the environment. Also, on this sixth day, human beings have been endowed with management and creative responsibilities – just as God ('in God's image') to manage the planet – flora and fauna. Humans would be nourished by fruit of every seed bearing herb and of the fruit-bearing tree, while living creatures from green herb plants All being vegetarians.

Day 7: **Dodecahedron: Pentagons: one bottom, five middle bottom, five middle top and one top = twelve. Part 2 of 2** *Genesis descriptions*: God completed all His work by the seventh day. He blessed, sanctified the seventh day, and rested. *Geometric interpretation*: The example here is that just as God worked six days, He also fulfilled the blessed and sanctified day of rest. This is the relationship - six plus one. Hybrid uniformitarians must not only account for 'billions of years' of God's rest period, but as Uniformitarians, recognize that the Big Bang model contradicts the six-day events, activities, geometric solids' infrastructures, and the realization that this Creative even occurs prior to two forthcoming singularities (catastrophes) a) drop of one energy density cycle making all creation starving for energy; and b) Noachian world Flood – its super initial and mega subsequent effects scars the Earth and Solar System.

In a similar way, engineering and logistics studies have been made in other biblical areas, i.e., plans and dimensions of Noah's Ark. This pre-historic engineering feat provides key features by which modern science can estimate what planners of Noah's Ark had to consider in order for him to help overcome challenges: fauna logistics, unprecedented radically changing global conditions, globally escalated tidal waves, temperature inversions, worldwide hydro-tectonic catastrophic events during an initial forty days and an additional eleven months of 'cooling' off. This included contrastive information on pre-, during, and post-flood conditions. This comprehensive picture is tracked through data history and corroborating scientific, geologic, and paleontological evidence, an ice age where oceans froze (Job 38) (2000 BC). Worldwide climate adjustments after the ice age resulted in droughts that covered lands, which in those latitudes which originally had abundant rains and wildlife (Jacob's time – Genesis 41ff) (1500 BC). Some have estimated that this brought about the beginning of large scale ice-pack meltdowns, which raised ocean water levels between 100 feet (north and south hemispheres) and 500 feet at tropical zones.

Christian Biblical history is not allegorized mythology. Ancient Israel's patriarchs, kings, and prophets had maintained genealogies to track and trace case histories, judgments, and compliance with the terms and conditions of the divine covenant; this allowed them to recognize the mission, identity of the messiah, and milestones through the annual holy days leading to resurrected life. An interesting sideline, for example, the Parthian wise men, which, at that time, were of the descendants of the dispersed northern ten tribes of Israel in Persia, recognized the glorious events that were to occur by having tracked the stellar calendar. The zodiac calendar was not an astrological tool for the Parthian, but a planning and scheduling tool of events and activities set from the beginning. The expected event in the Virgo sign did not only point to an event of historical proportions, but also foresaw the sacrifice, change, resurrection, and the removal of death from all of Creation.

After these Biblical events, one can also see the knowledge base (3DMM) maintained and expanded during the Christian era. Christianity that existed before, during, and after Constantine the Great (early 4th century AD) was quite singular in its makeup. Persecuted before Constantine and given imperial power during and after Constantine. During and after Constantine's period, Christians had the opportunity to re-create a world empire that removed pagan phallic worshiping anchors, addressed issues of pluralism, law, history, government, cultures, justice, commerce, and banking. Christianity, at that time, had substance and was set on establishing and developing an alternate world in contrast to the fallen pagan world. This substance seems to be missing from contemporary theological curriculums today. Today's Christianity must compete with modernism, competitive religious pluralism, and, after World War I and World War II, has been made next to impotent as moral authority.

How did the early Christians function in a secularized environment? In Western Europe, St Ambrose and St. Augustine in the fifth century, the Celtic Orthodox in the West, and in Eastern Europe, Cyril and Methodius in the ninth century – this was a time when Christianity was united. Christian missionaries, dispersed throughout Europe, interfaced not only with their church and monasteries but also with the city councils, kings, and people and tried to organize a quality living.

A debate about the relationship between holy traditions and holy scriptures can be viewed in terms of and effort to establishing a knowledge base - 3DMM, DMPS, and qualitative vertical change. Briefly, tradition has a <u>historical</u> value. The scriptures are just part of that long tradition along with Church <u>chants</u> and <u>art,</u> architecture, design, depiction of scriptures in liturgical 'principles of drama' that function as memory activators of Christian traditional world. We have a culture that reflects the works of the Holy Spirit. Above all, the very designations of the scriptures themselves as Old and New Testaments reflect the legal and management nature of this documentation. These are covenant designations and even more specifically, the marriage covenants between the eternal Lord God/Jesus Christ and the righteous bride of Christ. So when Christians talk about holy traditions and the scriptures, they actually are placing themselves – individually, as brothers, sisters, mothers, and fathers – within the body of Christ in a marital covenant. This covenant is functional and has a specific purpose in the world. As a body of Christ, these traditions and the scriptures refer to <u>precedents</u> that have been provided by the saints. In this covenantal marriage, Christians must talk with the Christian's bridegroom daily and support and encourage Christian families and members to do the same. All this is part of the true Christian tradition. Christians recognize this in the bulk of the scriptures. Both tradition and the scriptures become the Christian's very body, clothes, and atmosphere of their daily living.

Tradition is a social value. Tradition is the knowledge base from which Christians derive their intellectual, physical, spiritual and cultural nourishment. This knowledge base contains not only the best practices, examples, behavior, and communication among members of the body of Christ but also the standard values and decision-making exercises. The body of Christ must ensure that these precedents are flagged when a certain route is taken. All of this is known as wisdom. The proverbs and psalms contain a body of wisdom applied. King David constantly found nourishment from this 'wisdom' and it made him become a better king.

What is wisdom? It is the exercise of executive functions. The more Christians <u>remove</u> themselves from this tradition, the more they enter conditions described in Romans 1 and in modernism, and the more they lose the urgent and critical need for repentance. Christians <u>are</u> their brother's/sister's keepers. This is part of the Christian tradition. Christians are not rugged individualists who fight and take advantage of worldly opportunities. Christians must develop their professional and spiritual gifts to the highest level, and not only to become useful in the world, but also to invest into the body of Christ. This then improves the quality of the traditions for the future. Christian existence is to give, sacrifice, and love what Christians have for Christ and what he has for Christians. If Christians don't love Jesus Christ, then they won't love their brothers, sisters, mothers, and fathers – his body. The choices Christians make, the values they nurture, their highest priorities, must be in total conformity with the original traditions Christians have inherited and that which they will pass on. The language Christians use, the attitude, and behavior they have is their external sign of the traditions and scriptures they embrace daily (see also Style in 3DMM). The true Christian Church that is based on holy traditions and the Holy Scriptures must be the most wonderful place to be on Earth! Similarly, their contribution in the scientific, technological, bio, social, and political sciences are based on geometric natural law. It was the Byzantine Empire that maintained Greek discoveries and expanded them to the rest of the world and eventually also made them available to the Islamic world and Western Europe. In Europe, the Renaissance helped launch qualitative development in all branches of science, arts, and politics.

The holy fathers have continued the Biblical view that 'man is made in the image of God,' but the modernist 'scientists' and the media promote that man is made in the image of primates. Where the church fathers[242] have supported the view that God had created Creation in six days and rested on the seventh, the modernist 'scientists' provide alternate long-age

---

[242] This subject of Christian early church fathers had been addressed earlier, but, within this context of church fathers versus evolution, is well presented in the following article: "Genesis and Early Man: The Orthodox Patristic Understanding" – a response to Dr. Kalomiros by Fr. Seraphim Rose, http://www.orthodoxinfo.com/phronema/evolution_frseraphim_kalomiros.aspx.

versions that skip the 'seventh day of rest.' What this seventh day suggests in uniformitarian time (UT) is that God spent millions and billions of years 'resting' -- see hybrid uniformitarian interpretations.

How can we be sure that evolution is true, when in the school textbooks, evolution is 'proved' through outdated, disproved, and fraudulent 'scientific' ideas?[243] These scientific evolutionary proofs were disproved twenty years ago by honest evolutionary scientists. So, with this 'knowledge' of nonexistent scientific evidence or proofs for 'scientific' evolution, armed with a uniformitarian axiomatic posture that includes, luxury syndrome inversions, triple summersault logic, a reductionist three-to-seven-step scientific method, artificial or synthetic view of a simple-to-complex view of history, we have two generations of public school and college graduates who think in nonexistent realities and foundations. The uniformitarian method is the best one devised to 'self-brainwash' oneself. Convert all original historical and cultural evidence by primitivising and reducing it to naïve realism. Schools teach students to daily brainwash themselves with cynical reduced simple-to-complex thought processes. They use syllogistic processes to dismantle the 3DMM and misapply the DMPS. Today, we have a new self-promoting class of modernist priests who function like amnesiacs because they have a synthetic rather than actual knowledge of history, who have not been taught to reason from a third point of view and are satisfied with 'near certainty', not realizing that this is really uncertainty. How would such high priests that promote the uniformitarian gospel be able to distinguish between sanity and insanity when they hear ER edicts such as the notions that the 'theory of evolution has reached a point of almost being certainty and is truth?' It is like saying that a woman is almost pregnant, but everyone will consider her to be pregnant. When it is implied, and courts decree, that 'science' is synonymous with 'evolutionist realism.' That 'uncertainty,' which is inherent in the hypothesis and theory, becomes truth if this uncertainty sits around long enough. That anyone who disagrees or opposes this new 'scientific revelation' is hereby considered to be irrational and divisive. When it is decreed and enforced by the court that all institutions must reflect the UR/ER reality, and then all must be filtered through these filters. This includes education at all levels. Noncompliance must be

---

[243] Peppered moths, chemical evolution, embryonic recapitulation, the horse series, and a half dozen other examples

corrected or rejected. This is why we have social re-engineering, criminalization of Christian ethics, practices, worldview and the redrafting of the United States Constitution – not through majority rule but through activist court decisions.

When we examine UR/ER's abysmal result on the Scientific Report Card, its obsessive naïve realist 'nose close to the ground' view, its imaginary billion-year synthetic and artificial pre-history that has been erected upon uniformitarian axioms and not upon scientific evidence, it is clear that UR/ER members can only hope to qualify for membership in something akin to a subchapter in the HES[244] organization. Yet even here, the ER's low score and its relative's multimillion genocidal reputations will be enough to dismiss the ER's application. The HES will wish to totally disassociate themselves from any ERs, and even go so far as to burn this application to avoid being implicated in any future international tribunal proceedings. The uniformitarian 'evolutionist realism' is the foundation upon which World War I and II were substantiated; the Marxists[245], and Nazi[246] parties established their existence, their policies, and action. In less than fifty years during the first half of the twentieth century, this platform had been responsible for at least 500 million deaths in Europe alone. Other multiple millions in the Union of Soviet Socialist Republics and China died in court-legislated concentration camps, population movements, and adjustments. Today, ER stands in the forefront as the legitimizing foundation for additional millions of human lives in areas of abortion, contraception, and sterilization, as well as in the experimentation with human embryonic stem cells. This research is done within the parameters of two ER scientific 'uncertainties' - when human life begins and its limited mental model, which does not recognize information and nanobot functions at sub-chromosome levels.

With such an abysmal score on the 'Scientific Score Card', ER

---

[244] 'Horizontal earth society' is used here, not to involve the innocent bystanders of the "flat earth society."

[245] Karl Marx promoted through his *Das Kapital* an economic basis for dividing society between the exploitative bourgeois and working productive proletariat, thus justifying the dictatorship of the proletariat – international Socialism.

[246] The doctrine of National Socialism where the world is struggling between the superior and inferior, parasite races

members are appointing themselves to high social, educational and political responsibilities. Judges define what constitute science vs. pseudoscience, science vs. religions, and reality vs. insanity itself. All this is being exported under the umbrella of the 'USA democracy' to other countries around the world. Needless to say, big-money is promoting this pseudoscientific charade in all areas of social disciplines.

Upon yet a closer examination into history, it becomes evident that the 'uniformitarian/evolutionist realist' (U/ER) doctrine is designed to throw societies back to the pre-scientific dark ages. A Dark Age is a historical period where those in power ensure their future by keeping the economically controlled and disinherited masses at a hand-to-mouth bestial existence. The 'above-primates' have no rights and are collectively totally subordinate to the state's whims. On the other hand, *original Christianity* went beyond mere '*personal* salvation' or 'give one's heart to the Lord' syndrome. Original Christianity contained within its legal historical and 3DMM and DMPS structures the elements of social and cultural rebirth or Renaissance - recognizing that man is more than an advanced animal. Instead, man has executive (spirit) and supervisory (soul) management infrastructures that can manage and create perfection through geometric natural laws. Mankind is made in the image of the supra-natural eternal Lord God, and has the mission to contribute to the establishment of the Kingdom of God. This is mankind's mission - to daily qualify as a citizen of the Kingdom of God. Thus, the Christian Church had been moving humanity and civilization upward to that purpose.

The originators of the United States Constitution had recognized these Christian Renaissance geometric natural law qualities, and implemented them in the new Republic's framework. Yet it is these qualitative elements that are being criminalized in the new 'democratized' United States and European pagan and secular societies[247]. It is these re-engineered doctrines and laws that are being promoted as freedom from these geometric natural law views. We hear that we are 'progress' or 'free thinkers' out of *Christianity*

Now under the redefined umbrella of separation of church and state,[248] this allows for internal revolutionary social and cultural changes.

---

[247] George Orwell clearly foresaw and warned of the detailed methods by which social re-engineering was to occur: '*Animal Farm*' and '*1984*'.

[248] The 'separation of church and state' clause is not in the original United

Begun with the outlawing of prayer in school, the posting of the Ten Commandments and Christian symbols and Christmas in public places, there appeared Malthusian depopulation schemes, two children per family limits, contraception, sexual promiscuity and easy divorce. The passage of 'hate crime' legislation, opened the door to identifying anyone who opposes change - redefinition of marriage, abortion, fetus/embryonic stem cell research, court decisions on what constitutes science (UR/ER) versus cultism. Clearly such legislation and policy orientation demonstrates that secular initiatives are nothing more than the re-emergence of the religious practices known as 'phallic worship' within a Babylonian system[249]. A further and closer examination will reveal that numerous Executive orders have now been signed that would lead to the elimination of private property and human rights.

6.3. What's the Best Answer?

Uniformitarians are unable to provide scientific proof for their concept of evolution. For example, the book published in 1959 by Cardinal Ernesto Ruffini, *'The Theory of Evolution Judged by Reason,'* Joseph

---

States Constitution. This Constitution reflects the dynamics of a Republic that is based upon Renaissance, Apostolic Christian, and geometric natural law structures. This is what the 'Society of Cincinnatus' had been leading. Now however the United States has the United Nations charter to contend with – founded upon international Socialist Democratic rules, algebraic, subjective structure.

The United States Constitution specifically identifies the 'God' – as being 'nature's God' – i.e., the Creator of nature, and the state cannot escape being in the Creator's nature.

[249] Babylonian civilization had been an autocratic, authoritarian, and mercantile system. It maintained five social levels consisting of: (1) rulers,(2) aristocrats who are above the law, (3) military/security who are accountable only to the corporation; (4) temples with their intelligential casts of priests who were to maintain the (5) masses (serfs and slaves) under control, off-balanced, disciplined. This is achieved by allowing the masses to gratify their senses through promoted entertainment; drug-induced mysticism, fear ideologies, vice, phallic worship, institutionalized prostitution, abortion, child sacrifice, homosexual priesthoods, sports, wars, and ritualized cannibalism. The pantheist wizards ("scientists") research, promote, and manage the highest values and priorities - converting them into gods that included the rituals and organized practices. All this was the pantheists' heaven and sociology science.

F. Wane, Inc; New York, NY, becomes a marker of all that the debaters had to offer by 1960. From this marker it is now easy to see what has gone on in the sciences for the past 55 years. It is now easy to gauge scientific progress. We now can see that after juggling and tossing, the uniformitarians still fail to demonstrate scientific evidence for evolution. Issues that existed in 1959 persist and havenen been resolved today. In the 1980's Neo-Evolutionists received another blow when from their ranks many neo-evolutionists threw in the towel and initiated the Intelligent Design approach to help explain the unexpected high-tech information processes at nano levels. Clearly the 19th century organic uniformitarian model was never positioned to predicted or explain such phenomenon and such complexity. It is also tragic to see the means, strategies and tactics the highly financed uniformitarians who used to pass off a 'flat earth' pseudo-science during the past 150 years. They influenced the education system, destroyed professional scientists' careers, influenced Federal Courts, used legal processes and agencies to neutralize the American Constitution, became the foundation of the most genocidal ideologies in history and functioned like mafia to maintain the pseudo-scientific uniformitarian systems afloat for over 100 years. Clearly, together with Malthusianism and Monetarism the uniformitarian/evolutionary theory are used to introduce the dynamics of failed civilizations on a global scale. In addition, it is now easy to see that the three to four uniformitarian rules have become the most successful *self-brainwashing* technique yet devised. Fascists, Nazis, Communists and Masons came from its mold. This process promotes 'forget actual history and culture by using the simple-to-complex statistical progressive method – i.e., Big Bang to primates and man; from 'primitivism' to modernist pseudo-scientific simple realism.' From within a Christian civilization with its pursuit for an accurate knowledge base and investigative tools that overcome and find solutions to uncertainty; instead progress to uniformitarian's proposed truncated hands-on-materialist relativism.

In the 1990's it became interesting to realize that both the Intelligent Design and Creation science scientists after predicting and examining empirical evidence, raised questions of the origins of life. The dozens of evolutionary predictions and theories dramatically fell short in answering this question. After peering through the atomic microscopes two of the four debaters rejected the evolutionary pseudo-scientific implications. The DNA/RNA information and nanobot evidence was overwhelmingly against uniformitarian suggestions and contentions of 'almost certainty, and truth'.

Similarly, since the 1960's the *Creation Scientific Model* addressed and provided infinitely better explanations and predictions on issues of dating methods, geologic morphology and plate tectonics, fossil interpretation, speed of light and gravitation, mutational effects, etc. while uniformitarianism /evolution theories lagged behind for decades – none of the evidence pointed to billions and millions of years.

Those who address the pursuit of accurate knowledge, the scientific method must clearly:

1) Define what constitutes the 'objective or unfettered scientific method' (OUSM) in objective terms, such as those identified in the engineering project management approach.

2) Identify and formulate the current scientific methodology, its strengths and limitations. Clearly establish/document where this process actually leads. Recognize the difference between the subjective, relative, reductionist approaches that provide an ideological interpretation and method (e.g., dialectical materialism), in contrast to that which incorporates the 3DMM, DBSP and other features described in this book. To recognize that the evolution has yet to yield concrete evidence for qualitative (vertical) progression; while the Creation predicts qualitative infrastructural values at all levels of science, and seeks description, operations and validations.

3) Identify favorable conditions, where the scientific initiative thrives, and where the legal historical geometric natural law-based methods such as those worked on by J. Kepler and Riemann have produced qualitative progress. Recognize that today's Christianities are but shadows of what they originally had been during the past 2000 years - specifically, the favorable environments where we can recognize the pursuit for accurate science (3DMM, DMPS) and geometric natural law. We must re-assess historical data and information - much of which has been re-written or 'truncated'.

4) Re-assess the true nature and direction of the scientific effort – its infrastructure, education, high-tech-based investment and scheduled discoveries.

5) Recognize and assess the low, medium and dramatic impact that certain doctrines have had upon the scientific, technological, educational,

political, legal (philosophy and legislation), social, and faiths. Recognize the value of the shorthand formula:

Ideology, Religion, Cults

Geometric Natural Law, 3DMM Knowledge base, Standards, Filters, DMPS, OUSM

6) Assess and correct the damage incurred to the scientific community, careers paths and opportunities of millions. Re-assess initiatives in the education system curriculum and policies; as well as, the political, economic, social, international, historical, standards and judicial systems, that have succumbed to ideological, legal manipulative methods, disinformation that had been applied under the various doctrines, e.g., UR/ER and 'Christian' pantheism and cultism.

7) Objectively reassess the qualifications of scientists, their authorities; institutions' accreditation criteria and value in all areas of the Evolution-Creation-ID-Hybrid Uniformitarian arenas of the debate. The initial legally-oriented questions for these answers should help uncover a Pandora's Box that up to now was kept closed by: media, money and resources, politics and policies, courts – e.g., the precedents of seemingly insignificant mini case-histories (precedents) upon which the contemporary judgments are decided; the large-scale 'marketing' campaigns of disinformation; the behind-the-scenes special interests and lobby activities.

8) Recognize that in many cases the decision-making and problem solving process has been short-circuited in many areas. Here we have the re-/definition of terms, issues filtered through questionable non-scientific filters. Qualified and objective scientists and administrators must take a closer look at the Gap Depth Determination to identify where gaps appear. Figure 18 will help identify where the contemporary scientific method fails. Uniformitarian court procedures and decisions have polarized instead of resolved issues. Ideologically rigged courts will not solve but further polarize the positions -courts are notorious for not being the bedrock of 'scientific' truth. Find objective criteria and documented evidence for qualified court determinations? If courts were established upon the original American Constitutional Law then justice, true science and religion/ideology based upon geometric natural law would reign supreme in righteousness.

9) Re-examine to what extent individuals, group and all, have been contaminated by 'ER' - in their priorities, behavior, budget allocation, scientists' qualification and promotions. Re-examine to what extent a variation exists in the use of Executive, Supervisory and Functional faculties (see Figure 5) – DMPS exercise. Resize, re-purpose, cleanup, reassessment, and establishment of accuracy-based knowledge, purposes, objectives and strategies. What models of thinking are we using? How do we view and interpret history and the knowledge base? Why has Monetarism instead of the American Credit system prevailed?

10) Today, uniformitarian uncertainty causes never-ending debates in a pantheon of models: pantheism, theism, and supra-theism. One should ask who thrives in such an environment. It is clear that highly bankrolled relativists and Modernists have much to gain in their algebraic world-view and a depopulated dark age.

George Washington's Vision describes hope.

Appendix 1: Challenging Evidence

A perfect human footprint, a 14.5-inch-long track, found embedded in a rock that an expert calculated, from its location in the river's edge, to be at least 150 million years uniformitarian time (UT) – 'The American Anthropologist,' v. IX (1896): 68.

Dozens of other foot and shoe imprints have appeared up to that time; for example, in the Fisher Canyon, Pershing County, Nevada, on January 25, 1927 – discovered a shoe print in an excellent state of preservation, heel edges smooth, rounded off as if cut, right side appeared more worn than the left (right foot). The rock in which the heel mark was made was Triassic limestone - 225 million years old (UT). Furthermore, microphotographs revealed that the leather had been stitched by a double row of stitches, with double threads – a thread much smaller and refined than workmanship used by shoemakers in 1927.

E.A. Allen, 'American Antiquarian,' v. 7 (1885): 39, and further detailed studies conducted in 1930 by Dr. Wilbur Greely Burroughs, head of the geology department at Berea College, identified a total of twelve 9.5 inch man tracks among several creature tracks. The human prints were described as good-sized, toes well spread, and very distinctly marked - located sixteen miles east of Berea on Big Hill in Rock Castle County, Cumberland Plateau, impressed upon the gray Pottsville sandstone dating from the upper Pennsylvanian period – over 300 million years (UT). Doctor Burroughs was quoted in the Louisville Courier-Journal, May 24, 1953, of these, two pairs show the left foot advanced relative to the right. The position of the feet is the same as that of a person. The distance from heel to heel is 18 inches. One pair shows the feet parallel to each other, the distance between the feet being the same as that of a normal human being. Doctor Burroughs concluded that the prints were made by a creature that was exclusively bipedal, not quadruped, and without evidence of a tail acting as a tripod ('third leg') or signs of belly or tail marks in the examined stratum. Microscopic analysis of the human tracks, based upon grain count – "the sand grains within each track are closer together than grains immediately outside the tracks and elsewhere on the rock for the same kind and same combination of grains, due to the pressure of the creature's foot. The 'creature' exerted a weight pressure a little above that of a modern man. The clear impressions showed five toes, ball, and heel, totally unrelated to an amphibian's or reptile's physical makeup – only man has a foot like that. Albert G. Ingalls, Scientific American" January, 1940, stated, If man existed as far back as in the Carboniferous Period in any shape, then the whole science of geology is so completely wrong that all geologists should resign their jobs and take up truckdriving.

On July 20, 1968, the Cambrian shale (600 million years UT) revealed a five toe, child's 6-inch foot wearing a moccasin with trilobites for company - Dr. Clifford Burdick in Antelope Springs, Utah - Swasey Mountains and the Cambrian Wheeler shale.

Similar discoveries have been made in areas of metallic objects with properties that confound UT timetables. For example, the iron cube (2.64 x.2.64 x 1.85 inches, weight 1.73 lbs, specific gravity 7.75) was discovered at an Upper Austrian foundry in the fall of 1885, but in 1966-67, the iron cube was subjected to electron-beam microanalysis by experts at the Vienna Naturhistorisehes Museum. The results: no traces of nickel, chromium, or cobalt in the iron = not of meteoric origin. No sulfur detected = not a pyrite, a natural mineral that sometimes forms geometric shapes; low magnesium content. Doctor Kurat of the museum, and Dr. R. Gill of the Geologisehe Bundesanstalt of Vienna, concluded that the object was made of cast iron. In 1973, Hubert Mattlianer concluded from yet another detailed investigation that the object had been made from a hand-sculptured lump of wax or clay pressed into a sand base, this forming the mold into which the iron had been poured. Final conclusion: man-made, but was encased in coal dating to the tertiary - 60 million years old (UT).

Appendix 2: 21 Journalistic Assumptions

Some journalists' questions are 'loaded' questions. These are questions that may imply a conclusion and really require to answer multiple implied questions (e.g., twenty-one), yet this must be answered within a limited time frame (e.g., thirty seconds), or within one paragraph. In this case, it took a whole Chapter 5 to address such a question, because it implied twenty-one inferences. This would be a typical example of the violation of dignity, integrity, and self-determination (S8).

In this instance, the question is: Do you think that teaching evolution goes against religious beliefs? Here are the 21 inferences:

A clear contrast exists between evolution and religion.

Evolution is not a religion.

Religion is not science.

Evolution and religion are antonyms in their basic concepts.

Evolution is scientific.

Religion is mythological and subjective.

Religion may or may not include evolution.

Religion is not linked to reality as evolution is (origins, supernaturalism versus materialism).

Religion is potentially anti-evolutionary and anti-science.

Evolution is realistic, scientific, and rational.

True science cannot exist outside the evolutionary content or framework.

Religion is abstract, unscientific, and potentially irrational.

Evolution is potentially, if not actually, anti-religious.

Evolution may be included in religion, because of (#5), but evolution is not a religion itself.

Evolution describes a new reality, whereas religion has deep historical and cultural roots in mythology, folklore, work of fancy, or is a substitute for down-to-earth reality in the absence of evolution.

Evolution is a recent discovery and has never existed in history in an ideological or religious form.

Religion, in order to acquire a realistic foundation, must fully embrace evolution.

The purposes, objectives, and strategies of evolution and religion are dramatically different.

The purposes, objectives, and strategies of science and religion are dramatically different.

The policies, procedures, and rules of evolution and religion are different.

To use any hypothesis with non-materialistic or reductionist perspectives is to be seen as being religious.

Index

3DMM, 13, 55, 59, 81, 106, 117, 143, 155, 163, 182, 187, 193, 196, 204, 217, 230, 244, 249, 259

5 levels of qualitative change, 149, 195, 197

abortion, 81, 113, 172, 258, 260

adaptation, 20, 31, 34, 36, 78, 95, 149, 160, 165, 191, 211, 225-26

algebraic, vii, 7, 57, 64, 68-70, 75, 77-78, 82, 84-85, 121, 149, 152, 154, 182, 184-85, 191, 204, 209, 211, 217, 220-21, 224-25, 229-30, 234, 260

atheism, vi, viii, 207, 224

Babylon, 3, 13, 77, 83, 145, 186, 233, 235, 260

Baptist, 16

big bang, vii, 41, 93, 127, 137, 209-10, 253

Book of Job, 100-1

Catholic Church, v, x, 17, 86, 215, 226

Christendom, v, vi, 9, 13, 86, 142, 144, 147, 185-86, 188, 219, 246, 249, 251

Communism, 58

conditional certainty, iii-vii, x, 6-7, 53-54, 59, 89, 95, 97, 102, 104, 106-10, 114, 116-18, 120, 143, 145-46, 148-49, 153-58, 161, 167, 169, 172, 182, 183, 187, 196, 199, 201, 204, 208, 212, 217, 226, 229, 244-46

Copernicus, 4, 86

court cases, 11, 113, 174

covenant, 72, 75-76, 91, 132, 208, 216, 234-35, 255

Creationism, 19, 93, 136, 142, 146, 156, 167-68, 177, 248, 251

Darwinism, i, 17, 142

dating method, 136

Denton, Michael, 248

dialectical materialism, 31, 142

DMPS, iv, vii, xi, 34-35, 53, 59, 62, 76, 96, 103-4, 106-12, 115-17, 119-21, 143, 146, 148-51, 153-58, 161, 164, 169, 172, 175, 177, 180-83, 187, 189, 196, 200-1, 204, 209, 217, 226, 229, 231-32, 234, 244, 249, 251, 255, 257, 259

energy densities, 222

Evolution, i, ii, x, xi, 17-20, 24, 27-30, 32, 37, 41, 43, 62, 72, 88-89, 94, 98, 99, 102, 105, 113, 121, 134, 142, 146, 149, 154-55, 160, 167-68, 170, 174-76, 178, 180, 184, 187, 195, 203-4, 214, 218-19, 227, 243, 247, 256, 267-68

evolutionism, 87, 248

extraterrestrial, 24, 39, 40, 152

fossil record, 94, 174, 176, 178-79, 195

Galileo, 48, 86, 226

genocide, 8, 70, 172

geometric natural law, vi, xi, 6, 12, 21, 34, 41-43, 58, 65, 72, 75, 84, 107, 128, 145, 152, 156, 173, 181-82, 203, 208, 217, 223, 231, 247, 250, 259

Gish, Duane, 32

golden mean, 13, 222

Gould, Stephen Jay, 29, 88, 178, 248

Huxley, Julian, 15, 28

ideology, iii, vii, ix, 4, 51, 63, 66, 68, 84, 87, 97, 116, 150, 160, 161, 171, 173, 176, 185, 187, 191, 204-5, 213-14, 229, 243-45

Intelligent Design, i, ix, xi, 27, 31-32, 38-42, 62, 72, 75, 102, 113, 121-22, 142, 146, 148, 153, 156, 160, 164, 168, 170-71, 176-77, 180, 184, 186, 198, 203-4, 243-44, 246, 248

intelligent designer, 103

irreducible complexity, 38, 39, 102

Luther, Martin, v, 50, 86, 217

Lyell, Charles, 15, 27, 154

Marx, Karl, 28, 50, 58, 148, 258

materialism, vi-vii, 11, 15, 31, 50, 52, 58, 85, 87, 99, 147, 153, 155, 169, 172-73, 181, 184, 188, 211, 224, 230, 244, 248, 267

modernism, iv, vi-vii, 6, 16, 217, 244, 246

Morris, Henry M., 19-21, 32, 144

nano-robotic, 175, 195, 198, 248

National Academy of Science, ix, 159-60, 162, 167-68, 227

natural selection, 28-31, 58, 88, 155-56, 163, 175, 193, 198, 215 naturalism, vii, 154, 184

Nazism, i, 87, 144, 233, 246

Newton, Isaac, 49, 57, 134, 190

Noah's Ark, 92, 103, 253

Noah's Flood, 138

Omega Point, 17, 44, 218

Orthodox Church, v, 86, 218

OUSM, 122, 177, 249, 251

pantheism, iii, 44, 53, 99, 144, 182, 224

plate tectonics, 32

progressive, 27, 29, 38, 78, 86, 160, 168, 193, 195, 198, 248

punctuated equilibrium, 40, 178

qualitative infrastructures, 12, 149, 192, 222

qualitative vertical change, 255

re-design, 20, 31, 33, 38, 50, 84, 99, 108, 149, 160, 163, 175, 192, 226

reductionism, vi-viii, 39, 49-51, 57, 109-10, 154-55, 157, 172, 188, 204, 210, 212, 217, 244, 246

re-engineering, 1, 18, 20, 31, 33, 38, 84, 96, 98-99, 108, 149, 160, 175, 189, 192, 195, 225-26, 258, 259

religion, ix, xi, 9, 15, 39-40, 42, 50-51, 62-63, 66, 68, 82, 84, 87, 95, 142, 151-52, 167, 173, 175-76, 180-81, 185, 191, 203-5, 213, 216, 234, 243-44, 267-68

school textbooks, 17

scientific method, iii-iv, vi-viii, x-xi, 14, 32, 34, 39, 41-42, 49, 53-55, 59, 62, 89, 97, 100, 109, 111, 115, 117, 142-44, 147-49, 151, 153, 155-56, 158, 160-61, 164, 167, 177, 186, 204, 212, 225, 231, 234, 236, 243-49, 251, 257

Scopes trial, 17, 18, 231, 245

secularism, viii, 8, 234, 246

singularity, 35-36, 40, 41, 53, 73-74, 107, 178, 211

statistical progression, 6, 34, 39, 40, 160, 193, 210

Teilhard de Chardin, 218

teleology, 184, 248

uniformitarian realism, 110, 158, 182-83, 248

www.icr.org, ii, 20, 32-33, 37, 74, 93, 101, 136-37, 140-42, 156, 160, 163, 174, 181

young earth, ii, ix, xi, 21, 143-45, 155, 160, 163, 171, 178, 180,-81, 187, 203, 246, 249, 251

About the Author

George Grebens has studied and worked in the USA, Canada and overseas. He received his PhD at Michigan State University (1972) in Russian Literatures and Languages, with minors in international relations and other science and engineering subjects. He has worked in industrial project management with top multi-national engineering firms, conducted management development, and consulted in successful corporate restructuring. He held posts as Director of Education and Dean of Education Institutes, in Texas. He was presented with awards for his presentations at international conferences in areas of industrial management and leadership.

For over 35 years, Dr. Grebens has followed events, studied, written and debated on evolution, creation, intelligent design and hybrid uniformitarian scientific issues. This on-going science versus ideology debate underlies the continuing culture war in the USA and around the world.